Starting and Growing in the New Economy

Successful Career Entrepreneurs Share Stories and Strategies

Edited by

Sally Gelardin, Ed.D.

National Career Development Association

A founding division of the American Counseling Association

Library of Congress Cataloging-in-Publication Data

Starting and growing a business in the global marketplace: career entrepreneurs share
   stories and strategies / edited by Sally Gelardin.
            p.cm.
   Includes bibliographical references
   ISBN 1-885333-16-1 (pkb.)
      1. Vocational guidance. 2. Career development. 3. Entrepreneurship — Study and teaching.
         4. Counselors — Anecdotes. 5. Counselors — Examinations, questions, etc.
         I. Gelardin, Sally D, II. Title: Starting and growing a business: Successful career entrepreneurs share stories and strategies.

Hf5381.S7384 2007
658.1'1—dc22

                                    2007046895

Entrepreneurs are restless thinkers, impatient doers, and intuitors who hear the wants of those without a voice. They see resistance as opportunities to challenge accepted assumptions, operational rules and unexamined routines. More than most they understand that their only work role is to add value.

Rich Feller, Ph.D.
Professor of Counseling and Career Development
Colorado State University
Author, *Knowledge Nomads and the Nervously Employed*

Contents

Dedication

Just when I reached a place where I could take a breath, Ben Gelardin, my 98-year old father-in-law, captured my attention. Like the other fish he had played with throughout his life (as in the movie and book *Big Fish*), I floated in his web of stories.

During a recent visit to this forever charming nonagenarian, I discovered that Ben invented the first leak-proof dry cell battery, visited Albert Einstein at his home, and was hired by the state of New York at the age of 58 after being an entrepreneur for most of his adult life. In that position, he became an "intrepreneur" (an individual with an independent and risk-taking behavioral style who works within a formal organization), starting the first industrial condominium in the United States. He offered free tax consulting in his eighties, led hikes in his early nineties, and went deepsea fishing until the age of 98. Ben has demonstrated entrepreneurial strengths throughout his life and is always willing to share stories about his adventures.

I also dedicate this book to Dr. Garry Walz, who took a risk by publishing my first book, *The Mother-Daughter Relationship: Activities for Promoting Lifework Success* (2004). Like Ben, he has always been a self-starter, boldly adventuring into new territories. Garry chaired the counselor education program at the University of Michigan and started an online database of current counseling-related articles through the ERIC Counseling and Personnel Services Clearinghouse. Most recently, he developed (with Dr. Jeanne Bleuer) VISTAS Online, a project designed to continue the ERIC/CASS tradition of acquiring and making relevant counseling resources. Garry influenced me to offer readers ways, not only to acquire knowledge, but also to use it wisely and to share learning with others, which is the focus of this entrepreneur monograph.

Several years ago, Garry invited me to participate in a workshop on "Zen and the Art of Information Acquisition and Utilization." He asked me to present the "Zen" part, a role that I have subsequently developed in my life and work. He never told me what he meant by Zen, but I interpreted his request to mean maintain a sense of balance and peace of mind in one's work and life, especially important in this age of information overload, and doubly important when one is starting and growing a business. The seed that he planted is growing (view: http://www/lifeworkps.com/sallyg; then view "Owned Communities"), or to continue Garry's culinary metaphor in his Preface to this book, it is not enough to acquire information, but also to digest it, share it with others, and to clear one's palate after dinner so one can enjoy the fruits of one's labor.

As I reflect upon entrepreneurs who have had a particularly strong influence on me, my father comes to mind. He respected all his customers and was respected by them, in return. They trusted him. My father was the first automobile dealer in town to hire a woman in the 1950s. He was honorable in his business relationships, thereby serving as a powerful role model for his children. My father always placed his family first.

In this dedication, I have not included any female entrepreneurs as role models. In the process of building their businesses, most women who come to mind sacrificed relationships that are important to me, such as parents, partners or children. I discuss this predicament in my mother-daughter book (Gelardin, 2004), and offer examples of female entrepreneurs in this monograph who have consciously attempted to give quality attention to both personal relationships and business development.

As Ben reflects on a life fully lived, and as Garry enlists the support of the National Career Development Association (NCDA), the American Counseling Association (ACA), and the Association for Counseling and Supervision (ACES) to continue sharing current counseling research, programs, and practices, so I invite you to learn with me from these venerable entrepreneurs. Step into the doors of this monograph to read their stories, study what resonates within you, apply their experiences and exercises to your own lifework, and offer your unique menu of entrepreneurial treats to the world.

Acknowledgments

The speed and smoothness with which this monograph came together can be attributed primarily to the prompt responses of the entrepreneurs who contributed to this book. Within two or three months after I invited them to participate, all had submitted entries. The promptness of their replies amazed me, considering their hugely busy lives. Admittedly, I used an artful sales pitch, suggesting that they might like to reflect upon the development of their businesses over the winter holidays (about the only time of year that entrepreneurs might put aside a block of time to be reflective). Even Randy Miller, whose wife gave birth to twins at the same time that he wrote his contribution, came through within a few weeks of due date (I wonder if he wrote in the waiting room!).

As a multitasker, with a slew of entrepreneurial and organizational commitments, I could never have completed the manuscript on schedule without the careful editing of Marie Shoffner, NCDA Publication Committee member, the helpful suggestions of Judy Ettinger, NCDA Publication Committee Chair, the ongoing support of Mary Ann Powell, Publications Committee Administrative Liaison, and the typesetting and graphic wizardry of Wayne Sharp. Pete Hubbard provided hours of tutelage on how to continue the entrepreneurial dialogue on a free Internet platform that I describe in Exercise 2 of Appendix A.

I thank my husband, Bob Gelardin, who has guided me through the entrepreneurial forest and who patiently has shared with me his business experience and wisdom, as well as put up with my long hours coordinating the production of the manuscript. Between Bob and the experienced contributors to this monograph, I gained invaluable insight into the intricacies of entrepreneurship and am pleased to share this rich resource with you. I wish you the best in your entrepreneurial venture and invite you, not only to learn from the wisdom within these pages, but also to assimilate and apply the wisdom within yourself.

Sally Gelardin, Ed.D.

Preface

Prefaces, like hors d'oeuvres, are best when they are satisfying to your palate, but especially heighten your appetite for the entrée – the "feast" to follow. Hence, I will discipline myself to refrain from "serving up" my own views of and experiences with entrepreneurship. As the founder of ERIC/CASS, Human Development Services, Inc., the Life/Career Development System, CAPS, Inc., and Counseling Outfitters, LLC, I have many thoughts on entrepreneurship. Therefore, while I had to decline the invitation to prepare a chapter for this book due to previous commitments, I am pleased to have the opportunity to offer a brief overview of my perspective through this preface.

I first want to say that this book is long overdue. We have a prodigious literature on career development theory and research, but only sparse coverage of implementing interventions and services. To follow the food analogy, we devote too much time to discussing cooking methods and too little time to developing and trying out new recipes and serving attractive meals. Sally Gelardin deserves much credit for serving us this satisfying meal of practical ideas, action plans, and exercises. Both new and experienced entrepreneurs will benefit from using this book. It can help you become a successful entrepreneur, and it can help you sharpen your skills and identify actions and strategies that you haven't tried in the past. After all, good entrepreneurs are always looking for ways to improve their services and products.

If prospective diners were to ask you if you had a good meal at a particular restaurant, they would not be asking you for a bite-by-bite description. Rather, they would want your reactions on a few salient features, e.g., the food was great, the menu offered variety, portions were huge, or the prime rib is out of this world! *"Hey, you ought to try it!"* This book delivers everything that the editor promises in her introduction. I will add only a few salient points to help you decide whether or not to go there.

The first reaction one has in perusing this book is that the editor has chosen her writers wisely. They know their stuff. The speak from "having been there and done that." Their comments and suggestions have the ring of coming from people who know of what they speak and genuinely want to be helpful. A key factor! Without it, the book wouldn't be worth reading.

The order and movement of the chapters is logical and appropriate. You can read chapter by chapter or selectively pick just those that offer what you need. There is truth in the labeling – the contributors do what they say they will.

The coverage of the topic through the individual chapters is excellent. Each author responds to the question in the title so you know what you will receive early on. Although some readers may have preferred a more typical academic style, the chatty, person-to-person style makes for easy reading.

I especially like the activities and exercises at the end of the ten plus one chapters. There is a big difference between having an intellectual understanding of a task and acquiring the ability to carry through on it. These follow-up exercises reinforce what the reader has learned and increase the probability that he/she will follow through on putting the concepts into practice.

However, I do have one word of advice. This is a book of personal testimonials, not a review of the research on entrepreneurship. The contributors write with passion and conviction, and it's easy to get caught up in their enthusiasm. You must judge for yourself whether or not what works for them will work for you.

With what I've said in this preface and what Sally Gelardin has said in her introduction, you should be able to judge whether it s the right stuff for you. What do I think? *"Hey, you ought to try it!"*

Garry Walz, Ph.D.

Dr. Walz is Professor Emeritus at the University of Michigan where he chaired the counselor education program and launched the ERIC Counseling and Personnel Services Clearinghouse. Recently, he (with Dr. Jeanne Bleuer) founded Counseling Outfitters, LLC, which is under contract with the American Counseling Association to develop VISTAS Online, a project designed to continue the ERIC/CASS tradition of acquiring and making relevant counseling resources available to counselors.

Dr. Walz is a past president of the American Counseling Association and the Association for Counselor Education and Supervision, and chair of the ACA Foundation. Among his many honors are the NCDA Eminent Career Award, the Gilbert and Kathleen Wrenn Humanitarian Award, and ACA Fellow status. He is a highly prolific writer, having authored and co-authored countless books, articles, and research studies as well as overseeing the ERIC/CASS and CAPS Press publication programs.

Introduction
Sally Gelardin, Ed.D.

Objects fly through the air,
Stars wheel
through the universe.
All fall eventually.

If we become obsessed
with definitively mastering
the decline, we are lost.

If we achieve peace
within the intervals
of rising and falling,
we find grace.

Arthur Chandler

Small businesses meet the daily needs of most people. From dry cleaning services to hair salons, from an ice cream shop to the corner market in community neighborhoods, small businesses allow us to create, risk, and contribute to others while doing what we enjoy. In the following pages, career development professionals discuss their efforts to create small businesses. In addition to potential career entrepreneurs, the discussions and lessons can be applied to most people from a variety of settings who desire to start a small business. Millions of people around the world have created successful small businesses and many millions dream about having their own business. This monograph is packed with ideas, reflections, techniques, advice, and encouragement for those who want to improve their businesses, and especially for those who want to make their dreams become reality.

Career professionals are joining the international trend of creating small businesses, either as a sole source of income, or in conjunction with other work roles. Like our clients, many of us see growing a career development business as a viable way to meet the increasing demand for career services and products. For the purposes of this monograph, career development business refers to entrepreneurial career-related choices and transitions made over one's lifespan. An entrepreneur is *"someone who establishes a new entity to offer a new or existing product or service into a new or existing market, whether for a profit or not-for-profit outcome"* (Wikipedia definition of "entrepreneur"). Entrepreneurs bring something new to the marketplace and/or identify a new client base.

To provide you with a comprehensive overview of this topic, I invited successful career entrepreneurs to contribute their personal stories and business strategies. In addition to running private or group career counseling practices, the contributing entrepreneurs provide a range of services and products and target a variety of populations.

My personal goal for writing this monograph, *Starting and growing a business in the new economy: Successful career entrepreneurs share stories and strategies,* was to learn from contributors how to grow my own business into the best online job search strategies course available in the market today so workers in transition worldwide can find satisfying work. In addition, my intention was to provide guidelines, information, personal stories, experiential activities, feedback, and support so that you, an aspiring or current entrepreneur, could join with me to learn the secrets of successful career entrepreneurs. Together, we shall then be able to put into practice the lessons they learned and the business strategies that they generously are willing to share.

Just as I danced while my older and younger brothers played baseball, I encourage you to dance to your own music, picking and choosing what resonates with you from the wisdom of others who have danced to their own beat. In the 1960s, Bob Dillon was worshipped by the masses as a folk-singing idol until he added an electronic guitar and was booed off the stage at the Newport Folk Festival. Those who formerly denounced him now revere him. The famous 19th Century artist Vincent Van Gogh never earned a living through his art. Yet, Steve Jobs, Apple Computer CEO, has earned much more than most of us dream of attaining, doing what he loves.

Entrepreneurs are sometimes admired, but as often scorned by those who do not understand their vision. They build their reputations, not on the backs of established institutions or current forms of art or enterprise, but on their own visions, talents, and plentiful grit. To start and grow a business, read their stories.

You are welcome to travel with me to the "Home Depot" of career development – to build a business and a life (bricolage) that you can call your own. An entrepreneur, like a "bricoleur," is a person who creates things from scratch. "Bricoler" means "to tinker" or "to fiddle" or to "do-it-yourself" – building by trial and error rather than based on theory. An entrepreneur, like a "bricoleur," is creative and resourceful – "a person who collects information and things and then puts them together in a way that they were not originally designed to do" (Wikipedia definition of "bricolage").

Rationale

Start-up companies create most new jobs that fuel the economy. Who are the new entrepreneurs and why are they starting businesses? Entrepreneurs start an average of 550,000 new businesses monthly in the United States. Small businesses (independent businesses having fewer than 500 employees) represent 99.7 percent of all employer firms. Small businesses are the largest growing segment of the U.S. economy, creating 60% to 80% of new jobs. The majority of small businesses are entrepreneurs (without employees). Out of 25.8 million companies in the U.S., 18.6 million are entrepreneurs (SBA, 2006).

Leaders of the world's industrialized nations are seeking to promote a "global innovation society to thrive in a rapidly changing world" (Novosti, 2006: February 9). In the first global study of high expectation entrepreneurship, Autio (2005) found that "just 9.8% of the world's entrepreneurs expect to create almost 75% of the jobs generated by new business ventures." In this report, high expectation entrepreneurship is defined as "all start-ups and newly formed businesses that expect to employ at least 20 employees within five years." Because of their impact on job creation and innovation, these ventures will significantly influence the economies in which they operate.

Of the 25.8 million businesses in the United States, minority entrepreneurs are taking the lead in pace of growth, though Fairlie noted an increase in self-employment among nearly all U.S. demographic groups since 2000 (Kirk and Belovics, 2006, p. 51). Seventy-six percent of small businesses are owned by sole entrepreneurs with no employees. Women are the largest group of individuals who are launching their own businesses, and "immigrants have substantially higher rates of entrepreneurship than U.S.-born individuals."

Most workers in the United States and Western European labor market are in the middle age range. Members of this major age group will soon reach the age of 60. Older workers have a more difficult time finding work in large organizations. After working for organizations for most of their working lives, many don't choose to continue working for others. Corporations and government are cutting back on benefits. Therefore, financial necessity is forcing many older workers to set up their own businesses. The baby boomers are the largest age group in history who are retiring from public and private organizations. Since workers in this age group are just beginning to leave their organizational positions, and since many are

motivated to continue working, we have yet to discover what members of this upcoming population (including career and counseling related government and academic retirees) will do in their later years.

Most entrepreneurial start-ups are not forced into starting their own businesses by a lack of job opportunities. According to GEM's 2004 national summaries, "people with some post-graduate education and between 25 and 34 years of age are the most likely to start a new business." People who work full-time may also explore self-employment outside of their full-time work.

Corporations are adding to the potential entrepreneurial pool by laying off workers at a steady pace. Those who remain employed are more dissatisfied with their job during periods of high unemployment. As a result of outsourcing, technological advances, natural and man-made disasters, and corporate scandals, many young people, who are disillusioned with corporate ethics and goals and employer treatment of employees, also prefer to create their own way to earn a living and contribute to the world.

Career professionals are no exception. If you have been serving as a career counselor, career advisor, or career educator in an academic institution or government office, if you have worked in human resources, social work, or other service professions, or if you have worked in other capacities for public or private institutions for many years, you may be thinking about going out on your own. You may already be a career coach or counselor immersed in growing a business and would like to read others' perspectives on business development. The articles in this monograph are applicable to persons desiring to start and grow businesses in a wide variety of settings, from large cities to small towns to villages, nationally and throughout the world. Rather than leave you in a vacuum, trying to figure out the entrepreneurial process by yourself, I have compiled the collective wisdom of successful career entrepreneurs to support you in this process.

Special features

Since individuals learn in different ways, the book is organized in a format that allows you to progress at you own rate and in the way that is best for you. Some readers may choose to explore specific chapter topics. Others may prefer to progress from the first to the last chapter in a sequential order. Some may choose to perform all the activities and view all the Internet links. Others may prefer to jump directly to the topics that are of most interesting to them at the time.

This book was written in the focused, topic-specific format of a monograph so that you can begin to discover, through the eyes of experienced career entrepreneurs, how to create and build a career business. Each chapter is built around a question, answered by these experts. Woven within each chapter are the following elements:

- Personal reflections by contributors on their entrepreneurial process
- Stories about overcoming challenges with clients or work associates
- Mentors and models
- Suggested print and online resources for further exploration

(Resources and References for Exercises are located at the end of each author's contribution within the corresponding chapter.)

In the concluding chapter, I summarize what the contributing career entrepreneurs have shared in the monograph, and provide suggestions of what you can do after reading the monograph to build your business.

Appendix A contains exercises developed by contributors to help you apply their concepts and models. To further assist you in implementing your business, I suggest a way to organize your entrepreneurial process on your computer and describe an open-source Internet-based entrepreneur community that gives you an opportunity to communicate with other entrepreneurs about the concepts described in this monograph (see Appendix A, Exercises 1 and 2).

You probably won't read all the contributors' stories word by word or perform all the exercises in this book. That is understandable, since each contributor has a different perspective on what worked for him or her in building a business, and you bring your own perspective to the entrepreneurial process.

Delve into what you need, not necessarily what you desire. When you have learned all that you need to learn from this monograph, then you will have enough knowledge to write about your own entrepreneurial experiences and to create exercises that could be helpful to other potential entrepreneurs. The concluding chapter provides a way for you to share your entrepreneurial experiences.

In Appendix A, you will find 19 exercises. Perform Gail Liebhaber's "Gap Analysis" to discover what you need to know about building a business. If you need to increase risk-taking, perform Jack Chapman's exercise on overcoming barriers. If you need to explore ways to offer your counseling services, view Robert Chope's long list of consulting contracts or read about how Carolyn Kalil developed the True Colors business. Do you need to identify your values and prioritize the values that you bring to a business? Then immerse yourself in Jennifer Kahnweiler's Values Clarification Exercise. You may end up creating a business that no

one else every thought of, such as Donna Christner-Lile's vision for elders to age in their homes, near family and services. Jack Chapman guides you gently, but firmly, to the bottom line – how to make your business a financial success. Randy Miller adds a personal story about turning a challenge into a business opportunity.

I encourage you to examine, not only the content of what you need, but also the best way that you digest information. For example, if you would benefit most from a reflective approach to decision-making, read Ron Elsdon's, Gail Liebhaber's, and Edward Colozzi's stories and perform their exercises. Ed's chapter also includes a group feedback component. Do you prefer a methodical step-by-step approach? If so, read Dan Geller's theory and apply his exercise to your own business planning or follow Marcia Bench's instructions. Susan Whitcomb addresses both sides of your brain in a "two-track" approach that involves both inspiration and action. Lynn Joseph takes you on a guided imagery, Martha Russell guides you through an annual business check-up, and Michael Shahnasarian starts you thinking about exiting your business. In his straightforward fashion, Richard Knowdell suggests a quick and easy card sort to get you moving and takes you on a guided tour of his entire career. You may be intrigued by Marcia Bench's approach, which includes a spiritual component, especially since her educational background is in the legal field, and Ed Colozzi's multi-intelligence musings on internal and external sources of support.

If you are thinking about becoming a career entrepreneur, or if you are in the midst of growing a business, I invite you to "play ball" in the entrepreneurial playing field (as in the movie *Fields of Dreams*). You are welcome to join in this competitive, but exhilarating ballpark, where dreams become reality through long shots, foul balls, frequent strikeouts, far-reaching catches, dust and grime, trial and error, and an occasional home run. As the quintessential "Job Juggler," I invite you to throw your balls in the air and practice the entrepreneurial juggling act under the tutelage of experts. May you find peace and purpose between the rising and falling.

References

Autio, E. GEM 2005 High-expectation entrepreneurship summary report. Retrieved September 2, 2006: http://www.gemconsortium.org/document.asp?id=445.

"Bricolage" definition. Retrieved September 2, 2006: http://en.wikipedia.org/wiki/Bricolage.

Chandler, A. The moral and aesthetic implications of the mastery of falling objects, p.2. Reprinted from the *Journal of Popular Culture,* 25,3. Retrieved September 2, 1006: http://charon.sfsu.edu/JUGGLING/JUGGLINGSYMBOLISM2.HTML.

"Entrepreneur" definition. Retrieved September 2, 2006: http://en.wikipedia.org/wiki/Entrepreneur.

Fairlie, R.W. (2006). *Kauffman Index of Entrepreneurial Activity* 1996-2005. Retrieved September 8, 2006: http://www.kauffman.org/pdf/KIEA_national_052206.pdf.

Feller, R. (2005: October 28). Email correspondence with author.

Kirk, J. and Belovics, R. (2006). Counseling would-be entrepreneurs. *Journal of Employment Counseling* (June, 2006). 43,2.

Hopkins, J. U.S. entrepreneurial spirit remains steady, study finds. Retrieved September 2, 2006: http://www.usatoday.com/money/smallbusiness/2005-09-22-start-up-growth_x.htm?csp=34.

Novosti Russian News & Information Agency (2006: February 9). G8 leaders seeking global innovative society. Retrieved September 2, 2006: http://en.rian.ru/

SBA (2006: June), Frequently asked questions, SBA (Small Business Administration) Office of Advocacy. Retrieved September 26, 2006: http://www.sba.gov/advo/stats/sbfaq.pdf

I. Why start a business?

Making a decision to start a business can be based on many factors, such as need to make a living, put children through college, save up for retirement, create something that no one has ever created before, work at your own pace, work in your environment of choice (i.e., near adult children and grandchildren or in a fair weather climate), and/or resolve an early childhood experience. Identifying your motivation is an important step in starting a business. Starting a business is often a decision made during a transitional point in one's life. Who are your mentors? What is motivating you to start a business? Read what Robert Chope, one of the first private career practice entrepreneurs in the United States, has to say about starting a career development private practice. Perform his Exercises 3 and 4 in Appendix A to identify your motivation(s) for starting a career development business.

Robert C. Chope, Ph.D.

Establishing the Career and Personal Development Institute: Factors that Drove Me To Start a Career Counseling Business

As one of the founding associates of the Career Development Institute in San Francisco, I've been a principal of a private career counseling and consulting practice for over two and a half decades. I now have five associates. The group is called the Career and Personal Development Institute. We changed our name in the late 1980s when the Control Data Institute's Career Development Institute assumed our CDI moniker. Their business folded in the 1990s, but we continued on with the CPDI logo. The Institute is unique among career practices because our counseling model intertwines career and personal issues with a thoughtful developmental perspective. I am proud to be a founder of one of the oldest, private career-counseling firms in the United States.

At every career counseling conference I attend, people who know about the Institute query me about how it was started, what keeps it so successful, and how it accrued such celebrated tenure in the community. I usually give quick, cryptic answers to these inquiries because I haven't felt bold enough to deeply reflect on why I did what I did when I did it. In truth, I haven't wished to address the variety of different responses I could give.

Being asked to write about the motivation behind starting my practice has inspired me to develop this brief, personal career narrative. In so doing, I'm also able to explore the influence of the many contextual and relationship factors that gave me guidance and support over the years. Indeed, as Senator Hillary Clinton noted, it does take a village of support. I feel I've had that support in creating and sustaining my business.

Let me offer a few biographical tidbits. For the record, I've been a professor in the Department of Counseling at San Francisco State University since 1975. Prior to that, I served a year as a research associate at the University of Wisconsin Madison Regional Rehabilitation Research Institute, collaborating with George Wright and Ken Reagles, two major contributors to the rehabilitation research of that time. I joined their team three months before I earned a Ph.D. from the University of Minnesota Department of Psychology under David P. Campbell, my advisor, dissertation supervisor, and author of the Strong-Campbell Interest Inventory (SCII) and Campbell Interest and Skills Survey (CISS).

Why Did I Start a Practice, Especially Since I Was Already a College Professor?

I think that it's helpful for fledgling entrepreneurs to consider that there are a variety of factors in the decision to open an independent career counseling business. For me, these included the following: a lack of complete professional fulfillment as a professor, a degree of theoretical alienation from my colleagues in career counseling, a desire to make a difference in the world, the encouragement and support of other colleagues, the presence of entrepreneurs as role models, and a willingness to take risks. I will try to address succinctly each of these factors.

Lack of Personal Fulfillment as a Professor

The primary reason I embarked on a private career counseling practice was that teaching was not enough for me. I've always been a person devoted to service, a practitioner, and a counselor.

After graduating from Harvard in 1967, at the height of the Vietnam era, I served for four years as a counselor and senior counselor in a juvenile detention facility in northern California as an alternative to military service. During that time, I also earned a master's degree from San Francisco State University (SFSU) in the same department where I would eventually be employed for so many years. I figured that since I enjoyed the vigor of counseling disenfranchised and troubled youth, I ought to learn something about what I was supposed to be doing. Two years after receiving the degree, I became licensed as a Marriage, Family and Child Counselor.

I was accepted into the Ph.D. program at the University of Minnesota. During my three years at Minnesota, I was a psychology intern at the Minneapolis Veterans Administration (VA) Hospital. The VA gave me a stipend in return for 2700 hours of psychological service. With mounting interest in career development, I asked to be assigned to the Vocational Psychology Service of the VA. I believed, and still do, that the greatest impact any counselor can have, especially on those who are most difficult to serve, is through helping them obtain work.

David Campbell, originator of the Campbell Interest and Skill Survey (CISS), encouraged his advisees to graduate as expeditiously as possible and make a living. He didn't care what we did. Paul Meehl, on the other hand, thought that students should learn how to counsel in order to get a nonbookish feel for what a patient is really like and then return to the academy to think, research, write, and teach (in that order). As it turned out, both of these mentors influenced my career path.

Theoretical Alienation from My Colleagues

I founded the Career Counseling program at San Francisco State University in 1980. It has been one of the few CACREP approved programs in the United States. As successful as the program has been, I felt alienated in promoting career counseling because it always played second fiddle to the other, larger programs in our department. I wanted to bring more prestige to Career Counseling and regardless of what I did, students, faculty and administrators were all seduced by and gave attention to the larger programs like Marriage, Family, and Child Counseling.

The major idea I had for the career counseling program at SFSU was the incorporation of personal and emotional issues into the career counseling process. I've written two books about how these issues can affect career development (Chope, 2000; Chope, 2006). I felt that the emotional state of mind needed to be addressed during the job search. But this was very difficult to bring into the classroom at the time, and my colleagues thought that this material was better taught in other programs.

Establishing the Institute gave me an opportunity to take my ideas and test them out in private practice. I managed to get myself licensed as a

psychologist to avoid any scope of practice issues, and then I set out experimenting with my new model. With this clinical material, I was able to come back to the classroom with an approach that was quite different from that which appeared in most career counseling texts. In the meantime, I developed clinical models for other psychological issues that incorporated the use of family members into treatment protocols (Chope, 2001).

A Desire To Make a Difference

The serendipitous experience as a counselor in detention and probation services and as a psychology intern working with disabled veterans guided me in directions that continue to shape my professional career. These experiences forced me to recognize that I wanted to advance my work in a direction that would lead to social change. I've been caught up in social justice causes as a counselor and advocate for close to 40 years.

The Institute, unlike the university, gave me expanded opportunities for consultation on social justice issues. Rather than working from grants through the university, I developed contracts with people who were in need of services. Through the Institute, I worked with the Oakland and San Francisco police departments addressing employment discrimination issues among new recruits, and I assisted the San Francisco Fire Department in integrating women into the fire services. I also worked as an advocate with the Community Rehabilitation Workshop, World Institute on Disability, and the Community Alliance for Special Education.

Encouragement and Support of Colleagues

When I sought guidance from my professorial colleagues about starting a practice, I was startled that many were quite supportive. But the real joy of setting up the practice came from the students with whom I had worked. They were always chiding me to open a practice to add personal experiences with the cases taught in class. I loved the idea of bringing my own clinical material into the classroom.

When I finally opened the practice, it was with a group of colleagues and former students with whom I had maintained contact. While none of them are part of the group now, five of the six current members of the Institute were former students of mine. Beginning a practice with a group of trusted colleagues is an absolute joy. Not making decisions alone, sharing creative ideas about marketing and advertising, and sharing expenses made the early aspects of the private practice easy. Were I to do this again, I would do it in exactly the same way, partnering with colleagues who could enrich me. That support was crucial to my deciding to begin a practice, and it has remained a vital ingredient to our success.

Entrepreneurs as Role Models

I have had the distinction of being David Campbell's last doctoral candidate. He departed Minnesota and the Center for Interest Measurement after completing the 1974 retooling of the Strong Vocational Interest Blank, which he titled the Strong-Campbell Interest Inventory. Although I had little direct contact with Campbell, he has been a curious kind of role model for me throughout my career. He was a psychologist who enjoyed empirical test development, research, writing, teaching, and consultation, but also enjoyed the tangible fruits of working as an entrepreneur to create new products and service ideas for the clientele of the Center for Creative Leadership (CCL) in Greensboro, North Carolina.

Campbell was the quintessential example of a person who had a portfolio career before that word became fashionable as a part of the career counselors' lexicon. He was also willing to leave his position at Minnesota, still young and at the pinnacle of his career, and move away from academic life into a career filled with business consultation. While Campbell inculcated a spirit of entrepreneurial creativity in me, he also exemplified how many money making activities my education and training could provide.

A Willingness To Take Risks

For those of us who studied with risk-taking innovators, it's disappointing to work in a situation that does not allow for the chance to take your own risks and try out approaches that are distinctively your own without the critical, dictatorial eye of a senior supervisor saying that you can't do this or that. Many independent practitioners take an approach that moves beyond the conventional approaches of their time. These people should not only believe that they can provide a service to the public, but also believe that they can practice at a level that not only competes with but goes beyond that which is offered by other services.

Successful practitioners will always find gaps in the marketplace where services are needed, and they will capitalize on those gaps by offering new approaches. Moreover, practice changes regularly and those who are adaptable can continue to be successful. Practitioners need to maintain flexibility. The Institute today does not in any way resemble the Institute that was started 26 years ago. We have stayed in business because of that.

Deciding Whether To Start a Private Practice

My advice to those who want to assess whether to begin a private practice is to try Exercises 3 and 4 in Appendix A. The results of these may test your own creativity, so when you are ready to start a business, you will offer services that are new and different.

Summing Up

As I look back on the years that I've been in practice, I've had to make certain judgments about what it gave to me and how it limited me. Because my practice was part of a portfolio of writing, teaching, and public speaking, I never had the time to pursue work as an academic administrator. On several occasions, I was asked to consider being chair of my department. While I was willing to serve as the associate chair, I never accepted the chair position because it would mean that I would have to curtail my practice. I was unwilling to do that. The practice worked as a part of a portfolio career, but limited what I was able to do in the academic area.

That brings me to a second dilemma. I allowed the safety and security of the university to dictate how much I was able to practice. Make no mistake: I have enjoyed my 30 years in the classroom immensely. And with that enjoyment I have been able to have the comfort of a stable income with moderate wages, generous health benefits, sabbaticals, and a secure retirement package. The sabbaticals have enabled me to write.

On the other hand, the fees generated from my practice far outstrip what I am able to make as a college professor. I think that if I had this to do over again, I would leave the academy much like David Campbell did at the age of 42. At that time I would have had 12 years of teaching experience and been ready for larger training programs and newer opportunities. I didn't take that final risk. Knowing how successful we have been at the CPDI, that decision cost me financially.

For those who are thinking of creating your own business, you will have to decide what you're willing to risk in order to move on. My practice was an "add on," developed within elements of state-supported security. I think that it was a wonderful way for me to develop my practice because at no time was I ever totally financially dependent upon it. One might say that the portfolio career worked for me. But I still wonder how it might have been different had I created a large national firm like Right Associates or Challenger, Grey and Christmas. I think that while I had the know-how and inspiration to do it, I had some but not enough of the risk-taking personality. And I suppose that I will always wonder about what might have been.

References and Resources

Baxter, N.J. (1997). *Opportunities in counseling and development careers*. New York: McGraw-Hill.

CACREP. Council for Accreditation of Counseling and Related Educational Programs (CACREP). Retrieved September 2, 2006: http://www.cacrep.org/.

Chope, R.C. (2000). *Dancing naked: Breaking through the emotional limits that keep you from the job you want*. Oakland, CA: New Harbinger Publications.

Chope, R.C. (2001). *Shared confinement: Healing options for you and the agoraphobic in your life*. Oakland, CA: New Harbinger Publications.

Chope, R.C. (2006). *Family matters: The influence of the family in career decision-making*. Austin, TX: Pro-Ed Inc.

Hawkin, P. (1987). *Growing a business*. New York: Simon and Schuster.

Husch, T., & Foust, L. (1987). *That's a great idea!: The new product handbook: How to get, evaluate, protect, develop and sell new product ideas*. Berkeley, CA: Ten Speed Press.

II. What entrepreneurial strengths do you have?

More than 80% of small businesses fail within the first five years. They often fail because of lack of sufficient capital or lack of knowledge about what is needed to succeed in a business. Awareness of your strengths and transferable skills can be a great help in establishing a successful business in the first few years. This chapter will look at the key skills and strengths it takes to launch, grow and sustain a viable career business. It will present two entrepreneurs' experiences and an analysis of these experiences, along with the skills, values, and traits found to be key success factors. A model of career success as well as personal stories and illustrations will be discussed. Jennifer Kahnweiler and Carolyn Kalil designed Exercises 5 and 6 in Appendix A to help you uncover clues to your entrepreneurial profile.

Jennifer Kahnweiler, Ph.D.

Early Influences

One advantage of being a Baby Boomer is the chance to have accrued some years and hopefully a bit of wisdom under my belt (Brody, 2006). Over 15 of my 30 years as a working professional have been spent running my own business. This time has allowed me to accumulate a number of successes and failures along the way. While the years alone don't qualify me as an expert in starting a career business, I believe I have some insights from my experiences that may help others who are considering this path.

I grew up in a family of entrepreneurs on Long Island, New York. Both sets of grandparents were first-generation immigrants from Eastern Europe and began life in this country with no resources. My grandmothers both ended up as the primary breadwinners of their families. My paternal grandmother, widowed at an early age, raised her children on the income she generated from a small candy store in Brooklyn. My maternal grandmother took her husband's failing restaurant supply business and sold it for a profit years later.

My parents had a great influence on my attitude toward work. My dad was a successful radio, TV, and film screenwriter who wrote dramas on socially relevant topics (i.e., mental retardation, mental illness, drug addiction, etc.). He also worked at home, which allowed me to be shaped by both parents more directly than most of my friends whose dads were not around very much. My mom was a homemaker and volunteer who provided the stability and nurturing in our home. In addition to showing interest and curiosity about her children's lives, she also was influential in exposing us to great art, music, and theater. Another major influence was my aunt who carved out a career in the male-dominated film and TV businesses as a film editor.

Lessons I Learned

Following are a few of the lessons I absorbed in these formative years that set the stage for my entrepreneurial direction:

- Owning your own business or being a free agent is the way to make a living. I did not know many people who worked inside organizations and while this intrigued me on some level, it was definitely foreign territory.

- Women should be equal to men and no career direction is off limits. I had strong female role models as I watched my grandmothers and aunt make their own way. I remember my dad coming home from a parents' night when I was in junior high school and informing me that he had challenged the biology teacher who referred to scientists repeatedly as men. The idea that girls could be successful was part of the fabric of who we were. My younger sister, who later became a freelance photojournalist, and I readily absorbed this philosophy.

- Do work that has meaning to you. In my family, there was a great deal of discussion about work and the jobs and occupations people held, and how work could be a way to express who you were and how you felt. The creative nature of my family's business encouraged me to explore ways in which I could express myself in my work.

- Make a contribution. The work you do should touch people's lives in some way. Show an interest in them and understand what motivates people to behave the way they do. I think I was drawn to the helping professions because I felt this was the best way in which I could contribute.

I didn't start out as an entrepreneur. Once that I had decided on counseling as a direction, I gravitated towards the K-12 school system, and after that to work as a college administrator. I worked as an elementary school counselor for three years in the progressive school system of Amherst, Massachusetts, where I learned that while I could function in a bureaucracy, I was also constricted by rules, regulations, and policies. On the positive side, I liked the flexibility of my role, where I could develop and implement new approaches in working with students, teachers, parents, and administrators.

As I pursued graduate degrees, I kept the idea of being a consultant in the back of my mind. I had come across a few consultants in my work in education and the idea of calling the shots appealed to me. I later realized that I was a bit naïve in thinking that this role would give me a great deal of control. Ultimately, I was accountable to clients and forced to deal with the inevitability of unpredictable cash flow. I knew that further schooling would give me more choices in the type of work available to me.

Career Development as a Focus

Work in the career development field evolved from my time in graduate school and built on my foundation as a school counselor. As a graduate student hungry for both cash and experience, I welcomed the opportunity to run seminars for women who were returning to the workforce at the Continuing Education Center of Florida State University. I was fascinated by the resilience and possibilities of this work and even wrote my dissertation on how women in these circumstances moved through transition.

Under the tutelage of a professor with an organizational development background, I was introduced to group process and facilitation skills and found that I loved the work. The power, shared insights and support in-group dynamics was gratifying. I also found that I was energized when I could relate to the issues or life circumstances with which individuals were struggling. For instance, during this time, I was beginning to grapple with dual career issues myself and developed workshops to help other couples address some of the inherent questions such as "whose career do you move for?"

I loved the tangible nature of career counseling versus the abstract and slower process of what I knew about clinical work. I could see people take steps forward. I also was fortunate to connect with some pioneers in career development such as Dr. Robert Reardon, from whom I learned about the history and theory in this growing field. Both the group process and career counseling competencies I continued to learn were foundation skills for me.

I went on to eventually take the helm of a large university career center in Ohio. An equally busy role as mother of two toddlers in a dual career marriage and a need for more flexibility propelled my exit. I also knew that I wasn't expressing my creative side by becoming more heavily steeped in administration. I

relished designing and implementing innovative programs while also providing direct counseling and training services to individuals. I believed that there had to be a way to make a living performing meaningful career development work.

I could see that to do my job of managing over 30 people, meeting with recruiters after work, and leading our department forward, I needed to be more committed to long hours and life at the office. I knew then that I still wanted to express myself through work but that I wanted to be the one to have more of a say as to what those hours were and how they were spent.

Owning A Business, Act I

To pursue an emerging need to run my own show, I began a career consulting firm in Cincinnati, Ohio. However, I didn't just dive into an empty pool. For a period of over two years, I kept a notebook full of ideas, researched possibilities, and evaluated the risk with my spouse, friends, colleagues and family. I spoke with key company prospects and was selected for a leadership program in our local chamber of commerce. This helped me widen my network in the larger community, upon which I established an informal "board of directors," made up of finance, marketing, and legal professionals.

I then developed a comprehensive business plan and capitalized on a niche that the market was not addressing: spouse relocation programs for dual career couples that local companies were recruiting. Giving up a paycheck and benefits was both exciting and scary for me.

Kahnweiler Associates was born and grew. I hired employees, took new office space, and secured some outstanding contracts. It was a rollercoaster ride, and the firm had its ups and downs over a period of four years. The whole time, I remember feeling that part of the thrill was that I was steering the course. There is no feeling in work that replicates that. Four years later I sold the business and prepared to relocate to support my spouse in his career transition and new opportunity.

Owning A Business, Act II

In my new home of Atlanta, Georgia, the next six years were spent as an independent consultant working in government and industry. I participated in many downsizing projects, where I learned a great deal about a variety of organizational cultures and industries. Through many presentations, I honed my training skills. I also was fortunate to recalibrate my work and be able to participate in school volunteer activities with our daughters. I concentrated on integrating my work and family life. After playing many different roles and saying "no" to travel, my spouse and I assessed our positions and felt that because his job now had more flexibility and our daughters could take on more responsibility, that the time was right for me to enter a more fulltime organizational role. To round out my background, I needed to experience the world of organizations from an internal view.

The Corporate World

I mentioned earlier that when growing up, organizations felt like foreign entities. It was important for me to venture into this land of paychecks, office politics and a totally new lingo (I always like a challenge!). I accepted a terrific opportunity in training and development with General Electric (GE). After years in the world of education, government and on the outside looking in, it felt strange and oddly satisfying to be one of "them." The interesting thing was that I always maintained the psyche of an entrepreneur. I knew I would be all right even if (as happened twice) my jobs disappeared. As my family legacy had taught me so well, with hard work and drive I could make a living on my own. I always felt like this mindset was oddly liberating and gave legs to the mantra that was often shared with employees, "You, not the organization, are responsible for your career."

My time working inside the most highly valued company in the world helped me to broaden the scope and depth of knowledge in such areas as coaching, leadership development, change management, and organizational development. In the over four years that I worked for GE, I was in continual boot camp. This experience, more than any other, prepared me for future work as a career consultant. I was also able to bring credibility to my future work with a cross section of business professionals by understanding their language, how they are measured, and their key issues and motivators. While I would never be chief financial officer (CFO), I simply understood the world of business better.

Owning a Business, Act III

After a few short stints with human resource (HR) consulting firms and as a manager of employee development in a utility company, I was ready to venture out again. In 2000, I started About YOU, Inc., my current company. It is a firm specializing in providing career management expertise to individuals, organizations and the media. The variety and richness of the work that I do is very gratifying from the standpoint of career satisfaction and income. I am able to engage in career coaching, training and facilitation, writing and speaking. Using technology, such as a maximized website and email for communication with clients, has resulted

in increased revenues. Specialization in areas such as human resources, addiction recovery, and working with executives has kept me fresh. I hope to continue to guide the firm into new areas of discovery.

In addition to looking at experience, it is important to understand how self-knowledge can contribute to entrepreneurial success. Let's briefly review a framework of career success.

The Career Success Model

In the book I wrote with Bill Kahnweiler, called *Shaping your HR role: Succeeding in today's organizations* (Elsevier, 2005), we offer a model of career success that incorporates three key elements: achieving results, gaining knowledge, and applying knowledge.

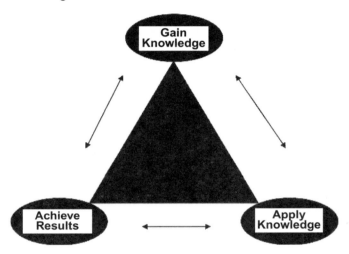

There are three elements of knowledge to gain: (a) self, (b) organization and (c) field.

In order to achieve results in your career it is necessary to first *understand yourself.* How do you know elements that go into the sum of who you are in the career world? What are your work and life experiences, your core skills, traits, values, and key likes and dislikes? It is only with this ongoing insight into yourself that you can make career choices that are in alignment with your needs. As you grow in your business, it is equally important to do a regular checkup on where you stand regarding this self-knowledge. As career counselors and consultants we need to practice what we preach!

Knowledge of the organization here refers to understanding the elements of running a successful career-consulting firm. Knowing how to manage the financial, marketing and sales, operations and administration, human resource, and general management processes (Strong and MBTI Entrepreneur Report, 2005), and knowing where you need to ask for support and guidance in these arenas are also critical and are addressed in other chapters of this monograph. In addition, *knowledge of the field* is key if one is to succeed. This includes knowledge of all aspects of the career development cycle from assessment to career decision-making to job search. It also involves specialty areas such as working with special populations (e.g., college graduates, career changers, senior executives, and retirees). Knowledge of current and future workforce trends, keeping up with business and industry developments on local, national and international fronts, and enhancing your technological skills are also critical in making you a more valuable asset to your clients.

The Career Success Model provides a clear framework for clarifying what areas you need to research and assess when considering a move into owning and operating a business. I have shared some of my career history and the factors in my personal and work life that I believe influenced me. I believe we learn through the stories of others. If my story has been even somewhat helpful to an aspiring entrepreneur, I am grateful. There is no one right way to do this. Owning a business of this kind is both art and science. There is a tremendous amount of creativity, variety, and unpredictability in the journey. At the same time, there are does and don'ts that can help prevent one from stepping onto some landmines. In this next section, I will reflect upon what key entrepreneurial skills, traits, and values I think have helped me achieve success in this role.

Skills

Skills such as marketing, operation, finance and human resources are often cited as necessary to run a business (Guide to the Strong and MBTI entrepreneur report, 1994). As I reflect on my different business ownership experiences, the skills I have found most helpful are marketing and public relations, counseling and facilitation, and networking.

Marketing and Public Relations

Wearing a marketing hat means that when I am delivering services, I am thinking about additional opportunities and needs that clients have. When I ran a spousal relocation program to help dual career partners find positions, I noted that they also needed assistance with other services. I expanded my line of offerings to provide tours and educational counseling in order to meet corporate clients' needs. Public relations have also been fun and a challenge for me. I figured out early on that it made more sense to get positioned as an expert than to pay for advertising space. I have seen many fruitful results throughout the years and gained a national media presence by pitching ideas to reporters and by being able to quickly and effectively respond to their needs.

Counseling and Facilitation

Through the foundation of my graduate studies in counseling and work experience in career counseling, I have tried to offer value to my clients by helping them discover the work they love to do and develop strategies to get there. I apply career development knowledge and a myriad of approaches to achieve results. Facilitation has been a skill that I developed through the years as I have led team meetings, retreats, and in more recent years, seminars for executives. The skill I am most proud of and that came from my experience on the front lines of companies is being able to handle resistance from participants.

When uncomfortable issues would arise in a group setting, I used to be concerned and anxious because I wasn't quite sure how to handle them. I realized that it was often essential to listen to these issues. Other consultants taught me tools to help bring negativity and frustration to the surface, and support people so they can move forward. In the setting of the classroom and counseling office, it is a continual learning process for me and one in which I must constantly be aware of my own feelings and attitudes in order to be effective. I feel that I do some of my best work when I am confronted with some of these more challenging scenarios.

Networking

Networking is the ability to build relationships for mutual gain. In my role as a career professional, I have always considered it to be essential to cultivate a dynamic and varied network of individuals. There have been many opportunities for me to learn from and lean on people for information, knowledge, and contacts. Likewise, I have found it gratifying to serve as a resource for others as they have challenges and problems to solve.

I have tried to be more strategic than haphazard in my networking. For example, rather than attend numerous networking events, I am selective about which events I attend and I follow up with pertinent people. I nurture relationships where I receive mutual gain and invest in those people who have strengths that I respect, who are connected, and who are willing to assist me. I also try to look for what I can learn from new people I meet. What type of work do they do? What are the current issues in their business or organization? Where do they see the opportunities for growth? The answers to these questions, whether drawn from an airplane seatmate or from a neighbor at a holiday party, all become part of my value as a career professional.

Every so often, I review my goals and see where I might have some holes in my network. For instance, several years ago, I was traveling frequently and I decided I needed to connect with some local professional women. I got involved in an executive women's group, joined the board and have built some strong connections from this move which ultimately have led to greater visibility and a number of business referrals.

The skills of marketing, public relations, sales, counseling, facilitation, and networking have been critical to me in growing my business ventures. The next section looks at how personality traits have come into the mix.

Personality Traits

Personality traits can be thought of as the style in which we perform skills. I have always found the Meyers Briggs Type Indicator (MBTI) to be the single best tool for use in understanding my traits and those of others. I will make the assumption that most readers are familiar with this tool. It is slightly amusing to me to learn how many of my colleagues, in the business of career consulting, possess the ENFP (extroverted, intuitive, feeling, perceiving) type. While I believe there is no one best type to fit the entrepreneurial profile, the preferences of the ENFP are well suited to this career. There are also challenges in realizing my goals if I neglect to attend to my auxiliary or nondominant preferences.

As Tieger and Tieger say in their excellent book, *Do what you are* (1995):

ENFP's are born entrepreneurs! They enjoy working for themselves because it gives them the freedom and flexibility, and the opportunity to choose the projects they wish to work on and the people they want to work with. They usually have an abundance of ideas that they want to see turned into reality, particularly those that will affect other people (p.143).

The Extroverted (E) side of me draws my energy from other people and outside stimuli and helps me to move from person to person, project to project and thrive on interaction. The Introverted (I) side of me is also important to use when I am engaging in writing and project planning.

I use my Intuitive (N) side daily in coming up with new ideas for my business through brainstorming career possibilities and options with clients. In my training seminars, I am constantly calling on my Intuitive side to convey concepts and help participants in connecting the dots. However, I call on my Sensing (S) side often when I am involved in accounting and office practices. I also need to use this side when dealing with clients who have Sensing preferences. I can only make headway with them if I try to see how they

are viewing our work and can translate my sometimes more abstract ideas into concrete, pragmatic points.

The Feeling (F) side helps me to tune into the relationships I develop with clients. I am driven to help people, and I obtain a great deal of satisfaction from using this preference. It also helps me attend to group process and dynamics, in addition to the goals and objectives, of a training class. Having a strong Feeling preference is a key driver for keeping me engaged and stimulated in the often ambiguous, business of helping people.

At the same time, I have learned to step over onto the Thinking (T) side as I plan for my business, work with my Thinking clients and create persuasive arguments with clients who approach life more logically than I might. I can present a business case with data, causes, and consequences, particularly when I am seeking to win new business. In my first stint in business, I expanded too quickly and found myself in a cash flow crisis. I would have benefited from taking Tieger and Tieger's advice to "focus your energy and attention on what really is in front of you rather than just what might be" (p. 146).

The Perceiving (P) function allows me to be spontaneous and maintain an openness to free flowing ideas. I am very resilient and actually thrive on most change (as opposed to chaos). Playing a variety of roles and working with numerous clients and individuals suit this flexible side. When clients have to change appointment times, I am not thrown into a tizzy. The Perceiving side of me allows new creative ideas to bubble up. This creativity (mentioned earlier in my family upbringing) is so helpful when supporting people in finding the work they love to do and in reaching their goals. Career counseling is seldom a linear path and the openness to let clients' journeys unfold according to their place and time is essential. In my writing, I find the possibilities are limitless when conceiving new ideas.

The Judging (J) side is also important for me. I have had to continually impose self-discipline in getting things done. The idea of closure and being on time for things are traits that are important in any role. They, like all nondominant personality traits, need to be consciously applied.

I have found that any career success I have had has occurred because I have used the different sides of my personality as the situation demands. In addition, values that fit with the role of entrepreneur have been extremely important. The next section focuses on how my key values are realized in my career.

Values

Values are the motivators that determine how you achieve satisfaction at work and at home (Kahnweiler

& Kahnweiler, 2005). Living by your values allows you to maximize your performance, job satisfaction, and emotional investment in your work. I have found that, like most people, my values have shifted over time. When I started on my entrepreneurial path, I was focused on achievement, recognition and independence. I was very highly driven and enjoyed moving up the ladder. I liked growing a successful business. I downshifted when I realized that my focus on work, while gratifying, was pulling me away from my young children.

The next value I had to find ways to incorporate was work life balance, so I put myself in an independent consulting situation that allowed me more flexibility. As I grew more confident in my work as a consultant, I found that creativity was a key drive for me. Coming up with innovative programs and stretching myself in new ways allowed me to tap into internal creative sources that I didn't know that I had. My move into writing a book and columns for national magazines and websites is one example of how this creative value has manifested itself.

One value that has emerged for me in recent years is contributing to the greater good. As my children have "left the nest" and become young adults, I have turned my attention to causes that mean a great deal to me, such as encouraging young women to pursue career options, developing women leaders, teaching English to recent immigrants, and contributing to professional associations. I also monitor my involvement so that I can reserve personal time to have fun, exercise, and spend relaxed time with my family. Spending quality time with my family is an important value for me, as is self-care. I have learned that I am a much more effective helping professional, business owner, spouse, and mother if I can take care of my own needs.

Conclusion

In this chapter, I have shared some personal history, experiences, character traits, skills, and personal values that have influenced my career path. In the spirit of my own self-assessment, I have shared the influences on my unique journey. I hope that even a fraction of this has been useful to you and allows you to achieve your desired results as a career entrepreneur.

References

Brody, B. (2006, January 16). From new kid on the job to tribal elder, *Newsweek*. Retrieved September 2, 2006: http://www.msnbc.msn.com/id/10753447/site/newsweek/.

Gerber, M. (1995, 2001). *The e-myth revisited: Why most small businesses don't work and what to do about it.* New York, NY: HarperCollins Publishers, p.2.

Hammer, A.L. (2001: March 19). Strong and MBTI entrepreneur report sample prepared for Pat Michaels *Consulting Psychologist Press*. Retrieved September 2, 2006: http://www.cpp.com.

Myers Briggs Type Indicator (MBTI). Retrieved September 2, 2006: http://www.en.wikipedia.org/wiki/Myers-Briggs_Type_Indicator.

Kahnweiler, W. & Kahnweiler, J. (2005). *Shaping your HR role: Succeeding in today's organizations.* Elsevier. http://www.elsevier.com.

Tieger, B.B. and Tieger, P. (1998). *Do what you are: Discover the perfect career for you through the secrets of personality type.* Boston, MA: Little Brown & Company.

Carolyn Kalil

Entrepreneurial Strengths

I was a very unlikely candidate to have a successful career development business, or a business of any kind for that matter. I lacked knowledge, experience, and even interest in running a business until recently. The first 30 years of my work experience has been in the educational field. I assumed that's where I would be until I retired. But when I discovered who I really am and what I am naturally good at, it gave me the courage to work independently of my job. I learned what I was passionate about and built my business around my strengths.

I am certain this is the key to others' success as well. No one has to know everything or do everything well to have a thriving business. I don't believe there is total truth in the cliché, "if I can do it, you can do it." You can't necessarily do something just because I can. But I am sure that if you do what you do well, and find others to assist you in areas where you have challenges, you can be successful. In other words, you can do it, if you lead with your own particular strengths.

Without the benefit of having a career counselor, I stumbled into an elementary teaching major and taught 5th grade immediately after finishing college. I didn't know why, but I instantly knew it wasn't a good fit for me. If I had understood better myself and my strengths, I would have known why I was in the wrong job. I grew up very mature for my age and always gravitated towards adults rather than playing with other children. I figured out that I preferred to work with adults and, therefore, belonged in higher education. After two years, I left the profession and went to graduate school and earned a master's degree in Counseling.

A year after my first counseling job at UCLA, I landed a counseling position at a community college in Southern California. This was really my dream job and an ideal career at the time. It was where I had the opportunity to truly use my counseling skills with the students who needed them most. Not only was I doing what I loved, but it was an enviable job in many ways. My hours were flexible. I felt very accepted and appreciated by my colleagues and others at the college. I had a great salary with generous benefits and an aesthetically pleasing working environment. What more could I ask for?

I was actually very content with my work for the first 10 years. Then I began revisiting old questions about "Who am I?" and "What is my real purpose in life?" I knew I would never be truly satisfied until I answered these questions. This pursuit led me on a journey of self-discovery and ultimately to starting my own business. It didn't happen immediately, but over a period of several years of reading books, taking classes and workshops, consulting others, and trying different avenues, I found the answers I had been actively seeking. All this occurred simultaneously while performing in my roles as a mother, wife, and full-time employee. Yet, at the same time, these experiences were extremely rewarding because intuitively I knew my search would eventually take me where I needed to go.

Mentors and Their Books

Mentors are invaluable resources that can save you from making costly mistakes as well as shorten your learning curve by many years. I have had far too many who have assisted me on my journey to mention in these few pages, but I shall name a few. Some I've met and others have no idea how life changing their influence on me has been.

I remember reading Marsha Senetar's book, *Do what you love and the money will follow,* back in the 1980's. I asked myself, "Am I doing what I love?" The answer was "Yes." But there was more that I wanted to do. I can't say that I was able to figure out what the "more" was from reading her book, but it was clear that my present work couldn't provide me with all of what I needed and wanted.

Are you doing what you love? If the answer is yes, maybe this chapter will not provide much new insight. But if you are either unhappy with your work or, like me, feel a need to do more than you are currently doing, I believe it is no accident that you're reading this chapter.

I especially loved reading nonfiction books for inspiration. Two, in particular, were extremely beneficial. Richard Bolles's 2005 edition of *What Color Is Your Parachute?* is one of those books. Before I began to write my own books, I would read over and over in the Epilogue of his early editions, a section called "How to Find Your Mission in Life." He stated that our third mission here on earth is to "exercise that talent which you particularly came to earth to use – your greatest gift, which you most delight to use." This powerful quote still has deep meaning to me today. He also said that career counselors will be the spiritual teachers of the future. I really related to this because I saw my work leading people to much more than a job or career. For me, it was more of a means of helping others fulfill their life purpose through their work.

Another book that gave me great inspiration and understanding of how to fulfill my dreams is *The Seven Spiritual Laws of Success,* by Deepak Chopra, a medical doctor from India. He discusses how we can consciously change our world and cause things to manifest through our attention and intention. Our intentions can create whatever we desire. Today I still use these concepts to keep me focused on creating my desires. I encourage you to do the same.

Dick Knowdell, founder of the International Career Development Conference, is another one of my mentors. I have spoken at his conference several times and worked on his conference planning committee. I also attended his Job and Career Transition Coach (JCTC) Certification Training. He became a role model because he showed us how to make a living as an entrepreneur in the career development field. I learned from him how I could offer my services to career counselors, coaches and others who assisted job seekers.

Turning Point and True Colors

The turning point in my life happened in 1988 when I took a position at my college as coordinator of our career center. I was using the Myers-Briggs Type Indicator (MBTI) and David Keirsey's Temperament Sorter as personality assessments at the time that I decided to attend my first Myers-Briggs Conference. It was there that I became familiar with a personality assessment called True Colors. Don Lowry, the founder, and the True Colors team became my ultimate mentors in teaching me temperament theory and True Colors. I became one of the first trainers for the program and introduced the system to my college. It wasn't long before we were all speaking in color language. The simplicity of this system really resonated with our students at the college. It soon became a popular and fun way to understand and apply who they were to career decision-making.

True Colors had a huge impact on me personally as well. As a result of using it, my life took a totally different direction. For the first time, I felt that I truly understood who I am. This happened in spite of the fact that I had majored in counseling in graduate school and had worked as a counselor for 14 years. I learned things about myself that I never knew, and I began to see my own strengths on a broader scale. I could see that I was more than just a counselor. My communication skills were really a natural talent that I had excelled at my whole life.

This insight gave me the courage to do something that I had only dreamed of – write a book. Without any formal training or previous writing attempts, I sat down and wrote. The book became my first publication, in the form of a workbook for students in the career planning classes that I taught on my campus. It was so well received that I got the idea to write a book for the general population. My book, *Follow your true colors to the work you love,* was published in 1988. It has made several best sellers lists for career books. Since then, I have written workbooks on the same topic for adults and youth. My book and workbooks are used in many high schools, colleges, and universities, and are sold in major bookstores. This was the beginning of my process of building a business around my strengths.

In addition to writing books, I had to think about how I wanted to use my strengths. Communication for me is not just about delivering information. I am passionate about inspiring others to be the best they can be. The key to the services that I would offer was to think of all the ways I could use my communication skills to inspire others. My business includes publishing, speaking, conducting workshops, providing certification training for professionals, and maintaining a website with a free personality assessment, as well as information about services and products. Today, I truly feel that I get paid to be who I am and do what I love.

You may be thinking, "This is all well and good for Carolyn, but how do I start my own business?" Exercise 6 in Appendix A can assist you in building your own career development business based on your entrepreneurial strengths. You are your best asset. The more you invest in learning about yourself and how to capitalize on your strengths, the more rewarding your business will be.

References

Bolles, R.N. (2005). *What color is your parachute?* Berkeley, CA: Ten Speed Press.

Chopra, D. (1994). *The seven spiritual laws of success: A practical guide to the fulfillment of your dreams.* Novato, CA: New World Library.

Kalil, C. (1998). *Follow your true colors to the work you love.* Retrieved September 2, 2006: http://www.truecolorscareer.com.

Keirsey, D. & Bates, M. (1978). *Please understand me: Character & temperament types.* Retrieved September 2, 2006: http://www.keirsey.com.

Senetar, M. (1987). *Do what you love, the money will follow: Discovering your right livelihood.* New York, N.Y.: Dell Publishing.

Tieger, P. D. & Barron-Tieger, B. (1992). *Do what you are: Discover the perfect career for you through the secrets of personality types.* New York: Self published.

True Colors free personality assessment. Retrieved September 2, 2006: http://www.truecolorscareer.com.

III. What are your business vision and mission?

Best-selling career author Richard Bolles suggests that you not only find something that you are passionate about, but also something that the world needs and desires. What is your unique vision and what unique contributions have you made or are you making in the development of your business? What did you do to implement your vision? What need of society have you tapped or do you think is waiting to be tapped? How have you contributed your unique gifts to fill a need or desire of society? Who are your mentors? Marcia Bench and Donna Christner-Lile share their stories, tips, and Exercises 7 and 8 in Appendix A to help you identify your business vision and mission.

Marcia Bench, J.D.

Entering the Career Development Industry

When I began work in the career development industry in 1986, research showed that 75% to 90% of people did not enjoy their work. My mission and vision was, and continues to be, to influence as many people as possible to do the work they love, including to help them clarify and implement the steps to get there. I have spoken, written, taught, trained, consulted and coached around the world toward that end. I have personally witnessed the transformation of individual clients, seminar participants, and others as they discover the work that will inspire them, and begin to do it.

How My Business Evolved

Interestingly, after 20 years of work in this wonderful field, speaking to tens of thousands of people, appearing in media, writing books and founding several companies, the statistics still haven't changed! Studies today still show that 75% to 90% of people don't enjoy their work. Maybe they are different people now, and certainly the pressures of the information age and modern life have intensified and perhaps led to more reasons for dissatisfaction, or even caused fulfillment to elude more of us. But regardless of the causes, there is still a lot of work for me and others to do to change these statistics!

Since I began my work, I have believed strongly that the key to fulfillment at work is identifying and fulfilling one's life purpose through work as well through one's life roles. In the 1980's, this notion was perceived as somewhat heretical, since most career professionals used skills assessments as the basis for their work with clients and, as a rule, did not consider overall life purpose in the mix. However, I chose to follow my heart and my own personal experience (good advice for the new or prospective entrepreneur too!) and continue to build my work around that notion. Writers such

as Marsha Sinetar and Nancy Anderson certainly influenced me in those early days, as they were conveying a similar message in their work. I later developed the Authentic Vocation Model of Career Design, which uses life purpose as its foundation.

Authentic Vocation Model

Part of the contribution I believe I make to the profession is to fill the gap with mid-career professionals who already know their skills and have indeed honed them over 5, 10, 20, or more years of work experience, but are at that point where competency isn't enough. They want to do "something different," but they aren't sure what it is. The Authentic Vocation Model helps them find that "something," and begin to move in that direction. I have also incorporated this notion into our Authentic Retirement Model for those who are approaching retirement and who want to design that stage of their life in a unique way that will be a perfect fit for them.

As the workplace and the career development industry have evolved over the years since I began my work, the coaching industry has emerged. One thing that nearly every coach (whether career coach or other specialty coach) addresses with clients at one time or another is life purpose. There are now an estimated 40,000 coaches in practice worldwide, with many other professionals incorporating coaching into jobs in human resources, career counseling, consulting, managing, recruiting, and related fields. Perhaps the notion, originally held by career coaches and counselors, of life purpose as a foundation for fulfillment, was just ahead of its time.

Often, it seems for midlife professionals (which may include many readers of this book) the expression of one's purpose at work means combining two seemingly unrelated parts of oneself in a new way. It may be a primary skill from one's job plus a hobby, or two disparate skills. In my own case, in my youth and throughout college, I felt as though there were two parts of me: the creative me that wrote stories, music and poetry and aspired to be an artist, and the business/analytical me that did exceptionally well in school, was very organized, and loved left brain activities. From the time I was 13, I was on a quest to find my purpose. And it was not until I discovered it in my late 20s that I could finally combine the seemingly separate parts of myself into one profession: self-employed consulting (and later, coaching). I expressed my creativity in the marketing pieces I wrote and in developing ideas for new classes and articles, and I used my analytical side in keeping the account books, writing the business plan, and developing business systems. A perfect match!

Career Coach Institute

That integration continues in my current work directing the Career Coach Institute, which trains and certifies career coaches worldwide. I have developed most of the course content, conceived innovative delivery methods such as blended learning and online e-modules, and learned and put into practice just enough about web site design to be dangerous (I now know to use experts on such projects!). Both analytical and creative tasks are involved in nearly any business. The new entrepreneurs need to surround themselves with support staff; for example, virtual assistants, and/or other professional staff that have strengths that compliment theirs. So if, for example, your strength is graphic arts and design, you may need a bookkeeper and/or technical writer whose strengths lie in the areas that are weaker for you.

Founding my businesses resulted from an "aha!" moment, or what I would now call a QuantumShift! moment. My consulting business resulted from literally being awoken in the middle of the night, shortly after starting my first attorney job after law school, and instantly having the idea for a new class I would teach for which I would write the text. I proposed that class to the local community college community education department, they accepted it, and my business was launched.

The Career Coach Institute developed through a somewhat similar process. Frustration with a current situation led to months of introspection. I was working in a "day job" I disliked, studying coaching at night, and trying to figure out what to do next. I thought I would need to leave the career development field, since nothing seemed to challenge me any more. When coming home from Thanksgiving weekend, driving through the Arizona desert with my husband, I was working on topics for teleclasses I would be teaching to earn my certification as a teleclass leader. Suddenly, it struck me: I could combine my then 15 years of experience in career development with the coaching skills I had been learning and teach people how to be "career coaches." It has been the most fun, rewarding, and lucrative career I have had so far. And I have had a chance to impact thousands of people in many countries to help them learn coaching, so that they could in turn inspire others to do the work they love. So it's back full circle to my mission: help people do the work they love.

Conclusion

To implement each of these businesses in start-up as well as development, I have sought out leaders in the industry, the best of the best, as my mentors. I encourage you to do the same, and to never stop learning and growing. I have found business ownership to be almost a spiritual path, one with ebbs and flows, ups and downs, but far more rewards than, for me, any corporate job could ever provide. I like being in charge of my destiny, and not having constraints of organizational politics, budgets, or procedures to slow me down. If you feel the same, perhaps your own business is the path for you to pursue too. If I can support you, feel free to email me at marcia@careercoachinstitute.com. I wish you well.

Resources

Print

Bench, M. (2001). The authentic vocation model of career design. *Career coaching: An insider's guide*. Mountainview, CA: (Davies-Black Publishing).

Bench, M. (2003). *Career coaching: An insider's guide*. Mountainview, CA: Davies-Black Publishing.

Bench, M. (2003). *Launch your practice*. Lake Havasu City, AZ: High-Flight Press.

Bench, M. (2003). *Discover your niche*. Lake Havasu City, AZ: High-Flight Press.

Bench, M. (2003). *Fill your practice*. Lake Havasu City, AZ: High-Flight Press.

Web

Career coach training and certification: Career Coach Institute. Retrieved September 2, 2006: http://www.careercoachinstitute.com.

Retirement coach training and certification: Retirement Coach Institute. Retrieved September 2, 2006: http://www.retirementcoachinstitute.com.

Donna Christner-Lile

What Is My Unique Vision?

I have the vision that my company model will be a common place for older adults to age either in their home or close to children. I call this way of living "Aging in Place." In this vision, the network of private and social services will be readily available to help older adults remain safe in their homes. My company will give outstanding transitional counseling service to assist older adults and caregivers at home or close to children. There will be no older adults living in unsafe homes with deferred maintenance, clutter, or electrical and structural hazards. I see them having access to funds and assistance to facilitate needed repairs or changes. Support services for their ever changing emotional, physical and social needs will be met.

What did I do to implement my vision?

I began a 20-year real estate career out of the need to provide for my family. Being a single mother at the time, I felt that the property market would be a satisfying and stable job option, even though I had earned an undergraduate degree in human behavior.

In 1994, after establishing a successful brokerage company, I felt burned out with my career choice. My son left for college and I started to question what I really wanted out of life. I knew that I needed a change and decided to go back to college for my master's degree in counseling psychology. As a counseling psychology graduate student, I co-facilitated caregiver support groups at the University of California, San Francisco (UCSF) for the university's employee assistance program. I quickly learned from the participants about the stress felt by caregivers. My counseling internship was done with Senior Peer Counseling at Human Services in Fremont, California.

After I earned my masters degree in counseling, I continued to work for Human Services. As a counselor, I followed up on referrals from the social workers of individuals in need of emotional support, and assessed the need for a higher level of intervention. I visited with the older adults in their homes and worked with them. I linked them with other city services available to help meet the transitional challenges they were having. Often I would make a referral to Friendly Visitors or the Senior Center for additional social support. Frequently, I would listen and work with older adults' issues on adjustment to aging, and other life circumstances. I was trained to watch for signs of needs not being met. During that time, I passed the National Certified Counselor (NCC) exam. Under supervision, I opened my own practice in 2000, and earned my NCC credentials in 2002. My practice focused on the transitional issues of elders and mid-life adults. Many times I provided caregiver support groups and mid-life support groups as a free service to the community.

Shortly after I started my practice, I became a part-time caregiver for my now 93-year old mother for five years. The experience of caring for an elder adult six months of the year for five years was a defining moment in the understanding the needs of older adults.

During the course of the next few years, the "Golden State" became flooded with counseling professionals while the real estate market boomed. I felt it would be best for me and for my clients if I combined my two careers. While working as a real estate agent, I realized that my clients needed more direction and information than I could provide. They were making major life decisions and reaching out for assistance and guidance. I focused my attention on counseling seniors in life transitions that pertain to their estate.

Since I have experience in real estate and mortgage lending, as well as counseling, I can make suggestions for older adults that the average counselor cannot make. I observed many older adults prematurely sell their homes because they didn't know how to adapt their homes to their current needs. With my past career knowledge and my new career experience and education, I formed a nonprofit counseling practice to assist older adults to safely and successfully age at home or near children. In practice, I also advise and work with caregivers. With the aging of America, boomers are now asking for advice on preparing for their future housing needs as they move toward older adulthood. My company has put choice back into the hands of the consumer, rather than the system.

What need of society have I tapped or think is waiting to be tapped by career professionals?

It is a challenge to meet older adults' needs of services, repairs, medications, and financial resources. In my experience in human services, I found that older adult clients often need more medication than their income will pay for. Often the client's home has deferred maintenance due to the tasks of finding and trusting good repair workers and of financing the repairs. Many times the home has become a cluttered firetrap. At times, the client is reluctant to move to a safer environment because of what feels like the overwhelming task of finding an acceptable and affordable living environment. It's unfortunate that, due to the fraudulent activities of a few service professionals, the help of financing, moving, organizing, or selling an older adult's home is an area that most human services professionals don't want to get into.

How have I contributed my unique gifts to fill a need or desire of society?

My knowledge and education from two careers has prepared me to meet these needs of older adults. I am the only Nationally Certified Counselor in the nation who also has experience in real estate and mortgage lending. By developing my own nonprofit organization, I can help older adults "age in place" in my local area. In time, I will develop a curriculum for professional counselors as well as internships to help counselors-in-training learn the human service skills, as well as learn how to access resources for helping midlife and older adults.

Having gone through some of those life changes myself, it seems like it has all come back together for me in a very worthwhile way. This has brought everything I knew and all my skills together. I can counsel and help these people. I can lead them in other directions other than what an ordinary realtor might suggest. I can look at the whole picture and help direct them to the resources they need to make the right choice for them and their family.

I often suggest to my clients that they should also consider advice from an estate planner, certified public accountant (CPA) and their family or support system. If necessary, I also contact the family members to get their input on the situation. As with any counseling relationship, I assess the situation of my client. I consider their mental and physical capacity and who can be their advocate in helping to make these decisions.

I work with them and present options, such as assisted or independent living facilities. Their need level will determine where they can go and should go. It's a very difficult decision to leave your home after you have been there 30 or more years. These people are overwhelmed and sad. They have built a lifetime of memories there. Often, they are left alone with all these wonderful memories residing in the home.

One of my clients is a recent widow and is determined to leave the home in order to avoid the memories. With her loss being so recent, she feels she can escape some of the pain by selling the home. My advice to her was to walk with caution — whenever you are making a decision that big within the first two years of the grieving cycle, you just need to be careful so you don't regret the choice.

I advise my clients and all seniors to stay in their homes for as long as they possibly can, safely, because that is where their happiness has been in their lives. But if it is unsafe or they are unable to do so, then we try to point out other possible options.

In some instances, a reverse mortgage is one way for the senior to stay in the home, and it could possibly allow for enough money to pay for a live-in nurse or housekeeper. The AARP defines a reverse mortgage as a home loan that gives cash advances to the homeowner and requires no repayment until a future time, as long as the borrower lives there. The loan can be paid at once, as a regular monthly advance or at times and in amounts the homeowner designates. The borrower pays the money back plus interest when he or she sells the home.

Especially in the state of California, many of these aging individuals have large assets with their home but are extremely reluctant to tap into those resources. Older generations grew up on the notion that they are obligated to leave something to their children, mainly their house. They were taught that their legacy is embodied in the family home. It's difficult to change their mind on that. I have to explain it to them that these assets are to take care of them, and if taking care of them means staying in the home, then we can find a way to do that.

I educate my clients on the various city and agency-provided services such as Meals on Wheels, senior services peer groups and church affiliates. By allowing these people into the home on a regular basis, their adult children are more confident and relaxed knowing that others are assessing their loved one's needs. Staying in the home ultimately depends on the senior's health and safety, which is often determined by the adult children or others in their support system. Many times the care-giving individuals feel strained and exhausted from hyper-vigilance and the need to be with the senior all the time. They will be more inclined to allow for space and freedom if they know they can count on the senior to open his or her life to others who care.

Who were my mentors?

My primary mentors were my parents. Both of them provided and modeled the ethics and morality I live by. My father was self-employed. His experiences and modeling instilled in me the courage to take a risk and start a business of my own. He was energetic, moral, and fair. As a child, I observed both my parents helping those who could not help themselves. If there were a death, my mother would be there with food for the family. If there were financial problems, my father would loan money. If there were a fire, they would be there to help rebuild. If there were older adults with needs, they would visit and support them in any way they could. Respect for older adults was expected and

16

cherished in our household. Whatever the need, my parents were always there for their friends and neighbors. They loved their rural life: my father hunting and fishing, my mother crocheting, cooking, sewing, and being active in her church.

References

Kennedy, A. (2004: July). Leaving home: Counseling seniors during life transitions. *Counseling Today.* Alexandria, VA: American Counseling Association.

Mulder, D.. (2006: Fall). Moving Forward, *Thrivent Magazine*, 104, 640. Retrieved September 2, 2006: http://www.thrivent.com/magazine/fall06/starters.html.

IV. How can you grow your practice with purpose?

How do you check, on an ongoing basis, to see how your goals are coming along? Do you reward yourself when you reach a goal or overcome a roadblock? How do you keep yourself motivated during this process? Do you forgive yourself when you don't meet a timeline and continually rework your schedule so that it works for you? How do you stay ahead of the trends? What is your secret for creating training programs on topics of interest to career professionals? How do you solve time-related problems? Do you run several business endeavors simultaneously? If so, how do you keep each business enterprise organized and flowing? Perform Exercise 9 in Appendix A, developed by Ron Elsdon, on how you can grow your practice with purpose.

Ron Elsdon, Ph.D.

Getting Paid for Loving Work

One of my most satisfying early moments was writing that first check to a colleague working with us as a contractor. This is a bit surprising really, for isn't being an entrepreneur all about making your own money? Perhaps there is some conflict here. As members of a counseling profession, career counselors tend to almost the opposite extreme. We are reticent about our entrepreneurial aspirations, maybe fearing a slide down the slippery, material consumption slope. I recall being almost apologetic asking for payment. "I love this work; you're kidding me, we actually get paid for doing it?"

Purpose

Let's explore how to resolve this tension between business and purpose, and what resolution of this tension means for growing our practices. To be sure, we must be able to support ourselves if those practices are to come into being and prosper for our clients and customers. And we need to do this without losing our way. Consider an example of someone who has grown an $18 billion dollar operation. That person is Howard Schultz, the founder of Starbucks. He was interviewed by the Road Trip Nation crew and spoke thoughtfully and eloquently about heart and purpose in his life. Here are some words from his biography (quoted by Terry Pearce in *Leading Out Loud*):

Years later, that image of my father - slumped on the family couch, his leg in a cast, unable to work or earn money, and ground down by the world - is still burned into my mind. Looking back now, I have a lot of respect for my dad. He never finished high school, but he was an honest man who worked hard. The day he died of lung cancer, in January 1988, was the saddest of my life. He had no savings, no pension. More importantly, he had never attained the fulfillment and dignity from work he found meaningful. As a kid, I never had any idea that I would one day head a company. *But I knew in my heart that if I were ever in a position where I could make a difference, I wouldn't leave people behind.*

Here is Starbucks first guiding principle: "Provide a great work environment and treat each other with respect and dignity." Starbucks lives these values, for example, in its provision of healthcare coverage for employees. And the organization has far outperformed the major U.S. stock indices over the past few years. So there's hope for us. It is possible to hold to principles that respect people and still build a successful business. I recall a colleague, who is active in the franchising area, once saying to me, "There are two types of people who start businesses – those who do it to make money and don't care if it's a hamburger stand or a real estate venture, and those who do it for a purpose. I want the first group." This article is for those in the second group, those who create a practice for a purpose other than just making money

In this second group, wonderful transformations can occur, just as they do in the career development process for clients. When people connect with their work on a deep level, the possibilities of personal transformation and fulfillment are actualized. When we build our practices with purpose, this also happens. Let's look at what we mean by purpose and then explore ways to realize those exciting growth possibilities.

My wife and I have two practices: (a) Elsdon Organizational Renewal (EOR), focused on organizations as primary clients, and (b) New Beginnings Career and College Guidance (NBCCG), with individuals as clients. They are connected by a common theme, that of renewal and growth, whether as individuals or as organizations. The theme of emerging growth is evident in the names and logos of both practices. The mission statements for these practices are as follows:

- EOR: "We support organizations in enhancing performance, productivity and effectiveness through revitalized workforce relationships and leadership practice."

- NBCCG: "We provide caring and personalized

help to individuals, students and families in career guidance, coaching and college planning services."

Central to each is a focus on the relationship of individuals to organizations. This extends also to the broader community as expressed in these words from EOR's approach and values: "With a scope that ranges from system and organizational interventions to work with individuals, our focus is on the heart of the relationship among the individual, the organization and the community." At the heart of this approach is a belief that "organizational and community prosperity are built on enabling each person to fulfill his or her potential." This infuses both practices and it is supported by our research (Elsdon, 2003) showing career development tangibly benefiting organizations as well as individuals.

In our organizational work, we intentionally tailor our approach to each organization based on an understanding their fundamental needs. We develop a broad range of capabilities, rather than using a laundry list of services off the shelf. Again from EOR's approach and values: "We tailor our engagements to the needs of each organization with a process designed to surface critical issues, identify root causes, build effective solutions, monitor progress and implement." This highlights content depth as another core value that we bring to each engagement.

Our purpose is not to be the largest in the field, nor to offer the same services for every organization in every geographic region, nor to enable one party to prosper at the expense of another. Our purpose is to enhance individual fulfillment and organizational and community prosperity by strengthening the relationship of individuals to organizations. This infuses all of our work. For example, we develop and describe the concept of affiliation as a foundation in the relationship between individuals and organizations built on a two-way partnership.

We incorporate the concept of inclusion, whether internal, external, community or global, into our descriptions of healthy organizations and in the variety of individual clients we serve. Purpose guides the choices we make about which business opportunities to pursue, and therefore it guides our growth. Let's now explore this fascinating area of growth further.

Creating a Climate for Growth

In financial terms, the value of a business is determined by two primary attributes: growth and profitability. While they are not completely independent, we can examine them separately. For the purposes of this exploration, we focus mainly on one of the two aspects of value creation growth. Growth occurs because strategies are sound and executed well. Let's look at some aspects of this. First, what kind of environment do we need to foster business growth? Let me suggest that there are several aspects:

Being open to learning, to new ideas, to serendipity and responding rapidly to opportunities

Openness to learning and new ideas encourages experimentation, which is central to growing a practice. It is through such experimentation that new areas emerge, and it is the lack of such experimentation that often hampers the ability of large, entrenched organizations to grow. Here is one area where the rapid response and flexibility possible in a small practice trumps the ponderous approach typical of larger organizations with disconnected senior management.

Being inclusive and welcoming different points of view

Growth often springs from the convergence of different points of view that result in the creation of something that was unanticipated. For example, the concept of building community around coffee shops in the U.S. as done by Starbucks, or the creation of a low-cost, efficient airline as done by Southwest, has sprung from this convergence. We too can find new approaches to serving our client and customer needs.

Creating a nurturing, trusting environment that values collaboration

Someone once said that new ideas are like new plants, you don't pull them up and look at their roots every few days to see how they are doing. Instead focus on building trust, well exemplified by Nordstroms' "Rule No. 1: Use your best judgment in all situations. There will be no additional rules."

Letting customers guide and support development

The best growth ideas invariably come from customers. In many cases they may be willing to support development of a new project for their use that can then be taken elsewhere (e.g., a workshop or system intervention). Our work in exit interviewing and demographic analysis sprang directly from a customer request. The challenge and opportunity is to listen well for customer needs.

Choosing the right time to grow

Choosing the right time means recognizing that there is a right time for acceptance of a particular approach that may be driven by a changing external environment or emerging capabilities. Today we are able to readily deploy survey approaches using on-line resources, often in conjunction with in-person contact, in ways that would have been very difficult 10 years ago. Frequently, technical advances converge so that a number of people see the opportunity at the same time. Be in the vanguard of that movement.

Avoiding applying old rules to new situations

I recall seeing an organization in the Human Resource arena try and force an organizational structure from its established (and declining) business into an emerging area with completely different needs. Not surprisingly the new effort quickly stalled. Different approaches, other than the traditional, would have been needed to address the emerging opportunity.

Building a Strategy for Growth

Having established a climate for growth, our next step is to build a strategy that can form the foundation for success. There are a number of aspects to this strategy. Following are some components:

What are the core differentiating aspects of your practice?

For example, in our case, it is a strong focus on customizing the process to specific needs, being highly flexible in structuring customer and client relationships, responding rapidly, and focusing on delivering more value than is promised.

What components should you include in the portfolio that constitutes your practice?

For example, does it include both work with individuals and organizations or just one or the other?

What types of customer are you seeking?

For a small practice it is not necessary to convert the entire world to the use of your services, it is simply necessary to find enough customers who value your services. For example, we focus on organizational customers who are supportive of their employees and who value partnership. We don't choose to work with organizations focused on price rather than on value, evident through such approaches as on-line auctions. Also critical is deciding what fraction of your time and resources to commit to one customer. It may be necessary to commit disproportionately to one customer in the early stages. Long-term sustainability requires diversifying your customer base. Set targets for this both in terms of the number of customers and sector breadth.

Skills You Need To Be Effective in Your Practice

One of the fascinating aspects of building a practice is the extent to which it draws on wide ranging skills. These include:

Content knowledge, such as proprietary expertise in analysis, approaches to building effective individual counseling relationships, and application and delivery of particular assessment approaches.

Consulting capability, or ways to effectively engage in conversations with clients and customers so that their needs are clearly expressed and understood, and you can build a bridge from these needs to the services you provide.

Effective selling, which is often a neglected area for those of us in the counseling community. This was a skill I needed to develop and the opportunity arose to learn much about consultative selling while with a large organization. Consider how you might do the same.

Financial and business acumen, which are important practical survival skills even though they may not be the most appealing area for many of us involved in the counseling, learning, or human resource consulting areas. Fortunately today there are excellent computer programs, such as QuickBooks Simple Start, that make some of the hands-on aspects readily accessible. There are also tools such as the One Page Business Plan that can make areas such as business planning more straightforward.

Marketing capability, that delineates how and with whom you make contact. This is another key survival skill. One of the most challenging aspects of building a practice for many in the counseling field is effective marketing. Just as we would advise a client about effective approaches to reaching prospective employers, so we need to decide how to reach prospective clients and customers. "Build it and they will come" does not usually work well. Resources such as the Small Business Administration (www.sba.gov) contain much valuable information and can help you make decisions about effective marketing, for example, whether it is through giving presentations, issuing a newsletter, advertising, or web outreach. Once you have established a foundation and reputation, then much business will come through referrals.

Allocation of your time. A key question facing most small practices is how to allocate time between delivering and marketing/selling. The neglect of either one at the expense of the other will expose the practice to short- or long-term risks. The balance is likely to shift over time with the marketing and selling component larger in the early stages of business growth. Also, decisions such as what work do you perform rather than outsource are important; for example, in web development or maintaining financial records.

Managing costs and determining fee structure. One key aspect of business success is managing your costs and building your fee structure so that your margins meet your financial needs. Be sure to conduct solid market research so that you know appropriate pricing levels that are neither too high to exclude you from key business, nor too low to provide sufficient returns. An effective process for tracking costs is central to maintaining business viability and guiding your decisions about allocating resources. Again, computer-based tools can make this process more straightforward.

Deciding on partners. You may find that engaging with partners can significantly expand your ability to provide services. These partners may connect with you on a contract basis to provide specific services, they may offer complementary services that are appealing to customers, or they may open doors to customers. The structure of each of these relationships will be different and it is important to think through options that may be open to you.

Giving how and to whom. One of the delights of building your own practice is the opportunity it affords for giving. This may be financial or it may be giving of your time, expertise, or knowledge. I well remember hearing Susan Packard Orr (the daughter of David Packard, one of the founders of Hewlett-Packard) commenting on how Hewlett-Packard was giving to philanthropic causes when it was first founded in a garage in Palo Alto.

We have adopted a similar approach with our practice. Meager as the financial contributions are, they reflect our thankfulness for all that we have been given. This might seem daunting, and I do wonder sometimes how it all comes together. But it does. These words from Kafka perhaps capture it best: "Just become still, quiet, and solitary, and the world will freely offer itself to you to be unmasked. It has no choice; it will roll in ecstasy at your feet." Here is where mentors can be so important. For me, mentors have included colleagues and friends who were kind enough to show me their expertise and give of their wisdom, customers who have been so supportive of a small practice, and family members whose constant support and presence make the journey possible and worthwhile. I wish you well on your exciting journey.

Print Resources

Brennan, A. & Brewi, J. (2000). *Passion for life*. New York: Continuum. An exploration of life purpose and meaning.

Chouinard, Y. (2005: October). Let my people go surfing. *Outside Magazine*, 70-78. How Patagaonia's CEO Yvon Chouinard built a company while staying true to his values. Connecting with meaning and purpose in our life and work. (Thank you to Carlos Gutierrez of John F. Kennedy University for this article.)

DePree, M. (1992). *Leadership jazz: The art of conducting business through leadership, followership, teamwork, touch, and voice.* Dell Publishing.

Elsdon, R. (2003). *Affiliation in the workplace*. Westport: Praeger. An exploration of how the relationship of individuals and organizations can evolve for the benefit of both.

Horan, J. (2004). *The one page business plan*. Berkeley: The One Page Business Plan Company. Retrieved September 2, 2006: http://www.onepage-businessplan.com/book.html.

Palmer, P. (2000). *Let your life speak*. San Francisco: Jossey-Bass Inc.

Pearce, T. (2003). *Leading out loud: Inspiring change through authentic communications.* San Francisco: Jossey-Bass.

QuickBooks Simple Start Edition 2006 for Windows. (2006). Retrieved September 2, 2006: http://www.provantage.com/intuit-296520~7INUT2E1.htm.

Web Resources

Small Business Administration (SBA): http://www.sba.gov. Many helpful resources for starting a small business.

Other Resources

The open road. DVD documentary by Roadtrip Nation speaking to purpose in work. (Thank you to Anna Domek for the gift of this remarkable DVD.) Retrieved September 2, 2006: http://www.roadtripnation.com/.

V: What Are Your Sources of Support?

Just like making any transition, starting a business requires the encouragement of others, as well as a strong internal support system. What are your sources of external support (i.e., professional colleagues, mentors, work associates, service professionals, family, friends, associational alliances)? Do you have a board of advisors, either formally or informally? What are your sources of internal support (i.e., meditation, exercise, listening to music or playing a musical instrument, cooking, reading)? Support in the form of "things" is also important, such as finances, workspace, materials, storage, and props. What physical sources of support do you need to allow you to do what you need to do? Include theories or models that relate to your sources of external and internal support. Who are your mentors? Ed Colozzi and Gail Liebhaber discuss sources of external and internal support. Read their stories and perform Exercises 10 and 11 in Appendix A.

Edward Anthony Colozzi, Ed.D.

Creating a Private Practice

In 1985 I decided to establish my private practice. It was an exciting and breathtaking moment in my professional life that, until then, was primarily involved with traditional faculty/counselor assignments at colleges and university systems in New York City and Hawaii for 15 years. I had never planned or even consciously thought about starting a private practice, but as I reflect back on that day, considering this venture felt like a deep-seeded dream just waiting for the right time to blossom. This was so much a part of who I was and how I needed to do the work I love so much; I just never realized at the time I could simply wake up one day and create it! My sources of external and internal support seemed to manifest from the very first day through the catalyst of conversation with a colleague.

I was speaking with a dear friend, Michael Gross, a colleague at Leeward Community College, where we both worked as counselors. At the time, I was the coordinator of the Career Development Center and a tenured faculty member. I had part-time teaching assignments at two local graduate counselor education programs. I also did some consultation for the Hawaii Departments of Labor and Education assisting career services providers to infuse career guidance into their school and agency settings throughout Hawaii and the Pacific Basin Area.

I was enjoying my work and the related activities that allowed me to teach and preach the passion I had discovered about career/life back in 1976 -1977. I first created the term "career/life" when I was teaching a small group of women called "displaced homemakers," as part of a newly established, federally funded program to assist women in transition. I discovered the rich stories of these women and began using narratives and guided imagery as a means of facilitating their career exploration and decision-making.

My intent was to stimulate the personal agency of my students and encourage more active involvement in their own career development. I also realized that the traditional focus of career planning was far too limited given the breadth of life experiences and angst of the women in my class.

I decided to change the name of the class from "Career Planning" to "Career/Life Exploration and Planning" and placed an emphasis on understanding the combination of life roles these women were trying to balance through all their difficulties. I spent several years promoting this new paradigm throughout the islands and the Pacific Rim area. By 1985, almost ten years later, I was thoroughly enjoying my work in a university setting and really hadn't given any thought to establishing a private practice.

It was during the early afternoon. Michael and I had walked outside to the plumeria-scented air to enjoy the sunshine and gentle trade winds for a brief break during a typical busy day. Michael is the type of close friend who is easy to talk to about any subject because he is so present with you as he listens and then shares. We were leaning over the railing gazing at several trees filled with dozens of chirping birds and quietly talking about our students, the world about us, and life in general. Michael and I would always enjoy these semi-philosophical discussions. Then one of us pondered out loud, "What would it be like to have a private practice and do more in-depth work with our clients?" The other quickly responded, "Yes, that would be so great! Let's look into it!" And we did just that with no hesitation at all. It seemed so natural and felt so right.

Michael indicated he had a psychologist friend who might rent us his downtown high-rise office overlooking the ocean for select evening and Saturday hours. Within two weeks we visited the office, shared the idea with our wives, and decided to start our private practice venture. Michael called himself Counseling Services of Hawaii and dealt with clients experiencing depression, family and marriage problems, while I focused on career and life counseling issues, with some obvious overlap, and created Career Development and Counseling Services (CDCS). Through word of mouth, we soon had our first clients!

My First Paying Client And Twenty Years Later

When my first client completed her first hour-session and pulled out her checkbook to pay me my $50 per-hour fee, I remember how different I felt, actually being handed a check for a service that up until then, no individual had ever paid for directly. I had spent my entire professional life as a salaried employee and counseled and taught classes for thousands of students over the years. I was not accustomed to receiving a fee from individual clients for my services. I remember thinking these thoughts; "This person is about to pay me money for listening to her and sharing some ideas that might help her with her situation. She is now going to pay me for our time together. This is so new and so strange, and yet feels so powerfully filled with potential! This is a good thing."

I do believe that had she asked me to wait and cash her check a month or two later, I would have instantly indicated, "Yes, no problem!" For many years I charged clients for one hour when in fact they might have been with me an hour and 15 or 20 minutes. This behavior is most certainly not conducive to the establishment and growth of a successful private practice! I have since learned to set my fees according to a "50-minute" hour and raised my fee considerably.

Within a few months of establishing our new private practice venture and renting space for select evenings and Saturdays, two facts were very clear. Many clients were finding us, and it became apparent that we needed our own office space. Trying to arrange times for clients around our limited available times and space wasn't working. We found a similar office suite in the same building and continued there together for another year, each of us having specific day or evening hours for our individual clients because there was only one private room in the office suite suitable for seeing clients in addition to a small open waiting area.

Soon Michael decided to leave his full time college counseling position and devote full-time effort to building his practice, and I tried to fit my client appointments around his schedule. Eventually I decided that I needed more space and moved my practice to another office suite in the same building. This evolution of my private practice continued, and in 1989 I left my tenured position and relocated to Boston, Massachusetts with my daughter after experiencing a divorce. I have since continued my private practice in the New England area.

I recently experienced my 20-year anniversary of CDCS in 2005. Over the years, I consciously expanded my practice to include corporate, education, and agency consultation projects in addition to individual career and life counseling. I deal with many different clients including doctors, dentists, lawyers, carpenters, actors, engineers, pilots, architects, sales managers, CEOs and CFOs, undergraduate and graduate students.

Many clients are in a category I call "baby-boomer bloomers" (Colozzi, in press), the generation of people born after 1946 who were raised thinking that they would retire in their late fifties or sixties and who now realize they either can't or do not desire to retire and are seeking meaning and purpose, as well as income, from their work role. They experience much stress and angst in their present jobs, have many unfilled dreams, seek more career and life balance, and are highly motivated to discover their passion and move on with the rest of their lives with new work and a new focus. This group alone will require the services of many private practice counselors. These "boomer-bloomers" are motivated to make changes, have a good measure of wisdom based on years of experiences, and have sufficient income to support their career and life transitions.

I have discovered the importance of diversification of services and focusing on specific niches that reflect of my interests and expertise. This has led to multiple contracts with schools, colleges, state agencies such as the Department of Labor or Department of Education, and nonprofit organizations. I assist clients in various states with their efforts to design or implement national career development standards and develop cost-effective systematic approaches to provide career guidance.

I also offer comprehensive trainings in a values clarification technique (Colozzi, 1978) called Depth-Oriented Values Extraction (DOVE) (Colozzi, 2003). I wrote a self-paced workbook, *Creating careers with confidence* (Colozzi, 1984), which eventually became the first career/life exploration workbook published in Braille (Colozzi, 1990). A primary focus in all my work is dealing with clients' callings (Colozzi and Colozzi, 2000), and helping people discover and realize more meaning and purpose as they balance career and life roles. I did not do all this alone. Mentors were and continue to be important in my life.

Mentors As Sources of Support for Success

Many people have influenced me over the years in ways that have increased my self-efficacy and helped me break through any barriers of doubt. There are far too many to fully describe here, and another book chapter sometime in the future will better acknowledge who these people are and what lessons they taught me that may be useful to readers. Yet I want to delineate several specific categories of influential mentor types to encourage readers to discern areas of potential sources of support for success.

Realizing success means acknowledging the buck stops with you and taking responsibility for your actions and all your decisions, those that produce both positive and negative consequences. Establishing a private practice is difficult because all the research and anecdotal stories remind practitioners that only one in five survive. How daunting! Realizing success also involves acknowledging that you are not alone and are probably being influenced by many people in ways that might be obvious or subtle, pleasant to hear or sometimes unpleasant, very supportive of your journey or perhaps distracting and taking you off your course. Real mentoring relationships keep you on course.

When you decide to start a business venture, you might imagine yourself as Columbus believing the world was round and that sailing toward the horizon could mean discovery, adventure, and experiencing many positive results. That enthusiasm is important and will fill your sails during those windless days. You will need others who also believe in you and help you generate the powerful winds of positive beliefs to sustain your journey. Some of these mentors may manifest their support through constructive critical thinking. This is important to hear and could be misconstrued as lack of support or just plain criticism. It is important to discern a level of constructive and supportive dialogue from a fear- based dialogue with others that can plant seeds of self-doubt and sabotage and potentially steer you away from your journey. Mentors are everywhere, and knowing how to identify them is very helpful.

Categories of Mentors

Mentors come in all sorts of shapes and sizes, ages, colors, positions in life, and often show up when you least expect them and most need them. Some are even disguised as total strangers whose path you cross for only a brief moment in time, a moment that provides you with a huge insight or much needed shot in the arm. There are the traditional older and wiser mentors who take you under their wing, treat you as a daughter or son, and take on the responsibility to "raise" you to new heights of realizing your potential. There are the "colleague" mentors who may be older or younger, clearly see your potential, and do whatever they can to facilitate your work and your journey

through dialogue and actual opportunities of involvement with them or through them with others.

There are "therapist" mentors who assist you in your own career and life "bumps" and are able to point out the pitfalls as you deal with your own career, life, and relationships. There are the "spiritual" mentors who encourage you to dwell deep within your inner soul and better listen to how God speaks to you. Counseling is soulful work and counselors always need renewal. There are the "stranger" mentors who suddenly are in your life on a particular day. They may almost seem to have "appeared" to you as you reflect on how you initially met them. Sometimes they are around for a good length of time, and sometimes your "mentor window" with them lasts only a weekend, a day, or even for a brief discussion as you wait for a seat at a restaurant or are at an airport standing in a boarding line.

There are "family" mentors, wives or husbands, mothers and fathers, other relatives, and even your own children. I have had blessings of insights from my immediate family and even some relatives. I have especially been blessed with my three children (Marc, Michael, and Kristen) who have supported my private practice when I first started it in Hawaii in 1985. They each take the time and effort to encourage me in numerous creative ways that make a big difference. My sons Marc and Michael have a small cell phone business in Hawaii and also do very creative projects with photography and video. We enjoy talking about business ideas, projects and strategies. They presented me with a Macintosh computer several years ago to encourage my video-editing projects that relate to some plans I have for my private practice.

My daughter Kristen works for Imagine Entertainment in Los Angeles and especially has believed in my life's work and my private practice. As a child of ten or twelve, she sometimes sat at the back of my classes observing me teaching my students about career and life topics. She has seen me make presentations from time to time and is always encouraging me to "grow" my business and do the work I consider to be my calling in life.

All my children have been powerful sources of inspiration in emotional ways with their creativity, sense of humor, and philosophical and spiritual outlook on life. They have taught me so much over the past 35 years I have been a parent to them, and I am grateful for the opportunity to be their "Pops." In special ways they have been my life-teachers and mentors along with many others. I believe all people have access to mentors in their lives. How do you recognize mentors and what are there characteristics?

Characteristics of Effective Mentors

Effective mentors have several important characteristics. They show up when you most need them. They truly understand who you are and what you are trying to communicate; they get it! They believe in you and your work. They are eager to help you achieve your goals. They have this uncanny ability to harness what is most needed to move you forward. They might say the right words, ask the right questions or provide the right network that results in real progress and in ways that you notice the difference, usually rather immediately. At times, initially you might sense only a little push forward, and the giant leap of progress occurs later.

Sometimes the giant leap of insight is immediate and almost overwhelmingly accurate. You may wonder, "How did they know?" or "How did we connect so powerfully and so quickly?" They raise your self-efficacy and help you listen more clearly to your own heart and be less distracted by nay-sayers, either real people who do not support you or those inner negative scripting tapes that erode confidence and cause you to stray off course. They are authentic sisters and brothers to your heart's energy who know your rhythm, honor it with a sense of unconditional belief and love, and do not seek praise or acknowledgement for their efforts. Your progress toward your goal seems to be their source of contentment. They are your breath of fresh air and enjoy your success because you are fulfilled and happy and on purpose. They are generous in their giving.

Internal Sources of Support

My efforts to develop a clearer spiritual awareness of who I am and how I relate to others provides me with my strongest domain of support for my private practice and my whole life. For me personally, this involves my relationship with God. I pray every day and have been facilitating a Centering Prayer group every Tuesday evening since 1991. This is based on the work of Thomas Keating and has proved to be invaluable to all who practice this (Keating, 1998). A small group of us spend about twenty minutes on a quiet meditation followed by a brief reading and small group discussion. In my counseling, I appropriately encourage clients to discover their spiritual support base whether it is the Buddha within them, their Atman, the Christ within them, or some source of energy or positive influence that allows them to have a clearer understanding of themselves in relationship to themselves and others over time.

Another source of internal support is taking the time to gaze and reflect on a beautiful picture of Planet Earth in my office and appreciate the vast area of land and ocean that unites all people, making us truly one human race sharing the Planet's resources and contributing to our planet and to each other. I also take time to play the piano, compose songs and enjoy video production and editing as a producer with my local cable access television station. I enjoy writing, and while journal or newsletter articles can be challenging and fulfilling, letters to the editor and creative short articles are most enjoyable and clear my mind and spirit very easily. Cooking and preparing meals for my family and friends brings me great pleasure (what can I say; I'm Italian!). Even cutting the grass and some gardening can be so peaceful, clears my mind and opens my spirit and creativity.

A practice I do several times weekly is walking up to one of my three office windows that face onto the main street and watching the grade-school children playing during their recess period across the street from my office building. They are always playing, laughing, skipping, and running about and seem to be totally immersed in joy, oblivious to everything else around them. This reminds me to take time to nurture myself and choose to take on projects that bring fulfillment, happiness and make me get excited and cause me to smile. Then I look to the right where I notice steady streams of customers rushing in and out of the dry-cleaning store next to my office. This reminds me to make sure I accomplish what is important and not to take on so much that I am rushing and under pressure all the time.

Then I look to the left where I usually see a hearse, a coffin and mourners as someone is carried either into or out from the Catholic Church funeral mass several times a week. This reminds me about the gift of my life and the opportunity to do my calling in ways that positively touch the lives of others. This also reminds me about the importance of having faith, living out my faith and trusting in a God who unconditionally loves me and all others and probably expects us all to just do what we are able to do – and to do THAT great!

Physical Sources of Support

Some counselors prefer to have their private practice in their home; I prefer to have a separate office space. This provides a sense of privacy and boundaries that leave my home life private and separate from my work life. I usually do not bring work home. My office is one of four main suites in a professional building that is easily accessible by car or the local public transportation and only five minutes from the center of town.

My suite is comfortable with two rooms: an outer waiting room with enough space for small group workshops and a large desk area for special projects that require lots of space, and an inner smaller office where I see clients and work on my computer. A microwave and small refrigerator provide opportunities for nourishment and hot tea for clients every now and then. Classical music is quietly playing all the time to create a peaceful milieu and also to provide some measure of additional privacy for my sessions if I am seeing a client in my inner office and a person happens to enter the outer office area.

Using Your Intuitive and Analytical Talents to Assess Potential Market Niches

All people have inner support systems that serve as compasses to guide them through life. Counselors must use their own compasses as they consider taking the leap to reinvent themselves as private practitioners. Identifying client niches is different in private practice compared with education or agency settings. Usually the clients or students are already on your campus or frequent your agency setting on a regular basis for multiple reasons. You must sufficiently engage them so they are aware of your services and hopefully choose to become actively involved with your career center's activities. In private practice you must do all this and more. You need to identify market niches and then develop strategies that will successfully penetrate that market with your particular brand or way of identifying yourself to potential customers. Does your business name include your own name or another name that connotes what you do and provides immediate brand identity?

Could a logo communicate something about your business? I use a pyramid with three slanted lines trisecting the figure as my logo. It represents self-knowledge (abilities, interests, and values) and somehow catches people's eyes and attracts the type of clients who want and need my services. I have used this symbol for many years in all my marketing and advertising, such as in the Yellow Book, a customer-friendly company that supports small business such as mine. They publish a local directory that many clients use from their homes and offices. The use of the Internet is obviously a very powerful marketing tool and needs to be used wisely and cost-effectively. Know your business goals and select your target groups before you start to advertise.

If you enjoy working with small groups, where can you find people who might want to join the small groups you will create? Are existing small groups ready to be cultivated, for example in a local church, synagogue, or YMCA/YWCA setting? Perhaps you prefer a focus on spouse relocation activities. Who deals with this on a national or international level and how can you network with them and become a

provider? Are you interested in designing your practice primarily around individual career counseling or some hybrid of this focus with some corporate clients? This is the path I have chosen with Career Development and Counseling Services. I work with individuals and couples, and provide a variety of consultation services to corporate, education and agency settings locally and nationally, and have a few international clients.

One of the main motivations for many private practitioners to initiate a private practice is probably the opportunity and freedom to concentrate primarily on individual counseling activities with clients and not deal with the many other activities that often are an integral part of the job responsibilities at most educational and agency settings. Counselors choose to be counselors because they enjoy the counseling relationship and believe that this one-on-one interaction can effect change. Research from meta-analyses informs us that the primary factors that effect outcome in career counseling are "... the type of treatment modality and the duration of time spent counseling" (Sexton et al., 1997). Individual counseling has been viewed as "the most efficient career intervention in terms of amount of gain per hour of effort" (Spokane, 1991), described as "the most effective" treatment modality based on meta-analyses performed by Sexton et al.,(1997). It is a "superior" career intervention based on a therapeutic alliance, that should be available in comprehensive career centers (Rayman, 1996).

We know individual career counseling works, but there are not sufficient numbers of counselors to provide such comprehensive services within the infrastructure of most education and agency settings. Since secondary school students' needs for career guidance "remain largely unheeded" as reported by Herr and Cramer (as cited in Sexton et al., 1997), they bring their unmet needs to the college environment, contributing to the estimated half of all undergraduates in colleges and universities who need some form of career assistance (Sexton et al., 1997).

The reality is that most career service providers in college and university settings are very busy and unable to meet the needs of their students. Career planning courses, workshops, the use of computer guidance systems and other activities cannot effectively reach the multitudes. In many such settings, "the prevailing treatment modality probably remains 'career counseling by appointment,' a familiar, comfortable, and proven intervention," yet student needs are not sufficiently met, and the use of systematic career guidance with small structured groups at least begins to cost-effectively deal with this demand (Colozzi, 2000).

Unfortunately, the majority of deciders will probably experience their college years without spending sufficient time and energy in committed career exploration activities (Colozzi, 2000). Their unmet needs will be carried forth into their first-time employment experiences from which they will eventually change jobs seven to ten times in two or three unrelated careers during their work history. This will result in a need for private practice counselors to assist with this growing demand for career/life counseling in our ever-changing global economy. This situation should be very encouraging to school, college and agency counselors who might be considering a career change and open to starting a business.

Seek Support for Your Dual Roles As Businessperson and Counselor

As you set out to develop your private practice, be ever conscious of the many important business tasks that are necessary to successfully function in this type of environment. Be clear on your goals as a businessperson and as a professional counselor. Seek out people or materials that will support you to do this. It will affect the way you structure your business and deliver you services. Up until several years ago, I used to think that to be successful in private practice, you needed to see yourself equally as a businessperson and a career counselor – a 50%/50% even split – not a businessperson first and then a career counselor.

I have shifted and now believe that to be successful, you must always see yourself and act as a businessperson first – at least 51%. This requires serving your customers/clients with integrity in ways that meet their needs and simultaneously allows a reasonable profit so you can continue as a private practitioner to do the counseling you thoroughly enjoy. Otherwise you can work for a college or agency setting primarily as a career counselor and not have to deal with the business aspects of running a private practice. In this context, you may decide not to take on a client because of their inability to pay, and therefore might refer them to some other appropriate service. Do not ever put your business agenda to earn income above meeting the counseling needs of those clients you do decide to take on. This compromises the counseling you are offering and moves your business immediately out of integrity.

An important support for your business is someone to help with finances. They didn't teach us in graduate school about running a business, so this is a major learning curve for most of us. Be sure to find a great accountant, and don't be shy about asking questions! My accountant Steve Walsh has been a staunch supporter of my business since my relocation to Massachusetts. He has guided and encouraged me to be successful by using a simple formula: increase income and decrease expenses! He is helpful in many strategic ways and also provides emotional support that has assisted me through those tough years of growth and sometimes low-income quarters that most small businesses experience from time to time.

As a Vietnam veteran, Steve has seen the best and worst of times and brings a faith-filled approach to his work and his life that is inspiring and effective. I welcome any calls from readers who may need a little advice, a nudge, or handholding to begin their new business venture or improve their existing business. During my 20 years, I have made many mistakes and have lots of "learning experiences" to share. As you continue your business venture, know that you will make mistakes, and that is one way to learn what to do and what not to do to be successful. Another way that will support you and your business is to pay attention to professional development activities that are important to your counseling skills and your role as a businessperson. Read a book or article, talk to a colleague, attend a workshop. It all helps.

Professional development is important to the work all counselors do. In education and agency settings, many opportunities for professional development are available throughout the year. In a private practice setting, it is very difficult to take advantage of such opportunities. Planning such activities around a client load can often be distracting. Dealing with finances can easily discourage planning and budgeting for such activities. Exercise #10 in Appendix A is a brief activity you can perform to assess your professional development pulse, to stimulate ideas, and to encourage you to set goals and realistic timelines for achieving your goals. Many of the activities listed are important for the professional development of all counselors, especially those who choose to work in a private-practice setting. These activities need to be consciously chosen and implemented if they are to be effective catalysts for professional development.

Colleagues and staff of my National Career Development Association (NCDA) "family" have been important to my personal, professional and spiritual growth. Attending the annual conference or reading Career Convergence on the NCDA website provides an immediate connect with the people whom I respect and want to share experiences. I love spending time with them, hearing them speak, sharing ideas, agreeing to disagree sometimes, and mostly, being passionate about promoting excellent career development for others.

Summary of Reflections

I have discussed how one person initially decided to set out and create a private practice. The experience will be different for each person. However, there are some common areas of the journey that most persons who start a business will probably traverse. Finding or creating internal and external support systems including the right mentors, discovering and penetrating market niches that match your special gifts and interests, creating brand identity, and learning how to be a successful business person while providing the counseling you enjoy are all important activities that contribute to the successful and fulfilling reinvention of yourself. This is also very possible to achieve. You only have to start thinking about it and believe that you can accomplish this. It really involves the power of positive belief and raised self-efficacy beliefs.

I have been especially blessed with mentors and colleagues who have raised my efficacy beliefs and supported me. These include JoAnn Harris-Bowlsbey, Don Super, Darrell Luzzo, Mark Savickas, Skip Niles, Michael Gross, Pat and Dale Cramer, Ed Pei, Mike Murakoshi, Bob Fishman, David and Dolly Langen, Sybil Kyi, Phyllis Dayao, Elsie Matsumura, Ken Hoyt, Larry Murray, Don Creamer, Elwood Chapman, Dick Bolles, Larry Murray, Henry Quill, Merle Jordan, Darlene Martin, Michael Regan, Julie Glowacki, Fr. Dick Messina, Fr. Thomas Keating, Fr. Frank McGann, Sister Rose Marie Lipke, Earl Nishiguchi, Pete Hubbard, Sally Gelardin, and Camille Gouldberg. These and many others, especially my children and my clients, all contribute to my growth in ways that really can't be measured or even adequately described. I am very grateful to them.

Finally, voluntarily offer your services using your special gifts to either select clients annually or to groups affiliated with an agency or non-profit organization in your community, such as JA Worldwide (Junior Achievement Worldwide, http://www.ja.org). JA is an organization that promotes entrepreneurship and develops materials and programs for millions of K-12 students annually, nationally and internationally and is always looking for willing volunteers. This type of community involvement will benefit the recipients and will surely support your own spiritual growth and spill over in positive ways to your overall business venture and lessons on being a successful entrepreneur. I believe we all have an obligation to share our gifts and talents to contribute to the improvement of others and this world.

The desire to create your own business, something that happens only because of your individual efforts and perseverance, comes from a place deep within your heart. This might be a product or a service, perhaps even a unique expression of your special talents or ways of thinking, doing, or interpreting. This urge to pioneer is as old as time and very much present in the very fabric of today's global economy. This important and timely monograph will reinforce your efforts and inspire you to reach your greatest potential!

References

Colozzi, E.A. (1978). *Values clarification process*. Oahu, Hawaii: Leeward Community College.

Colozzi, E.A. (1984). *Creating careers with confidence*. Hawaii: DELTA Rainbow.

Colozzi, E.A. (1990). *Creating careers with confidence*. Boston, MA: National Braille Press.

Colozzi, E.A. (2000). Toward the development of systematic career guidance, in D. Luzzo, *Career counseling of college students: An empirical guide to strategies that work*, Washington, DC: American Psychological Association.

Colozzi, E. A. (2003). Depth-oriented values extraction (DOVE), *Career Development Quarterly*, Broken Arrow, Oklahoma: National Career Development Association, 52, 2.

Colozzi, E. A. (in press). Callings and careers: A spiritual perspective of the career development process, *Career Development Quarterly*, Broken Arrow, Oklahoma: National Career Development Association.

Colozzi, E.A. & Colozzi, L.C. (2000). College students' callings and careers: An integrated values-oriented perspective, in D. Luzzo, *Career counseling of college students: An empirical guide to strategies that work*, Washington, DC: American Psychological Association.

Keating, T. (1998). *Invitation to love*. New York: Continuum.

Lent, R. W., & Brown, S. D. (1996). Social cognitive approach to career development: An overview. *The Career Development Quarterly*, 44, 310-321. Broken Arrow, Oklahoma: National Career Development Association. Retrieved September 2, 2006: http://www.ncda.org.

Rayman, J. (1996). Apples and oranges in the career center: Reaction to R. Reardon. *Journal of Counseling & Development*, 74 286-287.

Sexton, T.L., Whiston, S.C., Bleuer, J.C., & Walz, G. R. (1997) *Integrateing outcome research into counseling practice and training*. Alexandria, Virginia: American Counseling Association.

Spokane, A. R., (1991) *Career interventions*. Englewood, N. J.: Prentice-Hall.

Gail Liebhaber

Keys to Finding Guidance, Support and Encouragement in and around You

Congratulations! You have made the courageous decision to open the doors to your future as a business owner. You have reached your moment of truth and decided to start your own business and make your claim as a career development expert. You have crossed the line when you go from asking yourself such questions as "Why would anyone pay me? What do I have that is special and unique in my profession?" to that deep knowing that you have something of value to share which is worth charging for and will contribute to a person's career search. All your hard work of learning the theories, skills, and practices of our trade has prepared you well.

You are probably feeling exhilarated, scared, energized, overwhelmed and hopeful—all at the same time! Welcome to an entirely new world that has the potential to be amazingly satisfying and stimulating for your own growth, both in income and in fulfillment. Potential clients need your unique contributions and many will benefit from your services. What an amazing blessing to be paid for the work that we feel so strongly passionate about, and to participate in work that is so necessary for the health and wellbeing of the 21st-century workforce.

From an income standpoint, our business is a good business to be in - we are one of the few professions that can remain stable despite variable economic conditions. When the job market is robust, people call upon our help in finding a better opportunity with more money, recognition, and responsibilities. When the job market is weak, people need strategic job-search skills and in-depth knowledge of their transferable skills. I have found over the past dozen years that my client load has increased to a satisfactory level, meeting and even exceeding my business needs.

The satisfaction barometer has an even happier result. Over the last 25 years, I have created a portfolio career and arranged my work life with several income streams, resulting in diverse situations and roles, including manager, program director, counselor, educator, executive coach, and consultant. Far and away, the most satisfaction comes from working individually with clients in my office and feeling that I can independently (along with the client, of course) decide the best approach for their situation with no rules, regulations, or constraints from outside forces. I can take full responsibility for all aspects of my business, allowing myself to be as creative, spiritually based, and responsive as I feel it takes to be an effective and empowering guide.

As you have discovered in the previous chapters, your success will be determined by many key factors. The purpose of this chapter is simple but important: to present you with a selection of ideas to support and guide your entry into the multi-faceted world of entrepreneurship. I will do this on two levels.

First, I shall share how I have received much-needed encouragement and support in two very different ways. I shall then describe some of my experiences developing my own internal and external support systems so you can gain first-hand knowledge of how I set up structures to keep me inspired, creative and energized while at all times staying grounded in the reality of keeping my business viable and relatively stable. I invite you to learn by my mistakes and accomplishments.

Secondly, I shall involve you in the process of identifying, exploring, and cultivating your existing and potential sources of external and internal support. We shall start with creating a vision, use some mind mapping and gap analysis tools, (see Exercise 11 in Appendix A) and end with a short guide for finding more resources. This is a fun and creative chapter. You can choose to skim it for ideas for later thought or settle in with pen and paper and mine it for deeper benefits. If you choose the latter, you will discover your inner guides, create a mission statement, develop a discipline, identify your teachers/mentors/role models, invest in a community, and become a valued member of the greater career counseling community. Either way, it is an honor to be your guide. Let's start the journey.

Who Are Your Role Models? Who and What Have Influenced Your Development?

Two Examples of Internal and External Support

I immediately think of Richard Bolles and Barbara Sher. Before I met either of them in person, I had become totally enthralled by their respective books and took to heart their teachings of why I chose to be a career counselor and how I had a very crucial role to play in my clients' lives. Their stories captured my fantasies of how I wanted to help in the world. But even before I happened across these respected theorists and teachers, I had a serendipitous occurrence that came to me from an unknown teacher through her small xeroxed book on the shelves of a feminist bookstore in Cambridge, MA.

First a little bit of background about how I first became involved in our field. Growing up in suburban

New Jersey, I had never heard of the occupation of career counseling. I did go (only once) to my guidance counselor in high school. A kindly but scattered older woman prone to wearing her wig sideways, she absent-mindedly promoted the local state school and teaching occupations to all girls who crossed her path. My hopes, however, went beyond the small world around me. I was influenced by the media of my time - television. Weeknights I watched Patty Duke, starring and co-starring in a television program about high school twins with a father who cut a dashing figure as a cosmopolitan and intelligent foreign correspondent for a sophisticated city newspaper. This looked exciting, glamorous, and rewarding, and soon became my career goal.

I entered college with journalism as my major. Little did I know that the summer before my freshman year they eliminated that major, loosely substituting Mass and Human Communications as possible fields of study. I mostly ignored any need to explore career options. Serendipitously, a dean of students took an interest in me and took me under her wing as she pursued a vision that was extremely important in her role at an all-women's college. I tagged along when she conducted her research on how young women made career choices and soon devoted myself to the mission of helping them explore all possible options.

After graduation, I hitchhiked one cold January day to Boston. I answered a handwritten ad on the bulletin board outside the Boston University career counseling office: "Like to write and help people? Call Don at 555-7689. Without a plan, I had drifted into a job as an Activities-in-Daily-Living instructor in a sheltered workshop for emotionally disturbed and mentally retarded people on the grounds of a state mental institution. After four years and a series of promotions, I became the coordinator of employment services. I was helping to place people in transitional jobs outside the shelter but grew frustrated by the entropic systems and lack of resources. I left to travel, get married, and go to graduate school.

A turning point occurred when I was in my mid-twenties. I happened upon a small book in a Women's Words Book Store. The author was Patricia Fleming. When I picked up the slim Xeroxed volume, I somehow felt that this book was going to change my life. It opened up the world of counseling in a way that I had never imagined. I know that this might sound strange for you to read, but it was true! Beyond coping: How to form a vocational achievement support group for women provided me with a vision of how women could come together and support each other's growth. I had not yet had the experience itself of being a member of a powerful and supportive group, but here was a book that was going to provide all that I needed to envision the possibilities. According to Fleming:

The purpose of the group is to help its members gain the satisfaction of meaningful achievement. It provides its members with support, encouragement, and practical help in their effort to define and follow a vocation that is satisfying, remunerative, and useful. In addition, the group provides help in overcoming both long and short-term blocks to success.

I was launched into my chosen career.

Hearing the Inner Calling: A Winter's Night

Even though I had been in the career development field in a variety of capacities for over a dozen years, I had yet to find my specific place. Like my colleagues in the career development field, I performed all types of functions: program development counseling, staff training, and now, management. I vaguely knew that I wanted to be well paid and respected for my expertise but still felt unrecognized and confused about my best options. I wanted recognition, a substantial income, and independence. I often asked myself how I could possibly reach my goals.

With two young children and a full-time job, I did not have much free time. But through my Jewish community, I had found that meditation and Kabbalism offered glimmers of peace and deep fulfillment. I committed to weekly evening meditation classes. Here is where my story starts to get interesting.

I was looking forward to another night of my Jewish meditation teacher's Chassidic stories. True, I had not quite learned to meditate in a disciplined manner, but I certainly enjoyed the relaxation and warmth of being with fellow seekers. This particular night we were using the breath to lead us inwards. I took my usual position of lying on the floor with knees bent (to protect a bad back) with a pillow under my head. Perhaps it was the exhaustion of the day or the relaxing posture - soon I found myself drifting further and further from Martha Joy's voice to an inner empty space. In that small space a voice, unlike any I had ever heard before, spoke to me. Actually, I experienced it more like a command than a spoken word. The voice commanded me, simply and plainly, to become a career counselor. My whole body responded by relaxing into the moment, as if each cell had heard the calling. I did not tell anyone about this revelation for a very long time. It felt very precious and very private. Although it took a few more years before I started my business as a career counselor, on this night, I found my calling.

What Kind of Encouragement, Support and Structures Do You Need To Start a Successful Business?

"Isolation is a dream killer." (Sher, 1979).

When I first read these words, I thought about

my clients and how they needed my support along with their family and friends. I would make a practice of asking my clients, " Who is your support team?" Then I suggested, " Think about who you can turn to for help, ideas, resources, or information that will help move your dream along. Remember, it is extremely difficult to accomplish your goals on your own."

Soon I realized that Barbara Sher was speaking to me. I have a deep need to connect with others in an intimate way, so my chosen profession is perfect for me in this way. Her very strong message is that you need to build your support team before you start pursuing your goals. According to Sher, no one should even attempt to get there alone. And along the way, you might find yourself learning by giving to others.

Building Support: Colleagues, Community, Family, and Finances

Since my early college years when I helped to start the Women's Collective at my school, I have found tremendous value in surrounding myself with smart, articulate, and emotionally available people. Over the past 25 years of my professional life, I have continued to either find or create a variety of groups where I could learn about topical career counseling issues, share best practices, and feel a sense of belonging to group that was bigger than me.

In the early 1980's, I helped to create the Career Counselors Consortium in the Greater Boston area. In the early 1990's, I joined the Holistic Career Counselor's Group, meeting in each other's homes as we explored what we could offer as guides to career clients who were starting to recognize that they possessed spiritual as well as material needs. By the turn of the century, I was finding collegial support across the country as the Internet-based tools, such listservs, email, eforums, and blogs emerged as a way to stay in touch with people that I had met at national conferences and workshops.

Although I have not had a "mentor" since my college days, belonging to professional associations such as National Career Development Association (NCDA), Association of Career Professionals International (ACPI), and International Coach Federation (ICF) has provided me with a whole cadre of "peer mentors." These colleagues have offered encouragement, contacts, procedures, web sites, tools, etc. that I have incorporated into my counseling practices. We have referred clients to each other and covered for each other's vacations.

I trust that you will share in my experience that we career counselors are typically a noncompetitive crowd, eager to share resources and practices with other professionals in the field. Our commitment to our clients and our field gives us the perspective that when our clients benefit from good services, where they obtain those services is secondary. Teachers, coaches, and therapists are other possible sources of general support if they can help you to see your own potential. Journals, books, web sites, magazines, and newspapers are helpful in that they are available any time you need their inspiration, expertise, or suggestions.

Perhaps you are a member of other types of communities that provide the safety, warmth, and comfort so necessary when times get tough. My Jewish community has been a place where I can get hugs and sympathy during discouraging times. These friends are also eager to celebrate my successes and have watched me grow, providing cheers along the way. I have also created it into an environment where it is safe to try new things such as practice a new teaching style or share a heartfelt poem.

Family can be an equally valuable source of support, both emotionally and financially. If you are in a committed relationship, you will need your partner to recognize and value your chosen path. Seeking the advice of a financial planner would be an important first step in planning for ongoing expenses as you begin your business plan. Will you quit your day job or attempt to start small, devoting evenings and weekends to testing the waters? My first few years I charged $50 an hour, meeting during the evenings at my dining room table with friends and friends of friends. I wanted to see if I liked the process and if people would actually pay for my services.

I chose to keep working while my children were growing up. My strategy was to get health benefits for my family, a structured workplace, social niceties (holiday parties, lunch meetings with colleagues), and a steady income from a job.

Although I started out as a full-time employee for the Department of Employment and Training of the Commonwealth of Massachusetts, I parlayed my job into four days a week, managing to keep my benefits. For the past eight years, I have worked as the Director of Career Services at Harvard University graduate schools, devoting 24 - 28 hours a week to Harvard and the rest to my private practice. An important decision for my work/family balance was not to see clients at night or weekends, though there are certainly many hours of "back-office work" (including writing my book, *Purposeful listening: Spiritual coaching techniques for career development practitioners* and this chapter) that sneak into my off-hours.

Is this the right time to mention that I have a husband who actually likes to cook, clean, and otherwise nurture our family? Support in household tasks is crucial to allowing you to expend the energy you might otherwise need to get kids off to school, care for elders, and the myriad other demands on time. Negotiating all tasks with a partner or other available family members is a necessary step in smoothing the way for all the bumps that are sure to arise.

Nourishing Yourself from the Inside Out

What are your internal structures for keeping going? What do you have in place for developing a sense of "being"?

You have probably sensed by now that it is my purpose-driven mission that fuels my entrepreneurial aspirations. Being a career counselor in private practice feels natural, easy and essential - more like play than work. But it did not always feel this way. It took several years and many experiences before I could talk about my business with integrity and confidence. First I needed to access the part of me that felt wise, patient, practical, and authentic. Essentially, I needed to know myself so that I could trust myself to be a part of other people's development.

As early as 1980, I was envisioning my mission in the world. I found it recently on a business card that I had printed: to help people discover their options in the work world. Somehow, having an intention in the world has always seemed like the best road for me. My spiritual sensibility of being connected to something bigger and wiser than just me has provided me with this sense of purpose in my life. In my religion, the Hebrew word for soul is the same for breath. Following your breath leads you to your soul and connects you to the soul of the world.

There are many resources for getting comfortable with yourself. Journaling, writing poetry, doing yoga, meditating, dancing, and painting with water colors are some of the ways I have chosen over the years. Your own ways of spending time with yourself—music, cooking, carpentry, sculpting, photography, hiking, walks in nature—can be fertile soil from which your sense of being, honoring, and understanding can provide a fountain of nourishment and support. Putting aside the time to find your inner sources of support will release that flow so that it will be there whenever you might need it.

Just recently I have been making space and time to align my external sources of support with my internal structures. This might take the form of going on retreats with a spiritual teacher, such as Thich Knat Hanh or Parker Palmer, or simply getting away to a lovely place where I can do yoga, read, journal, walk, or simply rest. Being with a wonderful teacher is affirming and inspiring and is an example of an externalized source of support becoming internalized. My sources of internal support get recharged and my community of kindred spirits grows. Feeling more connected in the world then helps me feel support, and so the circle flows and grows.

This is a great time to develop a mission statement for yourself. Make sure your vision supports your essential self in a way that offers a clear picture of what you are trying to accomplish in your business in the simplest terms possible. Then, whenever doubts or anxieties arise, you can pull out your mission statement and reconnect with what brought you into your business in the first place.

Use this space to capture and honor your mission.

Reference

Gap Analysis Theory (2003 - 2004), as presented in Harvard University's Leadership Development Program. Cambridge, MA.

Print Resources

Anderson, T. R., (Fall 2005). *Not by ourselves, Buddhadharman*. Shambala: Boulder, Colorado.

Bolles, R. (2005). *What color is your parachute?* Berkeley, CA: Ten Speed Press.

Five practices to change your mind. (2005: Summer) *Tricycle: The Buddhist Review*. Burlington, Vt., 56).

Fleming, P. (1978). *Beyond coping: How to form a vocational achievement support group for women*. Cambridge, MA: Self-published.

Liebhaber, G. (2004). *Purposeful listening: Spiritual coaching techniques for career development practitioners*. Lexington, MA: Self-published. Retrieved September 2, 2006: http://www.yourcareerdirection.com.

Palmer, P. (2000). *Let Your Life Speak*. San Francisco: Jossey-Bass Inc.

Sher, B. (1979). *Wishcraft*. New York: Ballantine.

Web Resources

Performance Management. Retrieved September 2, 2006: http://www.manageyoursuccess.com/.

Experiences and thoughts about the idea and practice of spirituality in the workplace. Retrieved on September 2, 2006: http://www.workplacespirituality.info/.

Richard Leider. Assorted articles and resources. Retrieved September 2, 2006: http://www.inventuregroup.com/.

Mind-Mapping. Retrieved September 2, 2006: peterussell.com/MindMaps/HowTo.html.

VI. What is your strategic plan?

Marketing a service or product is often the most difficult task for entrepreneurs. Who are your competitors? How have you positioned yourself to your advantage? What are your revenue streams and what is your operating model? What marketing strategies have you found most effective in marketing your service or product? To develop your strategic plan, take the time to perform Exercises 12 and 13 created by Dan Geller and Randy Miller in Appendix A.

Dan Geller

Strategize or Eulogize

When I started my strategic planning consulting practice in 1999, my plan was to help small business owners develop their strategic planning process. Little did I know, at that time, that my small consulting practice would one day evolve into a much larger business that services thousands of customers every year through my website, line of products, and Business Planning Center in San Rafael, California.

How It All Started

Early in my consulting practice, I discovered two amazing facts that shaped the course of my business. The first fact was that, on average, one small business fails every 60 seconds! According to the Small Business Administration (Office of Advocacy, 2004), there were 589,837 small-business terminations in 2003. This figure includes 35,037 bankruptcies and 554,800 small-business failures. There are 547,500 minutes in a year. The second fact was no less astonishing. In a three-year study (Gibson & Cassar, 2000) conducted with 6,400 small businesses, the researcher found that only 19% of small-business owners practice business planning on a regular basis.

Faced with these two facts, I decided to explore the possibility that there might be some correlation between the two. I devoted the following few years to conducting research, as part of my doctoral dissertation, to find the answers to two main questions:

- Is there a relationship between lack of strategic planning and business success and failure?
- If there is such a relationship, why don't most small business owners engage in strategic planning?

The findings of my research were very revealing. Scientific studies in the field of small-business success have demonstrated a strong relationship between business planning and the prospects for business success. Moreover, studies have shown that practicing strategic planning, which is the highest level of business planning, can have an even greater impact on the financial performance of small businesses. As to why most small business owners do not plan, my research found that the main reason is lack of time. Simply put, the methods and system for strategic business planning that are currently available (with the exception of Instant Strategist) are too complex, cumbersome, and time consuming for a small business owner to deal with. As a result, most small business owners do not bother planning.

As an entrepreneur, this was the moment the light bulb went off in my head. If strategic business planning can impact the success or failure of a business, and if most small business owners do not engage in strategic business planning because there is nothing on the market that they can use, why shouldn't I develop a quick and easy methodology for strategic business planning? The solution was Instant Strategist, my current business, that has grown into a very profitable business that caters to thousands of small business owners worldwide.

Obviously, the first thing on my agenda was to develop a strategic plan for my new venture utilizing my newly-develop strategic planning methodology – Instant Strategist. After all, I should practice what I preach. This exercise was very rewarding and beneficial in focusing on my vision, defining my mission, and outlining a detailed action and financial plan for my new business. In the next section, I will outline for you the main steps of the Instant Strategist methodology so that you, too, may develop a quick and easy strategic plan for your new or existing business. Keep in mind that this is only an outline. You may obtain the complete methodology by visiting http://www.instantstrategist.com.

Instant Strategist – Quick and Easy Business Strategy Formation

What Is The Purpose of Strategic Planning?

The purpose of a strategy is to provide the audience with a top-level overview of your idea or concept. Moreover, a strategy should demonstrate the overall validity of a concept before you begin developing a business plan.

The central concept of a strategy is to validate

the proposed business, before any details enter the picture. The logic behind this approach is that if your strategy is invalid, no amount of details or planning will correct the basic flaws in the strategy. Consequently, such an undertaking has a very high probability of failure.

What Is a Strategy?

Simply put, a strategy is a way to pursue a vision by leveraging tools and tactics that will produce the desired outcome. The ultimate objective of any strategy is to lead the initiative in the direction that will most likely reach the ultimate destination. I use the phrase "most likely," simply because there are no guarantees, in life or in business, that proper planning will yield the desired results. On the other hand, be assured that invalid planning will always result in an undesired outcome. A valid strategic plan is one that contains the basic elements of motion - there is a destination, a means of getting there, and the ability to move in that direction.

Strategic Planning vs. Business Planning

I'm often asked the difference between strategic planning and business planning. This is a very good question because whenever I mention strategic planning to my clients or my students – they automatically think of a business plan.

To begin, we must understand what role these plans play in the early stages of business formulation.

Strategic vs. Business Planning

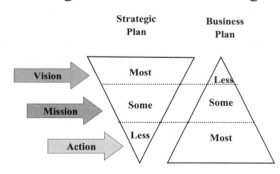

Both plans have the same starting point—an idea for a business that will become successful and profitable. Nevertheless, there are important differences between the role of the strategic plan and the role of the business plan in bringing an idea to fruition.

The simplest way to explain the differences between a strategic plan and a business plan is to equate them both to a person preparing for a trip. There are two major decisions a traveler must make before he or she can go on a trip: (a) where to go and (b) how to get there. The strategic plan focuses on "where" the traveler wants to go; whereas, the business plan focuses on "how" the traveler will get there.

The main reason you need a strategic plan before you even begin to work on your business plan is very simple: If you don't know where you are going, how can you know how to get there? The vision for your company, project, or program is the first step in the strategic planning of any successful initiative. This establishes the ultimate destination, and dictates the means ("how") and the actions ("what") required to successfully complete your plan.

Your Building Blocks

Developing a valid strategic plan is much like working with building blocks. First, you must place the foundation blocks—and only then can you put the other blocks on top. The most effective way to construct a strategic plan is to follow the same approach.

This process has three main stages:

- First, determine what you want to do (Vision).
- Next, figure out how you are going to get there (Mission).
- Finally, work out the details (Action).

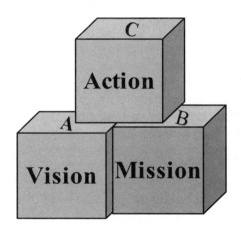

Consider our traveler planning a trip. First he or she decides on the destination, then how to get there (e.g., by car or by plane) and only then can the traveler work out the details (such as what to take along and when exactly to go). By following these three stages, you can stay focused on each part of the plan, while maintaining the sequence of the process.

The **Vision** block consists of three steps. Each of these steps must be covered and validated before you can continue the building process of your strategic plan. The three steps are:

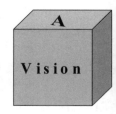

1. Desires (need, value and audience)
2. Drivers (connectivity, interactivity, and speed)
3. Landscape (competition, analysis, and advantage)

Now that you have defined and validated your vision (where you want to go), it is time to decide on how you are going to get there. Remember the rule: Knowing where you are going is not enough to guarantee that you will arrive at your destination. You now must decide on how to get there.

The **Mission** block consists of three main components. Each component deals with specific elements important to a well-defined route. Think of your Mission block as a road map, one you are using to plan the route to your selected destination.

The three main components of the Mission block are:

1. Models (business model, revenue model, and operating model)
2. Markets (size, selection, and targeting)
3. Marketing (positioning, posting, and programs)

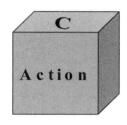

The **Action** block is the third and final phase of your strategic planning process. The purpose of this block is twofold. First, it helps to transform your previous two phases into a practical and "tangible" plan, so that you can see exactly how to fulfill your vision. Second, it enables you to view your vision through a financial perspective and check the financial feasibility of your final strategic plan.

Another important aspect of the Action phase is to provide a check-and-balance mechanism for your strategic plan. Often, when we are engaged in high-level planning, we let our minds and imagination float free – which is a necessary part of strategic planning.

The Action block consists of three major components:

1. Activities (priority, stages, and cost)
2. Personnel (responsibility, accountability, and measurement)
3. Finances (revenues, capital, and income)

Now that you know how critical it is to have a valid strategic plan for your business, it's time to start planning. Good luck.

Resources

Bracker, S. J., & Pearson, N. J. (1986). Planning and financial performance of small, mature firms. *Strategic Management Journal*, 7, 503-522.

Eisenhardt, M. K. (1989). Making fast strategic decisions in high-velocity environments. *Academy of Management Journal*, 32, 543-576.

Geller, D. (2004). *Instant strategist*. San Rafael, CA: Wizbizweb LLC Publishing Company. Retrieved September 2, 2006: http://www.instantstrategist.com.

Gibson, B. & Cassar, C. (2002). Planning behavior variables in small firms. *Journal of Small Business Management*, 40, 171.

Office of the Advocacy. (2004). *Small business economic indicators for 2003*. Washington, DC: US Small Business Administration.

Orser, B. (2000). Performance, firm size, and management problem solving. *Journal of Small Business Management*, 38, 42.

Perry, C. S. (2001). The relationship between small business plans and the failure of small businesses. *Journal of Small Business Management*, 39, 208.

Randy Miller

The Value of "When" in Setting up a Career Business

Are you an "if" or a "when"? The answer to this question is vital as you determine the current or next set of business choices that you will make. "If" you are truly thinking about this question, then "if" is your answer. If you did not hesitate, then you are more than likely a "when." "When" people give up a great deal; "if" people usually do not. "When" became my middle name when I embarked on bringing counseling, business, and technology together eight years ago. ReadyMinds has not only become my business, but my journey and my life.

Creating a Distance Counseling Company

Today, ReadyMinds is the most prominent distance career counseling and training company in the United States, and it has taken a leading role in advancing the field of counseling in the online technology sector. However, ReadyMinds was not founded as an online "dotcom" company. The initial model was built on traditional face-to-face (f2f) counselor/client relationships. With an entrepreneurial approach and the advent of the Internet, an entirely new model evolved.

Following is a narrative summary designed to show you the personal, business, and counseling insights that led to the creation of Ready & Motivated Minds (ReadyMinds). As the Founder and CEO of ReadyMinds, I believe the company was born largely out of my own experiences. It is the fibers of these experiences, woven together, that led me to create a private, for-profit company dedicated to counseling, training, and coaching.

ReadyMinds came about as a way to fulfill my need to nurture the passion of others, and to help people identify their potential, harness their strengths, and find courage in their decision-making. This is what others had done for me. The culmination of this mission in my mind was helping others embark upon and embrace career opportunities that would not only lead to a job, but would also fulfill and utilize their individual skills, talents, and personal vision.

Since the inception of ReadyMinds eight years ago, I have been asked on several occasions to share the ReadyMinds story. Namely, where did the idea to start a counseling "business" come from? Along with the personal inquiries, there are many questions about the field of distance career counseling. What exactly is it? I've heard of it, how does it work? How effective is it? How can I find out more?

September, 1985, Kingston, Rhode Island

Little did I know as I stood gazing at the pristine buildings of the University of Rhode Island (URI) quad that standing here on this day was the beginning of a journey that would take me down a path I never imagined, and set me on a course to help many others who would follow in my footsteps.

The crisp, clear fall day matched the exuberance I felt as a young freshman, born and raised in Philadelphia, who suddenly finds himself in a new world. Just being here was a miracle. My senior year of high school had been a turning point in my life. No, it wasn't acne, a prom date disaster, or problems in school. It was a neurological disease called Guillain-Barré Syndrome (GBS).

It came out of nowhere. Suddenly, I started having trouble getting up from squat position and walking up stairs at home. Assuming it was just fatigue, I used the lockers at school and stair railings at home for support. I was 18 and invincible. I believed that whatever this was would disappear as quickly as it had come. It didn't.

For eight weeks, I lay in a hospital bed as numerous doctors examined every nerve in my body, but offered no diagnoses. After much deliberation, the doctors performed a spinal tap that yielded a diagnosis: GBS, a disease that affects one of every 100,000 people. GBS is a debilitating disease that affects the central nervous system.

Once diagnosed, I immediately began physical therapy in the hospital to rebuild my muscles and regain control over my motor functions. Four to six weeks later, much to the doctors' surprise, I returned to school and resumed extra-curricular activities. This included playing basketball, my favorite sport, in which I excelled.

As I stood on the campus at URI, I was fully aware that I had been through something that could have derailed my life. Thankfully, this was not the case, and I was determined that this disease would not prevent me from living life to the fullest. Armed with a large briefcase-like duffle bag (as opposed to the typical student backpack), I found the nearest map, and proceeded to bob and weave my way through the maze of buildings to my destination, Roosevelt Hall, home of Career Services.

Career Services for First-Semester Freshmen

Behind the Career Services reception desk sat a kind elderly woman. "Can I help you?" she asked. "Yes, you can," I replied, "I'd like to speak to someone about my classes, my major, and my life plans." She smiled and said, "You'll need an appointment with a counselor but it's too early in the semester. How about three weeks from today at this time?" I responded, "Okay, I'll see you then…. thank you!"

You might be thinking, "How many students seek out Career Services as a first-semester freshman?" The answer is far too few. For many students, it seems to be completely overlooked until graduation looms. I have asked myself and others over the course of several years about this phenomenon. Is there anything that can be done to set young college persons on an early path towards self awareness, self evaluation, and decision making, skills that will serve them well in their personal and professional lives? I happen to believe there is.

Family Influences

Bounding down the stairs from Career Services, I thought of my parents. They divorced when I was seven years old. My mother was a former schoolteacher who became a full-time mom while my two siblings (an older sister and a younger brother) and I were growing up. She was always there for me, whether it was urging me on in sports, giving me advice on girls, or coaching me in my school work.

My relationship with my father was different, almost businesslike. He owned his own business, a clothing manufacturing company, and worked hard to grow the business. When it came to discussing college options, my mother said, "Go where you will be happy." My father agreed to pay the tuition each year, as long as I promised to work during the summer to cover all other expenses. This agreement with my father, plus the "investment" on my part, made me take college seriously.

My grandfather, a well-known speechwriter and voracious reader, was another source of inspiration to me. I could discuss anything with him – school, sports, music – and know that I'd walk away with an answer, or at least some clarity.

My mentors also played a significant role for me. These were the people who influenced my mission to nurture the passion of others: to help people identify their potential, harness their strengths, and find courage in their decision-making. All of these relationships strongly influenced my willingness to seek the guidance of adults who I thought could help me. As I look back, I see the developing pattern of seeking the guidance of mentors.

Back To Career Services

The next three weeks, as I waited for my appointment with Career Services, were a flurry of activity - getting acclimated, finding my way around, figuring out my classes (what was I getting myself into with Philosophy 101?), and making new friends. One of my closest and dearest friends turned out to be someone completely unexpected.

On the scheduled day, I returned to the Career Services Center for my appointment. "I'm so sorry," stated the same woman from behind the desk, "I didn't realize you were a freshman. You'll need to wait another three weeks for an appointment." My heart sank, and my face must have done the same. "Is this a problem?" the woman asked. "Yes, it is, I need to speak with your boss." "We don't have a boss," she replied," but I can see if the Director is here. Wait a few minutes please."

Ten minutes later, a distinguished man wearing a blue oxford shirt, tie and slacks, carrying a planner under his arm, began walking towards the students' area from the long corridor. With a firm handshake and unwavering eye contact, he introduced himself as Bill Wright-Swadel. "How can I help you, Randy?" "Mr. Swadel … [Interruption – "Please call me Bill"] … I have a few questions that I need answers to."

Without another word, Bill nodded and led the way to his office just down the hall. What started out as a "few questions", led to lunch, and what would become a "standing date" that took place at least once a month for the next four years. This translated into more than 48 lunches (sessions), and a great degree more mentoring and career counseling than most people get in a lifetime.

Bill remembers me asking him, "Bill, why wouldn't every student want to have what I have with you?" It is close to 20 years later, and I am happy to report that Bill and I have maintained a wonderful friendship and a stimulating professional relationship.

The Question That Is Not Asked

In my role as CEO of ReadyMinds, there is an old but effective saying I like to use when addressing staff, groups, and counselors: "The only stupid question is the question that is not asked." I have no doubt that my initial conversations with Bill showed my naiveté, but he always treated me with respect. Not once did I feel like I had asked a stupid question. He was instrumental in allowing me to understand and explore my entrepreneurial curiosities and plans. I worked all the way through college (more on that later), and in part because of my sessions with Bill, I gained confidence to try things that I may not have otherwise tried.

Soon I was approaching graduation. It was time to take the next step. Based on many of the conversations I'd had with Bill, I knew I wouldn't be happy working for a company that didn't offer a lot of freedom and growth potential. I was hungry for experience and success. I also knew I wanted to pursue something that really interested me, something that I was passionate about, although at that time, I didn't necessarily have the wherewithal to truly understand the idea of being "passionate" about work.

Career Landscape, 1988

The year was 1988. I mention this date only as a reminder that the Internet did not exist as it does today, and the career landscape was much different than it is now. I interviewed with Xerox, Colgate Palmolive, and IBM. All three seemed incredibly exciting to me. After a series of interviews, I received my first offer from Xerox. I could not have been happier. Yes, I would be living in Boston, which was not necessarily my first choice, but it was Xerox after all. What could be better? They had a great sales training program, the money was good, and I'd have opportunities to grow in the company.

My first phone call after I got the offer was not to my family or friends. I called Bill. He asked, "What will you be doing?" I said, "Weren't you listening? Xerox. Sales. Money!" He asked again (calmly), "What will Randy Miller be doing every day for Xerox? Please think about the question before you answer." I paused for what seemed like an eternity, "Hmmm, ok, I'll be selling paper, toner, and copiers … in Boston."

Suddenly it didn't sound so exciting. Bill always had a way of getting to the core of an issue in a very direct and easy way. It was never confrontational or judgmental. To this day, I think this is one of the most important skills a counselor or coach can possess – the ability to ask the simplest of questions and then listen to the real answer, not just what you or the client want to hear, but the real answer. The next trick (or skill) is helping your client (mentee) hear the answer also. These "Aha" moments may seem few and far between, but when they happen, it is rewarding for both the counselor and the client. Is this scenario really that different via distance? I was actually getting some telecounseling from Bill. However, at that time, neither of us would have looked at these phone communications in those terms.

Once I heard what Bill was saying, a weight lifted off my shoulders. I didn't really want to live in Boston or sell copiers. However, there was also some uncertainty. What was I going to do? I was confident that I would find something, and with my newly found, deeper understanding of what I was looking for, I was hopeful about my prospects.

Campus Connection

In 1987, as a junior in school, I had started working with Campus Connection. They published a national magazine distributed to schools all across the country. Each school had a sales representative who was responsible for getting local advertisers to place ads and coupons. This happened to be a very good fit for me. I loved people, and selling something I believed in came natural to me. I was also enterprising, convincing the corporate office to add a Fraternity/Sorority section. This strategy turned out to be a productive suggestion because all the different fraternities and sororities would take out ads too. Viola!

During my junior year, the URI edition became the largest grossing publication in the country. In my role, I met with numerous business owners, an exposure that enabled me to gain negotiation skills and helped me realize that business owners were just regular people like you and I. There was no reason to be intimidated by them. I embraced this experience and learned as much as I could.

After passing on the Xerox offer, I accepted a position as Vice President of Sales with Campus Connection. I was responsible for managing students all across the country. These students ran their own editions, and sold all the ads, just as I had done. The environment was more entrepreneurial than that of Xerox. The president/CEO of the company was a University of Pennsylvania graduate, and the other partner, a Stanford graduate. It was a tremendous learning experience. I saw determination, "guts," late nights, deals made, deals lost, right decisions, wrong decisions, successes, failures. These experiences allowed me to train, teach, and organize others. I also gained hands-on experience working with national accounts, such as Amex and AT&T.

This was my entrée into the business world and to my introduction to the college market. I learned how corporations targeted and spent money on this population. This experience would one day serve me well as I began to explore potential partners for ReadyMinds. Being in this entrepreneurial environment, seeing my decisions acted upon, and being involved in strategic planning and brainstorming was exhilarating, fun and inspiring. It was here that I really began to contemplate my own future as a business owner.

A Brief Sidetrack

The magazine was sold to another publishing company a year and a half after I started. At this point, I still opted against the corporate route, deciding instead to join my father in his clothing manufacturing business. I started in sales and worked my way up. Eventually my father and I started our own company, which I helped to run successfully for eight years, learning every aspect of the organization – sales, finance, marketing, and oh yeah, making the coffee and working on weekends! I did well in the business, but this industry was not where my heart was. The concept of building something that I was truly interested in stayed with me. As I reflected on my experiences and on those who had influenced me in my life, the idea of what is now ReadyMinds began to take shape.

The Birth of ReadyMinds

Thinking back to my time in school, I'll never forget the day, sitting in class reflecting on a recent discussion with Bill. Whether on the phone or in person, he consistently opened doors for me. He made me think of things I had not thought of before. He helped me to view situations and decisions in a different light. I began to get *ready* for every session. I would anticipate Bill's questions, and I realized how my sessions with him *motivated* me to follow up and explore all that we had covered in the session. While thinking of this, I wrote down *Ready and Motivated Minds*, thinking about how everyone should be ready, motivated, and of course, have the ability to be mindful, to think in creative and new ways. After I had written this phrase down, I realized *RMM* were also my initials, Randy Michael Miller. Something clicked and I knew this was a beginning …. of what? I just wasn't sure. I folded this piece of paper and securely stashed it in my wallet.

Reflections on Mentoring

What transpired during my four years at URI and in my sessions and talks with Bill, as well as with the start of my business career, made me realize that I had truly been given a gift – one of guidance and mentoring. In my work with Bill, I had come to know myself and also felt that I had gained an understanding of others. However, I wasn't sure exactly how I was going to give to others what Bill had given to me. I felt like I wanted to dedicate my life to finding a way to share these gifts with as many people as possible. In addition, I understood marketing and sales. This knowledge served to be a tremendous asset.

Towards the end of the eight-year period of working in the manufacturing business with my Dad, I methodically began to build a business plan around the idea of business and counseling. I began to apply the ideas and principles that I had learned during my sessions with Bill in order to build the framework. I was committed from the beginning to ensuring that the crux of this business would be the delivery of a quality counseling experience – something that had not been done before – at least on the scale I was imagining.

Launching ReadyMinds

I resurrected that scrap of paper from my wallet, jotted down Ready & Motivated Minds as the name of my business on the business plan 6-month project, and I "hit the road." I believed so strongly in my idea

that I was eager to share it, not just with my peers and others in the business world, but with students. I began visiting colleges and universities, such as Penn State, St. Johns, Rutgers, and Bryant, to speak to students.

I wanted to share my real world experiences and let students know, especially freshmen, that they had the ability to take control of their futures. I encouraged them to visit the campus counselors and utilize the campus resources as a way to evaluate their options – to think about their class selections and their future career goals. It was this "passion" to help others in their quest to find meaningful success that sparked the counseling business model. I finally understood the meaning of "passion." It was the thought of reaching as many people as possible that propelled this model into the "distance" space.

Tips for Potential Entrepreneurs

I recommend creating an easy-to-navigate website and clear, direct print literature explaining exactly what your services are. Understanding your own service will the content of your business will ultimately aid in marketing efforts. Viral marketing is the best form of marketing as it not only free, but it results in hundreds or thousands of people talking about you and/or your service without running an advertisement. Viral marketing is an Internet-based business strategy through which you share your message with others. Keep in mind that this does not occur overnight; it takes years to build, maintain, and deliver. You must first have quality services. Otherwise, what do people have to talk about or to refer to others?

Take your personal journey, embrace your truth, live your dream and mission, and it will come together. If you believe in what you do (and have your own story), it will be easier to market. It is also okay to bring in outside marketing people who can assist you. Following are steps you can take in developing a business strategy.

- First, understand and appreciate what your mission is.

- Then, research what else is out there, either by company or by category. For example, if you are interested in distance counseling, you could enter into a search engine on the Internet "distance counseling" or companies (like ReadyMinds) that provide such services. Before you position your company or practice, learn how to position yourself to your advantage. You must have a competitive advantage.

- Finally, understand your goals and objectives. Do you have a unique idea? Do others currently do what you are seeking to do? Are you copying what already exists? If so, are you going to do it better?

Conclusion

I hope my personal business journey has touched you in some way. It would be my pleasure to communicate with you. Let me know if I can be of further assistance with your marketing and business efforts. You will be writing a new chapter in your own life very soon. Whether it is read by many or read by you alone is insignificant. Keep your notes along the way, especially during the tougher days. I continue to keep all of mine! I wish you well in your strategic planning, your marketing plans, and your mission in life.

Resources

The following resources are both inspiring and sound. Some are dated, yet still apply.

Bloom, J. W., and Walz, G. R. (2004). *Cybercounseling & cyberlearning: An encore.* Greensboro, North Carolina: CAPS Press.

Bronson, P. (2002). *What should I do with my life?* New York: Random House,.

Brown, D. (1980). *The entrepreneur's guide.* New York: Ballantine Books.

Caples, J. (1994). *Tested advertising methods.* Englewood Cliffs, NJ: Prentice-Hall.

Drucker, P. F. (1972). *Concept of the corporation.* New York: John Day,

Farson, R., & Keyes, R. (2002). *Whoever makes the most mistakes wins: The paradox of innovation.* New York: Free Press.

Gottry, S, (2005). *Common sense business: Starting, operating and growing your small business in any economy.* New York: Harper Collins.

Iacocca, L. & Novak, W. , Eds.(1984). *Lacocca, an autobiography.* New York: Bantam Books.

Kaufman, B. N. (1991). *Happiness is a choice.* New York: Fawcett Columbine,.

Malone, J. F., Miller, R. M., & Walz, G.R. (2006). *Distance counseling: Expanding the counselor's reach and impact.* Dallas, TX: PRO-ED.

Sher, B. & Smith, B. Eds. (1994). *I could do anything: If I only knew what it was.* New York: Delacorte Press.

White, R M., Jr. (1977). *The entrepreneur's manual.* Radnor, Pennsylvania: Chilton Book.

VII. What challenges have you encountered?

How did you meet challenges as you developed a business? Describe a particularly challenging situation/client interaction that you have encountered and how you turned it to your advantage (or how you would resolve the situation if you could do it again). Include theories or models that relate to how you have dealt with challenges. Who were your mentors? To solve problems related to your business, try Exercises 14 and 15 in Appendix A created by Jack Chapman and Susan Whitcomb.

Jack Chapman

Building a Career Consulting Practice: My Story

I began my journey as a barely profitable, wet behind the ears, aspiring career coach eking out a living, and I finally made it to a seasoned veteran career consultant with high paying clients in a thriving private practice. It took me 27 years, and along the way I jumped over five big hurdles.

2006 marks my 27th year in the business of career advising. Today, I not only run a successful career coaching practice, but I have helped many other career advisors, people with ordinary coaching skills, to start from zero and achieve six-figure annualized incomes – no, not in 27 years – in as little as 12 to 18 months. Along the way, I have identified the five biggest hurdles and learned how to clear these hurdles easily in a sprint to a thriving private practice.

The five hurdles are:

- **Confidence**
  Achieving self-confidence, especially through the belief that there's enough business out there and enough competence inside me, that I can produce real marketable and sellable value.

- **Marketing Communications**
  Establishing channels of communications with enough people so they will refer people (prospects) in career distress to me.

- **Setting Appointments**
  Using my counseling skills to build a relationship with callers so they will come in to see me at least once.

- **Pricing**
  Pricing and packaging my services so that I thrive at 150k+ personally; it's realistic compared to other similar investments; it rewards speed and competence; and finally it's affordable by most people.

- **Support**
  Finding other committed, competent, career advisors so I don't have to do it all through expensive trial and error.

Join me in my journey. I hope that by sharing my steps, you can find your own path to personal career satisfaction and success by providing the same to others.

1. Confidence

My first obstacle in starting a private practice in 1979 was facing the fear that there wasn't enough business "out there." What I know now is: People are clamoring to pay for career help. They just don't know how to express what they need. If you develop the confidence inside yourself that you can help someone, they will believe it, too. If you're unsure you're worth $3000 – $5,000 to put someone's career on track, they will also be unsure.

The tougher the job market and economy become, the more individuals need to make decisions about how to succeed in their working life. When they gladly hire professionals to do their legal services, car repairs, and tax preparation, they do so because the "do it yourself" alternative would be risky if not impossible. They can be just as excited and committed to hire experts to help them not only do a resume, but also choose and find work that is well paid and satisfying. This is where skillful practice and management make the difference.

I remember my first foray into career consulting. I had taken intensive career courses, I had a master's degree in Guidance and Counseling, and I placed an ad in a paper for a 10-week career course. I got 10 participants. Only three of them made it through the whole set of sessions and only one of them got a new job. I thought something was wrong with me, that I had failed. I now know it's tremendously difficult to get someone to make a complete career move. Even at my best, I only get 85% of my candidates to complete with a new job. But it's not me. It is the nature of the beast; change is difficult, and some people just give up on making a change no matter how good you are.

A couple years after going out on my own, I became an employee with a national career development firm that had 50 offices across the United States and Canada. I got a glimpse into how big the market is, and how much people are willing to spend to get their careers in order. I rose through the ranks in that firm until I became owner of the Chicago-Milwaukee territory. I had 20 employees, 4 offices, 9 career advisors, and 30 new clients a month for whom we were responsible. I took on the task of national training and development for career advisors, and my offices pioneered innovative processes in career advising.

Eight years after becoming owner, I found myself spending 90% of my time administering the business and only 10% counseling. I'm a much better counselor than business manager, so I sold the business and went back into private practice. By that time, I knew unequivocally that this is a saleable product. Today, I look at people in private practice who are worried whether they'll "make it." They don't know what I learned in my years as a career search business owner: People are clamoring for our help. Why not? After all, it's free!

Unlike a lawyer, car mechanic, computer repairman, or tax accountant, career advisory services are nearly "free" to the individual. It's certainly fair to say that 90% of the time the service pays for itself. If you hire a lawyer to come to traffic court with you, you may save yourself some grief and higher insurance rates, but it doesn't actually put extra money in your pocket. If you help people figure out what they really want to do, besides being happier (there's no price tag too big for personal happiness), they also command more money. Also, they get paid sooner.

Consider two people. One flails around in the job market, answering ads, hoping that s/he'll somehow land in the right job/career. Another hires you so he'll not only know which jobs are their best fit, but he'll also know how to effectively reach decision makers in the "hidden job market." Compare their earnings: the hit-and-miss ad-answering person will spend more time unemployed, more time job searching, and spend more time in lower-paying jobs than the focused networker.

Add up the dollars. If all you were able to do was help job seekers get to work three or four weeks sooner than they would have on their own, that's $2,000 to $5,000 (or more) actual money in the bank. Add to that 10% higher pay because the job requires their real capabilities, and another 10% because you coached them in their salary negotiations, now you've added $5,000 to $10,000 (or more) to their coffers. And that's just in the first year. Over their 30-year career lifetime, your coaching could mean hundreds of thousands of dollars to them. There's no doubt you can be a godsend to any working person. Now, how do you attract interested people and turn them into paying clients?

It took me many years of learning the craft of career advising for me to get to a place where I could

charge hefty fees for hefty results. Along the way, I read every career book available, I attended personal growth weekends, encounter groups, seminars, and workshops because I knew that I could only take people as far as I myself had personally come. If I could not conduct my own networking interviews, make my own 5-year and 10-year goals, think big, negotiate well, and have many ways to communicate to and reach people, then that would be the limit of my career advising. Getting better was not just learning more tricks, it was personal growth and self-development. I took some pretty scary personal growth workshops, let me tell you!

Earlier I spoke about five hurdles. I didn't face them sequentially. They were all there, all the time. A better metaphor, perhaps, would be that I had to prepare five courses of a meal all at once. So, while I'm getting the flour ready for the bread, I'm also reading the recipe for the dessert, finding the spices for the sauce, fermenting the wine, picking and chopping the vegetables, and marinating the meat.

Along the lines of growth in competence, a personal milestone came one day when I was working at the career development firm. We had "client audits" once a month. Each counselor had to show progress on each of the clients in his/her caseload. The audit was done the first week of every month, so at the 25th of any given month, I'd go over my list and say, "Well . . . it's time to go round up my doggies." Meaning, of course, that I had to reach out and get the clients that were stuck and wandering around. It kind of implied that it was their fault. If they'd only quit getting lost, I wouldn't have to do this.

When I said it, I noticed that it was disempowering. By calling them "doggies," I implied that they were dumb cattle, and I, the all-powerful cowboy, had to go round them up. I realized, that these "lost souls" really represented my own threshold of incompetence. These clients had invested significant money in their careers with us. They were not wandering around because they were lazy, or obstinate; it was because I didn't have the communication skills, yet, to reach them and set them on the right track. So I changed their name - any difficult clients became my "teachers." By working with teacher after teacher, my skills got broader, deeper, and better.

Over the years I learned each piece of the career consulting process in depth, and applied and adapted it to each individual client I worked with. Frankly, when I began, I wasn't much better than the clients I served. Today, after 27 years, I consider myself A+ on most aspects of the work. I had the luxury of rigorous support, innovation, and training from my 13 years in the career management firm. To be successful in independent practice, I believe you must be able to deliver both aspects of the career advising process: (a) career focus and (b) job-search tactics. I came up with 18 aspects of our career advising work, but they fall into these two broad categories: career focus or choice.

Career Focus or Choice

Our work is half "art" and half "science." No one knows enough about the hundreds of thousands of different occupations and industries and myriad or unique qualities of each client to precisely pinpoint a client's career choice. However, you should be able to offer clients initial directions to pursue, and most importantly, a method for career exploration from that point on. For example, a burned-out teacher comes to you for career advising. You should be able to figure out if ENFP (Myers-Briggs) choices, like training and development, sales, motivational speaking, counseling, etc., are viable choices for her. Or maybe she is more suited to ISTJ meeting planning, event planning, event-based fund raising, and office administration.

Familiarity with tests like Myers Briggs, Sensory Integration Dysfunction (DSI), World-of-Work (WOW), Strong Campbell, 16 PF (Pearson self-report questionnaire that provides detailed information on 16 primary personality traits), a basic understanding of corporate functions like operations, manufacturing, sales, finance, and corporate trends impacting the workforce such as outsourcing and self employment are the "science" of career focus. The "art" of career focus is the ability to listen deeply to another person to impartially discover their passions, interests, visions, and dreams. What are the things they've always wanted to do, but gave up on?

For instance, I worked with a Human Resource manager who loved antiques, and eventually worked for and then purchased an antique store. Another one of my clients was a logistics supervisor who loved trains; he is now a train conductor. No aptitude test can give you this level of correctness. It's the "art" of helping someone discern his or her career focus. Beyond that, your work search method should kick in. You help clients pick one or two of the areas that appeal to them. Then your coaching should help them to discontinue "informational interviews," and to have more job-focused exploratory meetings. Then they can either decide among those choices or discover revised alternatives based on these interviews.

Job Search Tactics

Once they decide on an area, say, "technical sales," your coaching should be able to encourage them to have more job-focused exploratory meetings with hiring decision makers. We'll call those "networking meetings."

There is a fine line here. Once clients are focused, they no longer interview for information. On the other hand, they shouldn't approach a hiring decision maker expecting that the hiring person will have or know of a specific vacancy or opening at that time. So, you teach them how to identify, approach, and interview with hiring decision makers with the explicit purpose of being considered as a candidate, but not expecting a specific opening. If you don't feel fully competent that you can really zero in on which career choices would be best for people, then apprentice yourself to someone who can and learn it. The same goes for clients with the job search process.

Even if you do feel confident in these areas, you'll want to arrange a support structure so that you stay at the cutting edge of your field and have help when you get more challenging clients. Courses in career counseling cannot adequately teach you how to do this unless they include a lot of actual supervised experience working directly with clients. For more information on the 18 basic competencies, see Resources: #4 Private practice package.

2. Marketing Communications

This brings us to obstacle two: Establishing channels of communications so you will get referrals. The saying goes, "Build a better mouse trap and the world will beat a path to your door." I haven't found that to be the case. I have become more and more competent as a career advisor, but competence didn't automatically get people to beat a path to my door. A truer statement might be, "Cleverly market even a lousy mouse trap, and the world will beat a path to your door." When I was in the executive career-consulting firm, finding clients was expensive, but easy. They spent $10,000 in advertising, got 300 to 400 people to inquire, and got 15 to 20 new clients a month. Clearly that model wouldn't work in private practice.

My earlier experience with advertising made me realize that I could get the phone to ring by advertising, but the prospects I got that way were cautious, skeptical, and interested in comparison-shopping. This was a far cry from the people who called me up because of word of mouth, who knew what I did, and were favorably disposed to work with me from the beginning.

When I left the career firm and launched out on my own, I couldn't count on word of mouth to happen by itself. I learned marketing methods from a program I studied with Jay Abraham, a marketing genius. I paid $5,000 to do this intensive weekend, but it easily became the source of $100,000 worth of business over the years. There are three basic ways to be well known enough to get a steady stream of clients: (a) speeches, (b) newsletter, and (c) niche identity.

Speeches

Job-search clubs, libraries, service clubs, associations, college placement departments, and continuing education programs are all thirsty for career management presentations. I developed a few highly interactive presentations that gave people practical career tools and reached out to these organizations in order provide speeches. For more information on speaking venues and strategies, view Resources: Baker's dozen.

Newsletter

After a speech, I didn't just speak, hand out business cards, and walk away. I captured their names and addresses and "dripped" on them every month with a monthly newsletter. Without a newsletter, I would soon be forgotten. With a monthly newsletter, I'd be remembered month after month.

Niche Identity

I looked for organizations with 1000+ members who personally interact with each other. Remember the 80/20 rule. If you make yourself visible to 20% of the members, the other 80% will find out about you through them. I selected the "New Warrior Training Community." That's a community of men who completed a personal growth training (as had I). I gave free career advancement workshops to the members and developed a reputation as "the career guy."

Anyone can find a niche that fits his or her background and interests. For information on speeches, see "Home Run Speeches" in Resources. So now your phone rings, so what? If I couldn't turn an inquiry call into a paying client, it's all for naught.

3. Setting Appointments

Here's what I learned jumping over the third hurdle. I learned not to sell on the phone. When people asked, "what do you do," I didn't go into all the ins and outs of my career counseling services. I just listened, empathized, and suggested a small step - these were my natural counseling skills. I simply applied them to the prospect and got them in for a problem-solving meeting. I got them to take a small step.

The "small step" is the cornerstone of my sales process. In the big career development firm, I learned that it takes time to get some people to make up their mind about investing in themselves. I didn't want to give away my time, like coaches do, in a "taste and see" session. That seemed too expensive. So, I developed a session where, in an hour or two, I could make a big difference in how they understood their problem, and how they'd go about solving it.

One name for my small step is a Career Laser Session (CLS). I tell people that in an hour or two, we can get to the root of any career problem, and I give them a practical plan to solve it. I charged for this initial CLS session. I set the fee for this at a level high enough to indicate that my caller was serious, but low enough so that it would not pose any hardship. Specifically, that's above the amount they'd donate to a charity, and below a full hourly rate.

What did I do in a Career Laser Session? I listened to their career history, told them, broadly, what their strengths were, and let them know what's missing for them to reach their goals. Most clients benefited by meeting the following needs:

- systematic exploration of career options
- more interviews with hiring decision-makers
- better self-presentation
- more accomplishment-oriented resume
- better support and accountability in their search
- higher proficiency in job interviewing
- better management of salary negotiations

I crafted these needs into a chronological plan: step one, step two, step three, etc., and I gave them their plan of action. Finally, I suggested that if they wanted help with any of those steps, I'd be glad to help them further. Then I set another appointment to look at that. In the second appointment I laid out the plan, the price, and closed the deal.

4. Pricing

This is the most controversial aspect of building my successful practice. First, package pricing gets a bad rap in the media. Even Dick Bolles - a guru in our field – suggests in the back of *What Color is Your Parachute?* that job hunters be wary of paying big fees up front. The trouble is this: If a career advisor charges by the hour, then financially s/he is motivated to have the process take as long as possible, and the candidate is motivated to use them as little as possible. This is the opposite of a desirable state for both parties.

The other extreme, charging and collecting thousands of dollars up front, is not a "share the risk" financial arrangement either. So, I compromised. I set one fee, but I get paid over time. That way, I'm always "on the hook" to earn my monthly payment, but the client is "on the hook" for the whole fee; so I'm motivated to complete the work in an appropriate timeframe, and the client is motivated to use me as much as s/he can. Now the financial incentives are properly set. For information on speaking venues and strategies, see #7 "Package vs Hourly" and #42 "Cancel Hourly" in Resources.

When prospective clients returned to hear about the program I had for them, I laid it out and charged them a fixed fee, with payments spread out over time, and promised to stick with them through the several months of their entire job and career search.

5. Support

The most crucial component of building my private practice was the training and development I got in my 13 years with the career development firm. I was always talking with the other 25 franchise owners; I was always problem solving with my own career advising staff; I was constantly absorbing every good idea and dumping every bad one I could. If I had spent those 13 years alone, I'm sure I'd have 1 year of experience repeated 13 times. I would never have learned sales; I would never have understood the demand and the prices executives were happy to pay. It was support, interaction, training, problem solving, and conversations with others that ultimately account for 27 years of experience in 27 years of time.

In 1996, when I sold my franchise and went back to private practice, I looked for others with whom to make a mastermind group. I searched the country to find other peers so I could progress by trial and success, not trial and error. I couldn't find them, so I built my own network. I also created the "Guild of Career Excellence," a mastermind group of career advisors in private practice, who can not only master the basics of a hundred-thousand-plus private practice, but can also use each other to make creative innovations in career counseling work. For more information about "Guild of Career Excellence," see Resources.

I can't emphasize enough how you must walk your talk if you want people to buy your services. Would you trust a surgeon who had no affiliation with a hospital? A fitness trainer who smokes? A publicity consultant who had typos in his brochure? Would you hire a career counselor who had not mastered making a prosperous income in his or her own career? Support gives you the know-how to earn any amount of income you wish, part time through full time, from your career counseling.

When a member of the public is considering hiring you, what will you say if they ask you, "Do you have...

- A thriving career doing what you love?

- A career plan for where you want to be in 3 to 5 years?
- A program to learn, grow, and maintain the leading edge in your field?
- A close group of colleagues who are "best in class"?
- Accountability for implementing your career and business growth activities?
- A "hallelujah chorus" to encourage you and guide your success?

I hope my story can give you confidence and inspiration to explore career advising as a lucrative private practice. You are welcome to email me any questions, observations, feedback, and disagreements that you might have about my ideas.

Resources

Chapman, J. *Twelve biggest mistakes job hunters and career changers make and how to avoid them.* This free 34-page booklet covers the difference between "opportunities" and "openings" in the job market. It also doubles as an advertorial for career services. *jkchapman@aol.com*.

Chapman, J. #4 *Private practice package.* Detailed list of the 18 basic competencies such as testing and skills analysis. jkchapman@aol.com.

Chapman, J. Guild of Career Excellence. jchapman@aol.com.

Chapman, J. #7 *Package vs. hourly* and #42 *Cancel hourly.* Explanation of why package pricing works better for a private practice. You'll learn why it's better for your private client, it's better for you, it's crucial to your success, it's crucial to your private clients' success, it's the only practical way to make a good living as a private career consultant, it's the only way to generate private referrals, and it's the only way to get private clients to use you fully. *jkchapman@aol.com*.

Chapman, J. *Home run speeches: How to get one speech to pay off four times.* Jkchapman@aol.com.

Chapman, J. #32 & #33: *Baker's dozen speaking venues.* Information on speeches, especially how to get one speech to pay off four times. Jkchapman@aol.com.

Susan Whitcomb

It Takes a "Two-Track" Mind for Entrepreneurial Success

In writing this contribution to the monograph, I considered carefully the different challenges and opportunities I have faced over the past two decades as an entrepreneur. I thought, "So many to choose from!" Before I share a few of them, let me offer a brief history of my entrepreneurial journey.

I never had childhood dreams of being an entrepreneur. My college major was music therapy, and I had every intention of being a music therapist and making extra spending money by teaching flute lessons. After an internship and short stint as a music therapist in Dallas, nationwide cutbacks in mental health spending made me realize that this might not be a career track with great job security.

In order to be closer to my family and, not clear on what I wanted to do with my life, I returned to California and picked up a job as a secretary, which I was quite good at. I had always been great at spelling and editing, was a whiz at the keyboard (125+ words a minute), and, with a preference on the Myers-Briggs Type Inventory (MBTI) for Judging, enjoyed planning and organizing. (For any MBTI enthusiasts out there, I know you'll be curious about the full four-letter code – it's INFJ).

I soon moved to being an executive secretary for a commercial real estate broker and then a legal secretary for a partner in a law firm. I became fast friends with one of the word processing specialists with whom I worked. She was the one with the entrepreneurial vision, not me. Her dream was to open a secretarial and resume writing service, but she wanted a partner so she didn't have to go it alone. The next thing I knew, I was writing resumes nights and weekends and within a year or so, quit my legal secretarial job and jumped in with both feet. I had a home-based office, with very campy office furnishings (a sewing table for my computer table and a television stand to hold my printer and paper supplies).

My only business debt was a monthly computer payment – back in the 1980s, desktop computers cost three times what they do today. I lasted all of six months with my partner before we went our separate ways. First entrepreneurial lesson learned: Think carefully when choosing a partner! Long story short, I found myself on my own as an inadvertent entrepreneur (with house payments to make, which was very motivating!). I soon realized I absolutely loved being my own boss. Some might call it coincidence or fate.

I like to give credit to the hand of a loving God who orchestrated the chess pieces of my life into a plan that far surpassed what I ever dreamed or hoped for.

As I look back, I realize that the business grew only to the degree that I grew. I read everything about careers that I could get my hands on, attended professional conferences, and stretched far beyond my comfort zone when opportunities crossed my professional path (and there were plenty!). Early on, membership in a professional association was probably the best investment I made in my business because it connected me with like-minded people who were willing to share their painful entrepreneurial mistakes, as well as success secrets. Later, my investment in working with an experienced business and life coach was the ingredient for success. I soon dropped clients that needed secretarial work and honed in on a resume writing niche and later, an expanded career management niche.

The opportunity to write my first book, *Resume Magic*, came because of a casual conversation with David Noble, then editor at JIST Publishing, during the cocktail hour at a resume writers' conference. With no intentions of authorship, I simply asked, "Have you ever thought about doing a resume book that featured before and after samples?" His response was, "No, but you'd be the one to write it! Get me a proposal." And the MAGIC series was born. *Interview Magic* followed in 2005, and *Job Search Magic* was released in 2006.

In 2001, I discovered the dynamic discipline of coaching. I felt I'd come full circle from my original career focus on music therapy, except that coaching allowed me to work with people who were whole, naturally creative, and resourceful. My love of coaching led to founding Career Coach Academy, where I teach an interactive program via teleclass that is accredited by the International Coach Federation for 30 hours of coach-specific training. More recently, my business life took another leap as I acquired Career Masters Institute in 2004 and now create a culture of information and innovation for hundreds of career practitioners, many of whom are "solopreneurs" (solopreneurs are entrepreneurs with no partners or employees) and entrepreneurs.

So, there you have it – a fast-forward tour of my 20-plus-year entrepreneurial journey. I'm the first to admit that none of these progressive steps was carefully planned out years or even months in advance. Instead, they all were the result of opportunity intersecting with preparation and the courage to step up to the plate.

Now let's talk about the subject of this chapter challenges!

The Mechanics and Mindset of Turning Challenges into Opportunities

Life is relentless in tossing us opportunities that stretch our character and our competence. These situations often come with different frames, such as computer problems or difficult clients, but at the heart of each challenge is the ever-present Journey Of Becoming. To turn challenges into opportunities, I have found that a two-pronged approach works best. One track tackles the "Mechanics" of the situation—this is the "frame" mentioned above. The other track addresses the "Mindset"—this is the character and competence component (see Appendix A, Exercise 15). Addressing the mechanics of a challenge without taking into account the mindset will not overcome the problem, and vice versa.

The Mechanics

Let's start by looking at the Mechanics. The diagram below, entitled the "I CAN Entrepreneur," pinpoints 10 different frames within which your problems/opportunities will likely come:

As an entrepreneur, I've encountered my share of challenges in each of these areas. For instance, early in my career, I fell flat in Category 4: Market, Secure Strategic Partners, Network, and Close Sales. Because of my preference for introversion, I cowered when it came to traditional networking. I also had trouble closing sales because I felt sorry for everyone and didn't want to take their money (I bet many of you can relate to this)! In time, I discovered ways to network that felt authentic and meaningful, and I learned how to package and price my services based on value, sell

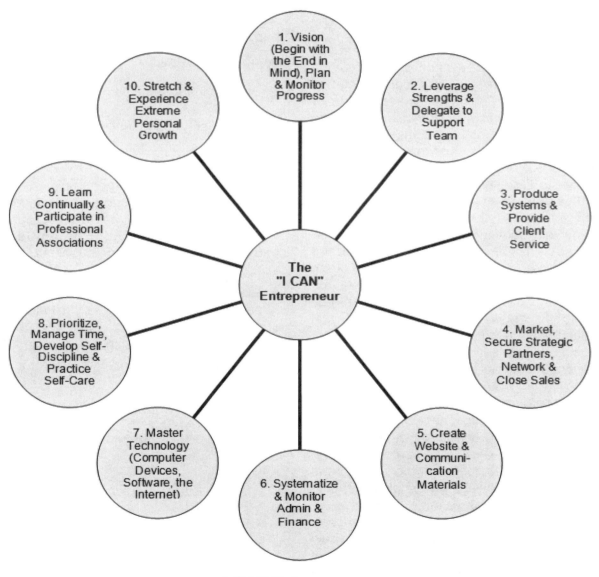

I CAN Entrepreneur

from a permission-based model, and create a realistic budget to help me remember just how much it cost to be in business. Interestingly, the more confident I became, both in myself and my clients' ability to take ownership of their success, the more I seemed to attract clients who understood the value of my services and were happy to pay!

Another Category 4 challenge for me was finding the time to write articles for my client newsletter. Because of this, I created something that I wish had been around when I was building my business. In each of the Career Coach Academy e-newsletters, there is an article that you can take and use for your own newsletter. (See the Resources section to find out how to access and receive these articles.)

One of the biggest challenges I still face is a crossover between Categories 2 and 8: Delegate and Prioritize. With responsibilities as executive director for Career Masters Institute, trainer for Career Coach Academy, author, and coach for a limited number of career and entrepreneurial clients (not to mention roles as wife and mother), it takes deliberate intention to stay focused on what's most important and to delegate daily. As your business grows, surround yourself with support and excel at delegating. The saying, "It's hard to find good help" rings true for most entrepreneurs. And yet, you must trust that the right people are out there and will be just as happy to find you as you are to find them. Fortunately, these days you can work virtually with people located across the country and world.

My support team has slowly grown over the years. It definitely takes an investment of time and patience to train others, but the payoffs can be great. Currently, my support staff consists of an accountant who comes to my home office twice a month to pay bills, track margins, and keep books in order; a virtual assistant (she lives one time zone away) who handles things like processing membership renewals; another virtual assistant and database programmer (she lives two time zones away) who handles technical and web-based matters; a program manager (she also lives two time zones away) who handles marketing and administration for Career Coach Academy; an on-call technology whiz (he actually lives in the same time zone) who helps keep me up to speed on technology; and a college-age personal assistant who helps with anything from running business errands to bathing my dogs. There are also a number of talented and committed industry leaders who volunteer their time to help make Career Masters Institute all that it is. And, of course, I have a coach! Clearly, success as a solopreneur/entrepreneur is a team sport!

Resources

Branton, N., and Whitcomb, S. B. (2006). *Certified leadership & talent management coach training manual.* Career Coach Academy, CareerCoachAcademy.com.

Rotter, J. B. (1966). Generalized expectancies for internal versus external control of reinforcement. *Psychological Monographs*, 80. (Whole No. 609).

Whitcomb, S.W. (2005). I*nterview magic: Job interview secrets from America's career and life coach.* Indianapolis: JIST Works, Inc.

Whitcomb, S.W. (2006). J*ob search magic: Insider secrets from America's career and life coach.* Indianapolis: JIST Works, Inc.

Whitcomb, S. B. (2006). Certified career management coach training manual. Career Coach. Academy. Retrieved September 2, 2006: http://www.careercoachacademy.com.

Web Resources

Career Coach Academy newsletter with free articles. Retrieved September 2, 2006: http://www.career coachacademy.com/subscribe.php.

Career Masters Institute entrepreneurial teleseminars. Retrieved September 2, 2006: http://www.cminstitute.com/teleseminars.html.

Free locus of control assessment. University of North Carolina at Charlotte, Department of Psychology: Retrieved September 2, 2006: http://www.psych.uncc.edu/pagoolka/LC.html.

Free locus of control assessment. McGraw-Hill: Retrieved September 2, 2006: http://www.dushkin.com/connectext/psy/ch11/survey11.mhtml.

International Virtual Assistants Association. Retrieved September 2, 2006: http://www.ivaa.org.

VIII. How do you evaluate what more you need to do to reach your goals?

Have you had to change gears at various points? If so, how have you refined your marketing and operational strategy as you developed the business? Do you have computerized scheduling, sales, operational, and/or database systems? If so, have they been helpful in developing your business? In Appendix A, find Exercises 16 and 17 designed by Martha Russell and Lynn Joseph, that you might try in evaluating what you have accomplished and what more you need to do to reach your goals.

Martha Russell

What a Ride It Has Been!

As I reflect on my professional journey, I realize that each and every step has led to this moment. And what a ride it has been. I would like to begin with a bit of history that I believe frames the work I have done. My bachelor's degree was in speech/theater education and my first career job was overseas running a service club for the military and organizing a German-American theater group. Then came love, marriage, and children.

When I decided to reenter the job market after several years of part-time jobs in theatre and elementary schools, I turned to what I believed I knew best and what was available at the time – working with people. I became a placement consultant for a temporary and permanent placement agency, and I stayed in that industry in one capacity or another for several years. I loved working with people and their employment needs, but there were two major elements missing. One was the process used in working with a job seeker and the underlying difference between finding a person a job and helping them develop and grow so they could do it on their own. The second was working for someone else when I really wanted my own business. I had always been on the borders of "free lance" work and special projects even while I was not in the career job market. I had a variety of experiences, knowledge that I had some skills, and a strong yearning to do something special.

That yearning led to graduate school in human resources in a school of business. After struggling for several years, I switched back to education and took my first course in career development. I was hooked. Before completing my master's degree, I took the plunge and opened my own placement agency with the idea that I could combine placement and career counseling, and help people reach their goals. However, the differences between placement and career development, as well as partnership issues, led to selling my share of the agency, completing my degree, and opening my own career counseling

practice. From the beginning, I knew it was the right thing to do, from a business perspective as well as a personal one.

From a small, one-desk, two-chair office and a primary focus on individual client sessions, to a large office with a library and a staff, and now a home office in a rural setting, my business has changed. I now communicate with individual clients via phone and email with no geographical boundaries. My laptop is my constant companion as I travel across the globe to deliver training, conference presentations, and consulting services. Russell Career Services and I have grown, changed and evolved in ways I never would have imagined. And after 19 years, I still know it's the right thing to do.

Goals and Evaluation

Many changes in the operations of my business have made it even more crucial to build on a solid foundation of goal setting, planning, and a continuous evaluation of personal and professional goals. Setting goals is paramount to success in any business.

As I look back on the first few years of my practice, the goals I set and the way that I evaluated them was a fairly simple process. It was based on numbers. Did I meet my predicted number of client sessions, number of training days, and number of presentations. Did I meet my projected revenue? I focused on short-term goals, rarely setting up numbers and systems for more than three to six months ahead. At some point, I settled in and trusted that Russell Career Services was a successful business and would be around for many years. I relaxed and accepted that the focus of my work would be different, the delivery methods would change, and that the way I evaluated the challenges and celebrations of the business would set the stage for a renewed vision and reenergized goals.

Evaluating and setting new goals became an annual exercise as well as part of ongoing long-range planning. Attention was given to vision, mission, and the development of a professional logo, tag line, and marketing plan. I hired a consultant and a graphic designer and got ready to expand into my dual dream of international work and a retreat center in the mountains. Websites had not become the norm, and my plan for growth was simple and low tech.

Challenges

Some of the reasons I cherished being in business for myself also presented some of the greatest challenges. I am motivated by flexibility and independence. Setting my own schedule is important to me, and as I have found through the years, can mean working around the clock. My excitement about multiple projects adds to my continuous challenge of having too many activities, too many interests, numerous deadlines, and a constant struggle to integrate all of the areas of my life. For me it is not a balance between my personal and professional life but rather an integration of who I am with what I do and how I want to do it all. At one point, I expanded my practice, rented larger office space, hired staff, and took on even more projects. And found myself losing time and energy for evaluation. I became so busy "doing" that I had no time to experience "simplicity" and reflection.

An evaluation method that continues to work for me, when I let it, is taking the time to journal and reflect on my struggles and my celebrations. When I take the time to record my feelings and outline where I am with my interests and projects and multiple commitments, I find ways to get organized, renew creativity, and reenergize. Julie Cameron (in *The Artists Way*, 2002) suggests using morning pages, which I have found very helpful. Annie Lamott's books (Lamott, 1994) have provided activities that help me focus on getting thoughts and feelings from the jumbled mess in my head to the written page. When I fail to pay attention to my need for reflection, I can easily get lost and overwhelmed. Rather than my evaluation process being productive, it then becomes negative self-talk.

My process of reflection requires time and space. I find that sometimes my best evaluation times are on plane trips and the hours I can spend in a hotel room. My preference is being surrounded with green trees, blue skies and the quiet of the countryside. I prefer being away from the clutter of my world. Clutter is an accumulation of the past; hanging on is fear of the future (Russell, 2002). Letting go is one of my challenges. Knowing when it is time to terminate a contract or stop providing a service is difficult but necessary.

In addition to the quiet time and space for reflection, it is also crucial for me to have the time and space to talk things over with others. My need for affiliation and connectedness shows up in many ways. Talking it over with my support team as part of my evaluation process is essential. My support team over the years has included mentors, my accountant and business advisor, colleagues, and my husband. Although I cherish them all, I also find that it is difficult to stay in touch as much as I would like.

Project Management

Another evaluation tool that is much more concrete is an organizational process I developed for myself a couple of years after starting my practice. It grew from the struggle between my entrepreneurial desires for flexibility, independence, service and excitement and the financial need to make sure I was adding to the family income. I began working with a formula that made sense of the way I was receiving revenue. From the beginning, I subcontracted with a community agency to provide training and employment counseling services. I also saw private clients and began delivering training seminars. I recognized the need to be both a contractor and a subcontractor in terms of the projects that I was involved with because of the revenue differences and the development of new skills.

Contracting meant that I handled all tasks, administrative and operational. Contracting also meant that I needed to handle the entire process. That included responding to a Request for Proposal (RFP) and understanding the federal and state bid process. Each year it is my goal to have a specific number of RFP contracts, which I am then able to consider as my base income.

The number changes, depending on the amount of work and the projected revenue. I set an annual revenue goal at the beginning of each year and then begin the formula of identifying projects, contracts and new sources to fit that goal. Geoffrey Bellman (2001) suggests using a formula to identify the number of days one wants to work. For me, it is more complex than that and often centers on the folks with whom I want to work. Focusing strictly on a dollar amount doesn't work either, but I know that in order to reduce stress and panic each quarter, I need to blend the revenue, the type of work and the time it takes to design, develop, organize, produce, and deliver.

Being visual means I need some sort of flowchart or diagram to have on my wall for the upcoming quarter, 6 months, and/or year. Basically the design covers the following:

Revenue Source	Projected Revenue	Projected Time	Projected Expenses	Energy*
Contracts: • Federal agency • State agency				
Sub-contracting projects: • Internal training company • Training seminars through vendor				
Teaching assignments: • University adjunct faculty				
Consulting projects: • Curriculum design • Job evaluation project				
Miscellaneous projects: • Counseling clients • Sawdust Press products				

* My energy column is my own way of identifying my enthusiasm and level of excitement about a project and is usually ranked according to the people I am working with and the amount of creativity I can be involved with. If a project depletes my energy and becomes stressful, it means I need to evaluate whether to continue or share with someone else.

Challenge

It is extremely important not to become contract dependent, spending all of your hours with a single contract and little or no time to continue marketing. When the contract is over, you are then faced with panic and anxiety about your future. Because much of my work has been with government agencies and a lengthy bid process, I make a concentrated effort to continuing marketing as I deliver services. Marketing is the key to success of any business. And because the integration of my personal and professional identities has been at the foundation of my business, marketing is an ongoing process. My marketing plan involves visibility, connectedness, and collaboration (Russell, 1997).

Connectedness

For me, none of the business practices and success would be possible if it were not for the people in my life. At the core of everything I do are the individuals that have supported, mentored, challenged, and walked with me on this journey. I have been incredibly fortunate to have a husband who has been with me every step of the way and who has spent the past eight years being my administrative assistant, my publications person and my main supporter. Harry has developed a small publishing firm, Sawdust Press, to produce the products that have developed from the activities and projects of my business. Small in size, we have exhibited at conferences and have plans to grow this business in the future.

Many individuals have served as mentors during the past years. Their greatest contribution has been a caring relationship that supports me and challenges me at the same time. Perhaps one of the most incredible feelings for me is when I read through a new career book and realize that I know many of the authors as colleagues and friends. That is an unexpected gift that I truly cherish. I have been privileged to meet many dedicated professionals along the way who have supported me and challenged me. They have believed in me and helped me discover strengths I didn't know I had.

Through that support and encouragement I have achieved a level of leadership that goes beyond any expectation or any goal I set for myself. As the 2005–2006 president of the National Career Development Association, I have been honored to devote my time and energy to our profession.

Professional Affiliation

The inclusion of professional affiliation is very important whenever I plan or evaluation my business, because it is very much a part of who I am as a professional career counselor and an entrepreneur. Organizational involvement and being part of a community has always been important to me. Affiliation is high on my list of values. Coupled with independence, this has translated into being in business as a sole proprietor while being surrounded by those who encourage, motivate and help me frame the work I do. Just as I have used the numbers formula for my contract work, I also have done that for my association work. I restrict myself to belonging to a specific number of organizations each year, and in those organizations, I identify how involved I am willing to be. Because of my leadership role in NCDA these past few years, I have had to reevaluate the level of participation in other organizations and the impact that has on my own work. At times, it has been a challenge and yet the rewards are great.

One of the questions I am often asked is, "Does being a leader in a professional association help my business?" For me, the answer is yes. However, this affirmation is not in the direct business sense that one might be asking about. Because one of my values is integrity, I try to be very careful of and cognizant about the separation of my entrepreneur role and my leadership role. That has meant removing myself from a revenue-producing project if it poses what I see as a conflict of interest. The important message here is that I believe you can contribute to your profession, stay true to your values, and behave in a professional manner without jeopardizing your income. Being upfront and honest with all concerned parties has worked for me. Basically, it translates into taking a "leave of absence" from a contract with the ability to return when my professional role changes. I strongly believe that being an active member of my professional organization is crucial to my feelings of competency and connectedness, and therefore it does help my business.

Unexpected Redirection

A major business redirection occurred quite unexpectedly when Harry and I moved to the state of Washington after 23 years in the Sacramento community. Although we made a fairly rapid move after a difficult job loss, the planning and the implementation had begun a year earlier when we began looking for property. Our search was intended to fulfill a long-term plan to build a career retreat center in the Pacific Northwest. The job loss sped up those plans by several years. However, in preparation for the long-range transition, I had already opened a second office in a small rural community outside of Sacramento and had begun to have small three to four person weekend retreats. The integration of our personal lives and professional exercise, short-term and long-term dreams became overshadowed by fear, self-doubts, and confusion. Although it was probably not the best time to act, we did, and within a year our lives and my business underwent major transformation.

Moving my business to another state was made easier because of the work I had been doing nationally, and the fact that my entire business focus had become training, outplacement, and contract work outside of my office space. It also pointed out the strength of my connectedness with members of NCDA. I had colleagues I could connect with no matter where I lived. I relocated the office and spent almost all of my first two years in Washington at airports, hotels, and training centers. I discovered that lots of folks had commuter lives. Publicly I laughed at the notion that I had given up my car for an airplane, but on the inside I struggled with constant travel and working seven days a week. There were many changes requiring flexibility and willingness to move into new directions. Keeping focused on a vision, community, and values allowed me to continue successfully.

My vision continues to be the integration of personal and professional activities. My mission continues to be to provide ethical and quality services with integrity, commitment and dedication to our profession. The ways I accomplish those things continues to change and that change allows me to grow and develop. For me, one of the major elements is to focus on the long-term, rather than the short-term goals. I know that I will continue to be in business in the years ahead. That business may be different, and I am confident that I can continue to be the enterprising entrepreneur, which is at the very core of my professional being. The confidence comes from taking the time to plan in a way that encourages a new beginning with energy and enthusiasm for the year ahead.

Evolving Professional Self

Several years ago, I was introduced to a resource that has been helpful to me in framing where I am headed both in terms of my business and my own career. Skovholt and Ronnestad (1995) outlined an eight-stage career model for counselors with 20 broad themes of development. Development implies change. I embrace change with more enthusiasm and greater success when I can understand the reasons, the structure, and possible outcomes. The authors focus on professional competence and evolution for each stage. I would like to say that professional competence means honoring that which directly relates to my business and my practices.

Stages of the Evolving Professional Self

(Brief overview of eight stages adapted from Skovholt & Ronnestad, 1991)

Stage	Theme
Conventional	(No formal training) Uses what one knows naturally (common sense, life experience, etc.). Learns experientially and plays the role of the sympathetic friend.
Transition to Professional Training	(First year of graduate school) Experiences both enthusiasm and insecurity. Assimilates information from new and old sources, and feels an urgency to learn conceptual ideas and techniques.
Imitation of Experts	(Middle years of graduate school) Maintains openness while imitating experts at a practical level. May feel bewilderment, then later calm and temporary security. Learns by imitation, introspection, and cognitive processing.
Conditional Autonomy	(Internship, 6 months to 2 years) Functions as a professional with variable levels of confidence. Has refined and mastered conceptual ideas and techniques. Learns by introspection, cognitive processing, and by continuing to imitate experts, but with alteration.
Exploration	(New graduate, 2 to 5 years) Explores beyond the known, with mixed confidence and anxiety. Modifies externally imposed professional working style, and rejects some earlier mastered conceptual ideas.
Integration	(2 to 5 years) Develops authenticity, with satisfaction and hope. Approaches work with a mix of externally imposed rigidity and an internally imposed loosening.
Individuation	(10 to 30 years) Experiences deeper authenticity, with both satisfaction and distress. Primary sources of influence are accumulated wisdom and experience-based generalizations. Becomes increasingly one's self in working style, within competent professional boundaries.
Integrity	(1 to 10 years) Prepares for retirement, with acceptance. Being one's self is primary.

The seventh stage of Individuation is where I am at this point. I have put aside the retreat center goal and continue to focus on the goals of expanded international work, writing, development of products, and delivery of services, using more of my consulting, counseling, and leadership development skills. One of my major areas of interest is to expand in the area of helping individuals understand how aging impacts career choices, career decisions, and career management. Perhaps, in some ways, that is also preparation for truly accepting and cherishing the integrity of my work. I feel blessed to have been able to follow my entrepreneurial dreams and cherish the roles presented to me.

Martha's TIPS

- Know your limitations but do not let them limit you.
- Know where your passion is coming from and how to keep it alive.
- Understand the need for, the reason for, and the steps in a strong marketing plan.
- Build on your strengths and your skills.
- Stay focused on client needs but don't ignore your needs.
- Know how much you can give of yourself, where you need to draw boundaries, and don't be afraid to ask for help.
- Stay in touch with your overall design, direction, vision, and mission.
- Identify the pace of your business and your lifestyle, and how they can be integrated.
- Keep focused on high quality, ethical, and professional service.
- Enjoy the journey and celebrate along the way.

Life is no brief candle to me. It is a sort of splendid torch which I have got hold of for the moment, and I want to make it burn as brightly as possible before handing it on to future generations."

George Bernard Shaw

Over the years, I have developed a reflective evaluation method that continues to work for me, when I let it. Each October I begin putting the pieces of the puzzle together for the following year. I have found that I generally need the three months before the end of the year to evaluate whether the contracts and sub-contract goals need to be increased or decreased and to determine what I need to do in terms of marketing. I also need to add in my own professional development and commitment to building my professional community, which are my nonrevenue producing activities. While they may not produce revenue, those activities are at the heart of who I am and what I do.

Resources

These are a few of the books that have been helpful to me along the way:

Andrews, C. (1998). *The circle of simplicity: Return to the good life*. New York: Harper Perennial.

Bellman, G. M. (2001). *The consultant's calling: Bringing who you are to what you do*. San Francisco: Jossey-Bass Publishers.

Bloch, D. P., & Richmond, L.J. (Eds.). (1997). *Connections between spirit & work in career development*. Palo Alto: Davies-Black Publishing.

Cameron, J. (1992). *The artist's way: A spiritual path to higher creativity*. New York: GP Putnam & Sons.

Campbell, S. M (1995) *From chaos to confidence: Survival strategies for the new workplace*. New York: Simon & Schuster.

James, J. (1996) *Thinking in the future tense: Leadership skills for a new age*. Simon & Schuster.

Lamott, A. (1994). *Bird by bird: Some instructions on writing and life*. New York: Pantheon.

Russell, M (2002) *DreamWeaving: Meeting the challenges of the helping profession*. Battleground, WA: Sawdust Press.

Russell, M (1997) Visibility, Connectedness and Collaboration: Keys to Marketing a Private Practice. *Career Planning and Adult Development Journal*, 13, 61-79.

Senge, P. M. (1994). *The fifth discipline: The art & practice of the learning organization*. New York: Doubleday.

Seuss, Dr. (1990). *Oh, the places you'll go*. New York: Random House.

Skovholt, T.M. & Ronnestad, M. H. (1995). *The evolving professional self: Stages and themes in therapist and counselor development*. New York: Wiley & Sons.

Lynn Joseph, Ph.D.

How to Expand Your Vision, Assess Your Results — and Light Your Fire!

I have found that the most practical way to evaluate my accomplishments is against my previous goals and objectives. In setting goals, I typically follow the classic SMAC guidelines: (a) Specific, (b) Measurable, (c) Achievable, (d) Challenging.

I set long-term goals first (one year or more) and then short-term goals that are stepping-stones to the long-term goals. I evaluate my progress on a regular basis (i.e., weekly and monthly). But it wasn't always that way!

Vague Goals

Many years ago I was in business for myself, selling poster art of my nature and wildlife photos. I was both financially and emotionally invested in my products, and had an intense desire to make a good living in this venture. For many previous years, I had worked in sales and sales management for two Fortune 100 companies, where my work had been driven by goals and objectives. Yet now I resisted creating a business plan and chose only vague goals. Thinking back, I may have been challenging the "establishment" way of doing things. After all, I had left my ideal establishment job to strike out on a new business adventure and I was determined to find my own path. What followed was a hard lesson in business planning, goal setting, and objective evaluation.

I intended to test market my posters at a trade show where I had a booth. The posters attracted encouraging attention, yet I went home with few orders. I loved those posters so much, however, and I was so convinced that they would ultimately sell that I focused on the attention and positive comments rather than the actual sales. Because I had no sales goals against which to measure the success of the project, I fell into the trap of making excuses (e.g., poor booth location, etc.). If I had objectively evaluated the results against goals, I would have understood what the disappointing sales signaled. I don't mean to imply that at the first sign of disappointment one should throw in the towel. On the contrary, the success of any new enterprise depends upon: (a) Intense Desire, (b) Positive Expectation, and (c) Imagination/Vision.

These qualities have been powerful influences in my life and the critical key to achieving my goals over the years.

Evaluating Events and Results Objectively

I have since learned to evaluate events and results more objectively against my goals, and to understand when my vision is manifesting as planned, or more importantly, to recognize when it has failed and to research the reason(s). It might be possible to revise the business plan and/or take steps to regain control. I ask myself tough questions like these:

- Does my product or service fit the needs of my target market?
- Does my marketing plan need reevaluation and revision?

Scientific research is one excellent, though not always practical, way to evaluate a product or service. While studying for my doctorate, I developed a mental image technology (MIT) protocol designed to get displaced workers back to work significantly faster than if they used traditional outplacement methods alone.

I passionately believed in the use of MIT for goal achievement. And what better way to measure the effectiveness of my MIT protocol than against the goal of reemployment? It was specific, measurable, and, I felt, achievable, yet definitely challenging. It became my dissertation research project. The results were so conclusively in favor of MIT that the research was published in the *Consulting Psychology Journal,* a peer reviewed journal of the American Psychological Association. The study and its research became the basis of my book, *The job-loss recovery guide: A proven program for getting back to work — fast!* This is not to say you should perform a scientific study to evaluate your counseling or coaching practice, unless you are academically inclined. But you can be creative.

At one time, I believed the journey or process mattered more than the goal. I have since discovered that the goal significantly influences the tone and development of the process, and facilitates achievement. For example, when I set a goal to write a book on job-loss recovery that would be published by a national publishing house, I learned all I could regarding about how to write a great book proposal. With proposal in hand, I attended selected events to meet agents and publishers. Nothing seemed to gel. It was when I was presenting my study results to a group of psychologists at a California Psychological Association annual conference that a publisher, who happened to be in the audience, approached me to ask if I had considered writing a book based on my study. I believe that my desire, clear intention, and positive expectation, along with the actions I had already taken to reach my goal, became attracting, magnetic forces for this unexpected means for achieving the goal.

Evaluation is also more accurate and thorough if you are not doing it alone. If I had had a team of trusted colleagues to consult with about the success (or lack of success) of my poster market test, I may not have been so quick to make excuses for meager sales. So consider asking trusted colleagues, family members, or friends to serve as your advisory board. Submit your plan to them. Get ideas and feedback

from them on a regular basis. Get feedback from your advisory board about your mission and vision as well as marketing and selling plans. And then listen to their advice! Some questions you might ask are the following:

- Is the mission unique and client focused?
- Is the vision compelling and motivational?
- Are the markets, companies, and customers defined?
- Are goals set and realistic?
- What do you like best about the plan? Least?

Helping Clients Cope with Loss

Sometimes new marketplace developments can lead a business/practice down an unexpected path to meet new needs for which the business members have the skills and resources to fill. For example, following the Katrina and Rita hurricane disasters, many companies in Louisiana and Mississippi found themselves faced with many employees that had sustained significant damage to their homes, or lost them entirely, and were living in temporary FEMA tents or trailers. Many had also lost family members to the storms or ensuing violence, and most were experiencing various levels of anxiety, grief, depression, anger, and trauma. Others felt guilty for having come through the storms and floods with no damage. Most were performing their jobs at about 50% productivity levels.

In short, they were in need of coping skills to deal with the losses, and to begin the recovery process, and to regain hope and positive expectations as well as new vision. These skills were not unlike those that I wrote about in my book and also co-developed in the Parachute Career Transition Program to move displaced employees through the trauma of job loss and on to the new job or career of their choice.

After meetings in which every member of the Parachute management team expressed the desire to help those in need on the Gulf Coast, we decided to create a half-day workshop called Focus on Recovery: Coping With Disaster, and offered it to companies in the damaged areas. When faced with these shifting market needs, Parachute's marketing and operational strategy shifted with them. We developed the new workshop, took concerted action to get the word out, and were soon delivering the workshop to employees of businesses in New Orleans and along the stricken Gulf Coast. Facilitating those workshops with colleague Amy Frost was one of the most personally fulfilling experiences of my career.

Yet no matter how fulfilling for the facilitator, the impact and effectiveness of all services delivered (whether a workshop, or group or individual coaching/counseling) should be evaluated by the participants. The most efficient way to achieve this with consistency is to have each participant complete a written evaluation at the end of the workshop or series of coaching/counseling sessions. These evaluations contain a wealth of information about what worked well and what may need improvement.

As I complete this chapter, I am again in career transition. Along with any significant change comes the feeling of chaos, and I have accepted and made peace with that. In fact, it is good to dive into the chaos for a while because there lay my source of creativity. As I think of all the exciting decisions and choices that lie ahead, it would be unfortunate to limit myself. I would like to leave you with a favorite quote of mine by Brian Tracy:

> Dream big dreams!
>
> Imagine that you have no limitations,
>
> and then decide what's right,
>
> before you decide what's possible.

Resources

Baum, K., & Turbo, R. (1999). *The mental edge.* Berkeley, CA: Berkley Publishing Group.

Bolles, R. (2006). *What color is your parachute?* Berkeley, CA: Ten Speed Press.

Johnson, S. (1998). *Who moved my cheese?: An a-mazing way to deal with change in your work and in your life.* New York: G. P. Putnam's Sons.

Joseph, L. (2003). *The job-loss recovery guide: A proven program for getting back to work-fast!* New Harbinger Publications,.

Joseph, L. (2005). *The job-loss recovery guide. Supplemental guided exercises.* Discovery Dynamics, Inc. http://www.discoverydynamics.net/.

Joseph, L. (2003). *The job-loss recovery program. Use the power of your imagination to get back to work —fast!* Discovery Dynamics, Inc. Two-CD set of guided imagery.

Joseph, L. M., and M. A. Greenberg. (2001). The effects of a career transition program on reemployment success in laid-off professionals. *Consulting Psychology Journal,* 53:169-181.

Orlick, T. (1990). *In pursuit of excellence: How to win in sport and life through mental training.* Champaign, IL: Human Kinetics.

Peale, Norman Vincent. (1982). *Positive imaging. The powerful way to change your life.* New York: Fawcett Columbine.

Peale, N.V. (1996). *The power of positive thinking.* New York: Ballantine Books.

Tracy, B. (2002). *Create your own future: How to master the 12 critical factors of unlimited success.* New York: John Wiley and Sons.

Ungerleider, S. (1996). *Mental training for peak performance: Top athletes reveal the mind exercises they use to excel.* Emmaus, PA: Rodale Press.

IX. Do you have an exit plan?

Family businesses often have legacy agreements. Like family businesses, procedures for closing a business or selling the business to others can be most effective if planned in advance, not at the last minute. What succession plan, if any, do you have? When will you exit your business – when you reach your goal(s)? When you find someone who can do the job as well as or better than you? When others make the decision for you? When you decide to pursue other goals? No matter where you are in your business development, it can be helpful to plan your exit strategy. To learn more about how to exit your business, read Michael Shahnasarian's story, examine his case study, and perform Exercise 18 in Appendix A.

Michael Shahnasarian, Ph.D.

Introduction

I suspect the evolution of my private practice is typical of most. Although I desired to pursue self-employment in a career counseling practice while in graduate school, like most young professionals, I lacked both the necessary experience and finances. After completing my training, I secured my first job, saved some money, wrote a business plan, began providing career guidance services while holding down my "day job" and, when the practice grew to generate sufficient business, made the leap and pursued private practice career counseling full time.

Over the years my practice grew, diversified, and specialized in various service areas, and began employing associates and support staff. While I invested great amounts of energy to nurture and develop the practice, I only recently began considering how it would succeed me. I suspect this, too, is typical of most career counselors – as well as small business owners – who tend to prioritize client service, day-to-day operations, and other business survival details over long-term business planning. Of course, I would be remiss not to acknowledge that often the thought of exiting one's practice rouses feelings akin to those a parent feels when anticipating the imminent separation of a loved child grown into a young adult, ready to embark on an independent life. Simply put, letting go is not always easy or natural.

In my case, a prime reason to focus on the process of exiting my practice was the stark economic realization that an asset I had developed would become greatly devalued when my involvement curtailed or ceased. The practice grew too dependent on me. Other factors prompting my consideration of this important matter – including both my desire for my practice to succeed me and my commitment to refocus on objectives for the next phase of my career development – caused me to develop an exit plan.

Consider the following questions as you assess whether your present exit plan from your practice – assuming you have one – is sufficient:

- Could your practice survive financially without you?
- Do you have a qualified replacement(s) ready and able to assume the work you currently perform?
- What would be the economic impact on you and your practice if your involvement in it suddenly ceased or were to greatly curtail?
- Would you be personally affected after your departure from your practice if it ceased to operate?
- How long would it require you to position your practice so it could continue to function and prosper in your absence? What specific actions have you undertaken or do you plan to take to facilitate this positioning?
- Have you focused your career objectives beyond your involvement in your practice? Is this necessary?

This chapter explores challenges that private practitioners encounter as they plan their exit from their practice. It culminates with an exercise to help you manage this transition.

Exiting Challenges and Options

Exit planning involves leaving your business on terms you orchestrate, based on your objectives. This concept is deceptively simple. In many ways, planning and executing an exit from a successful, established practice – a milestone objective that hallmarks what many career counselors aspire to attain – is among the most difficult career development tasks a private practitioner encounters.

A private career counseling practice, like other entities that provide human services, often realizes success because it consistently attains fundamental business operations requisites: providing quality services, establishing solid business relationships and partnerships, maintaining focus and commitment, containing costs and developing reliable revenue sources, applying sound management, and happening upon a dash of luck. These ingredients seldom transfer spontaneously or effortlessly.

Most private practice career counselors develop specialties – career coaching, outplacement, working with special populations, organizational consulting, or involvement in forensic matters, to name a few – that grow to define a mature, profitable practice. Unfortunately, few career counselors possess the talent, interest, drive, professional standards, and business savvy that likely fueled the success of your practice and that requires it to perpetuate. While assessing the feasibility of developing a successor(s) for your practice, your selection of an exit strategy is among the first and most important decisions you must confront.

Exits need not be awkward and abrupt. Some of the best and most memorable exude verve that, rather than mark an ending, punctuate a pithy message and hint at a new, more spectacular future, whether historical, like Douglas MacArthur's farewell address at West Point or cinematic, like Ashley Wilkes' goodbye in *Gone with the Wind*.

For better or worse, a finite number of exit plan strategies are available; these are some of the most common:

- Ceding the practice to family members, colleagues, or other trusted, qualified individuals
- Hiring and training successors
- Merging and blending the practice with a related practice
- Selling the practice
- Gradually phasing out, without any succession plan

A detailed discussion of these strategies eclipses this chapter's scope. Your career objectives and idiosyncratic factors will again dictate the course you take. Ultimately, like other career decisions, finding the exit strategy best suited for you is a personal decision. Few are better equipped than career counselors to apply proven career decision-making processes while evaluating viable exit plan strategies. Schlossberg (2004) and Shahnasarian (2006) provided guidance on gaining insight and formulating plans to facilitate career decision-making and life planning. Reviewing publications of this sort can help you gain perspective on your personal and work values, interests, skill set, and life circumstances as you assess your exit options and cultivate an exit strategy.

I hope that your private practice provided you a comfortable livelihood that other counselors qualified to assume your practice would intuitively perceive as both desirable and worthy of financial investment. Unfortunately, private practices offering human services are challenging to sell - even if they have a proven record of profitability. Henley (1997) identified 12 principles in the context of valuing a psychological practice. He concluded that, when coupled with the problem of finding a buyer, the sale potential for a psychological practice is bleak, and the typical psychological practice has minimal, if any, property value – as opposed to being viewed as an income source.

For many career counselors, exiting a private practice involves developing a succession plan. Garman and Glawe (2004) defined succession planning as a structured process involving the identification and preparation of a potential successor to assume a new role. The reference to "structured" infers a planned and managed process, thereby excluding from the definition the more ad hoc identification of successors.

Citing statistics indicating that most of all family-owned businesses fail before reaching the second or third generation, Marshal (2002) attributed the problem to lack of adequate succession planning. In an article committed to technical succession planning, Poduch and Rothwell (2004) emphasized that succession planning involves more than just finding replacements. A successful transition of technical positions, according Poduch and Rothwell, includes developing talent, "bench strength," and preserving the organization's institutional memory. According to the authors, institutional memory can be preserved by veteran performers at all levels who possess specialized knowledge about the organization's operations.

Exit Planning Factors

Like any career decision, the planning associated with your departure from your private practice will likely rely upon both objective and subjective factors. Focusing on two primary exit planning factors can help you gain perspective on your situation: (1) your personal career objectives and goals, and (2) your desired degree of future involvement in your private practice.

Personal Career Objectives and Goals

Ironically, private practice career counselors sometimes neglect their own career planning, similar to the adage "the shoemaker's children have no shoes." Naturally, the practice that became intertwined with your life and, in many cases, served as your raison d'etre has consumed you to the point where you have not considered your career development in its absence.

The factors that initially prompted you to pursue private practice work may have grown less important over time, influenced or supplanted by new work and personal values. One colleague, for example, disclosed that what initially inspired him to establish a private practice – namely, the bane of his former bureaucratic corporate position, which offered scant autonomy – ultimately became less of a sustaining motivating factor for remaining in private practice. After almost two decades of private practice work, he reinvented himself and assumed a school counselor job at a local high school.

Your exit-planning trek should begin with earnest reflection on the reasons for your planned exit. Only then will you be adequately prepared to prudently explore your future career objectives and goals, and establish an integrated exit plan.

Degree of Desired Future Involvement

Quite likely, en route to establishing your private practice, your career evolved or is evolving through maintenance and withdrawal phases of career development proposed along the lines of Tiedman (1961), Super (1990), and others. Often, one's phase of career development prompts consideration of an exit plan.

Several factors will likely drive the degree to which you wish to remain involved in your practice, including your fulfillment with your practice work, financial need and potential for remuneration your practice offers and, of course, your present career development objectives. In some cases, health and personal commitments may govern your practice involvement level and exit plan timeframe.

Some career counselors incorporate in their exit plans a swift, clean break from their practices. Others opt for longer transitions, gradually reducing their involvement and remaining at least tangentially active. The sample exit plan presented below (after the exercise) illustrates how a practitioner integrated this latter objective into an exit plan strategy.

Conclusion

There is no "right" or "wrong" way to formulate an exit plan. Personal factors typically are the greatest influence on the selection and implementation of an exit plan. Business and logistical issues often complicate the process. Of course, related legal and ethical considerations, including transferring client records and assuring continuity of services, complicate the process. I advise referencing relevant codes of ethics and state statutes for these details.

Resources

Garman, A. W., & Glawe, J. (2004). Succession planning. *Consulting Psychology Journal: Research and Practice*, 56, 119-128.

Henley, R. H. (1997). Valuing a psychological practice. *Professional Psychology: Research and Practice*, 28, 77-80.

Koocher, G. (2003). Ethical and legal issues in professional practice transitions. *Professional Psychology: Research and Practice*, 34, 383-387.

Marshall, J. P. (2002). The impact of business owners' conflict management and leadership styles on succession planning in family-owned businesses. *Dissertation Abstracts International Section A: Humanities and Social Sciences*, 62.

Poduch, S., & Rothwell, W. J. (2004). Introducing technical (not managerial) succession planning. *Public Personnel Management*, 33, 405-419.

Schlossberg, N. K. (2004). *Retire smart, retire happy: Finding your true path in life*. Washington: American Psychological Association.

Shahnasarian, M. (2006). *Decision time: A guide to career enhancement* (3rd ed.). Alexandria, VA: National Career Development Association.

Super, D. E. (1990). A life-span, life-space approach to career development. In D. Brown, L. Brooks, & Associates (Eds.), *Career choice and development: Applying contemporary theories to practice* (2nd ed., 197-261). San Francisco: Jossey-Bass.

The Institute for Exit Planning. Retrieved September 2, 2006: http://www.exitplanning.com.au/xpe/survey/whatIs.

Tiedeman, D. V. (1961). Decision and vocational development: A paradigm and its applications. *The Personnel and Guidance Journal*, 40, 15-21.

X. What, in your opinion, has made you a great entrepreneur?

What is YOUR personal definition of business success? In his straightforward, no-nonsense fashion, Richard Knowdell discusses his path to success. Explore Exercise 19 in Appendix A to learn how to grow a spectacular career development-related business.

Richard L. Knowdell

The Career Counselor as Entrepreneur and Intrepreneur

In the 35 years that I have worked as a career counselor, I have consistently been an Entrepreneur or Intrepreneur (an Intrepreneur is an individual with an independent and risk-taking behavioral style who works within a formal organization). In my 20 years in the workforce before becoming a career counselor, almost none of my 30+ jobs could be described as entrepreneurial. What made me an entrepreneur? I never took a course in it or set out to become an entrepreneur. The answer, I think, involves the following four points:

- In my 30+ jobs before becoming a career counselor, I took a job and just accomplished what was asked of me, not for any personal satisfaction, but just to earn a living.

- In every job or position (or business) that I have engaged in since becoming a career counselor, I have taken the lead in accomplishing the tasks I wanted to accomplish for inner satisfaction, and not to earn a living.

- Every one of these entrepreneurial (or intrepreneural) jobs or projects that gave me inner satisfaction involved "recognizing a need and striving to fill the need."

- Every one of these jobs or projects in which I filled a need, required the use of my "Motivated Skills" – those core strengths that emerged early in life, rather than skills learned in graduate school (such as active listening or statistical analysis).

In order to illustrate these four points, I will need to go back to the 1960s when my entrepreneurial behavioral clearly emerged. When working with clients, I frequently ask them to write an autobiography of accomplishments that they did well, enjoyed doing, and took pride in. They are then asked to select their accomplishments over a 40-year span so that the reader can see clear evidence of a strong and consistent pattern of behavior.

1967: Big Sur Camping Trip

I was living with a group of impoverished college students in a rooming house and doing nothing but cramming for tests and hanging out every night at the local pizza and beer joint. We were all looking forward to a spring break where we could get away from our routine. But, we were all going to school on the G.I. Bill and couldn't afford to travel to Fort Lauderdale for the break. About two hours south of our college was a small state park on the rugged Big Sur coast. I decided to organize a four-day camping trip for up to 20 students. I arranged transportation in four old cars that we owned. I developed a menu that included barbequed steak, hot dogs, hamburgers, bacon and eggs, and plenty of beer and wine. I was able to charge each person $25 for the entire four-day trip. Clearly, there was inner satisfaction in organizing and implementing this trip that met the students' need to get away with without spending a lot of money. My Motivated Skills of designing, planning, organizing, directing, coordinating and implementing the camping trip were central to its success.

1969: College Rooming House

While in graduate school, I was able to rent an 80-year-old two-bedroom house in the student ghetto that had a large attic, large basement, and a detached garage. Four of us shared the house. I was able to purchase the house for no money down and payments of $100 per month. Using scrap lumber and used plumbing fixtures (and no building permits), I spent the summer turning the two-bedroom house into a seven-bedroom place. With six graduate students paying me $30 each, I was making $80 a month more than I needed for the house payment. I also charged each individual $30 per month for food, and each of us took turns preparing the evening meal. Since I was able to purchase enough food with the $180 I received from my housemates, I was able to eat for free. Yes, I felt an inner satisfaction from operating the rooming house at a profit. I also met my housemates' needs for an inexpensive and comfortable place to live. My Motivated Skills of planning, organizing, improvising, building, and implementing were key to the success of the project.

1970-1971: Master of Science in Counseling Psychology Focused on Careers

In graduate school, I was working on a master's of science in counseling psychology and taking additional courses in clinical psychology. Most of my peers were preparing for employment as school psychologists or school or college counselors. Their main focus seemed to be on mental health counseling – figuring out what is wrong with a student and coming up with a cure. The professors were all experts on how to "heal' or "fix" these students. I became aware of an emerging subspecialty of counseling psychology called Career Counseling. It seemed that none of my peers were interested in this. And there were no courses offered on career counseling. Since I did not start college until age 30, I had worked in a wide range of jobs in business, industry, and government and found that choosing and progressing in a career was just as important and interesting as diagnosis . Since all of my professors were Ph.D. psychologists who spent all of the time teaching and advising students who would be entering employment in clinical and educational settings, I felt like a "fish out of water."

Luckily, I had one professor who had been an engineer and cartographer before getting his Ph.D. on the G.I. Bill. This professor was very supportive of my focus on "career" counseling. He let me design my own master's program and complete my thesis on "Career awareness of eighth-grade boys." I got a lot of satisfaction from developing more expertise than my major professors in this new area. At that time, there were very few trained career counselors, and I filled that need. I also had a need to be involved in something very practical, and career counseling is very practical. Developing my specialty focus required the Motivated Skills of recognizing a need, planning, organizing, developing, promoting, selling, and implementing.

1971: Guidance Consultant

My very first professional job after graduate school was as an Industry Liaison Coordinator with the Santa Clara County Office of Education. That job required knowledge of business environments (I had 15 years experience) as well as a counseling degree and credential. The County Office of Education served the in-service training needs of counselors at 32 school districts and six community colleges. My job was to obtain accurate information from local employers on what skills and knowledge were required for successful entry of new employees into the workforce. The other professionals on staff provided career consultation and career development training to counselors at the 32 school districts and six community colleges.

One week after starting this job, the state drastically cut funding to the project, and both of the guidance consultants resigned in order to return to "tenured" and more secure positions as counselors at their former organizations. Even the journalist whose job involved writing the project newsletter and developing promotional flyers resigned. Only the project director, project secretary, and I remained. But we still had a lot of work to be accomplished.

I started taking on many of the tasks that the departed staff had done. I spent less time interviewing training and employment managers in local industries and more and more time conducting in-service training, in-group career counseling techniques, and interest inventory interpretation to high school and community college counselors. I took over writing the monthly newsletter with career counseling tips for the high school and community college counselors. Since none of the high schools or community colleges had yet set up career centers, I took the initiative to build a model career center next to my office that I filled with the latest career information books, films, and pamphlets from publishers throughout the country. In this project, I filled the counselors' needs for training in career development techniques and current career information. In the project, I used my Motivated Skills of planning, organizing, developing, building, and teaching.

1972: From Employee to Consultant

As the County Office of Education project wound down, the director came to me with the news that our project budget category for salaries was close to empty. While this meant that my position would be abolished and that I would be laid off, he also informed me that there were still funds in the "outside consultant" category. He indicated that he could retain me as an external consultant, and I would be able to continue my work. To my surprise, the external consulting fee was twice my current salary. The project needed a consultant and "presto," I was one. This would permit me to continue using my Motivated Skills of planning, organizing, teaching, and training. This is also a transition from "intrepreneur" to entrepreneur.

1972-1976: Private Career Counseling Practice

Even with my training duties for the County Office of Education, I missed using my newly acquired career counseling skills with real clients, rather than with the professional counselors that I was training. I believed that there was a significant need for career counseling services by individuals who fell between the cracks. That is, if you were not enrolled in an educational institution, a downsized worker, or poor enough to be collecting public assistance, career counseling was not readily available. One particular group that I was most aware of consisted of college-educated wives of doctors, lawyers, engineers, and managers. They were considering returning to the workforce when their child-rearing responsibilities began to diminish. But they were not sure of what direction to take. Having access to an upper middle-class income, they could afford to pay for private career counseling.

In 1971, I hung out my shingle as a (part-time) private practice career counselor. I put together a package of five or six individual counseling sessions where I would administer and interpret a battery of career assessment instruments, assist the client in exploring a range of career options, guide her to developing a clear goal, and write up a report outlining her career strategy plan. I would work with this population, off and on, for the next 20 years. While there was a significant need for career counseling for this group, the need was not clearly recognized by enough clients in the early 1970s for me to quit consulting to make a living as a full time private practice career counselor. So, I did what many private practice career counselors do – got a "day job."

1975: Employee Career Development

Lawrence Livermore National Laboratory, a nuclear weapons research and development facility, was seeking a professional career counselor to develop and manage a career development program for their 5,000+ employees. They needed a career development professional who was familiar with an industrial environment. I met their needs is both areas. I was able to put my private practice on the back burner (seeing occasional clients on evenings and weekends) and assume the role of Chief Counselor and Manager of the Employee Assistance Division.

My initial efforts in this job involved designing a career development workshop, researching and selecting career assessment instruments, and conducting individual career-counseling sessions for employees and managers. Since the concept of employee career development was new, there was a need to get employees to sign up for the services. Consequently, I designed and wrote descriptive flyers for employees and conducted presentations at department staff meetings and brown-bag presentations in the company cafeteria. Even inside an organization, my entrepreneurial need had emerged – now as an intrepreneur. I continued to use the Motivated Skills of designing, developing, presenting, and teaching.

1976: Juggling Three Jobs

While working full time at my internal job at Lawrence Livermore National Laboratory and operating my private career counseling practice after hours, I was approached by the U.S. Veterans Administration (V.A.) They wanted to contract with me to provide career counseling to veterans who were receiving benefits through the G.I. Bill. The local state university had been operating a guidance center for the VA for the past 11 years, and the VA regional office wanted to make a change. I decided that I could just as well juggle three jobs as two, so I said "yes".

I quickly leased office space, purchased typewriters, transcribing machines, desks, and filing cabinets. I then hired a secretary/office manager and two counseling psychologists. In less than three weeks, we were up and running. I received a fee for each veteran that we saw. My expenses were rent, staff salaries, taxes, and office supplies. What was left over each month was mine (and I didn't have to put in any "billable hours." Here I was again meeting a real need as an entrepreneur and using my Motivated Skills of planning, organizing, directing, coordinating, and implementing.

1977: Career Assessment Instruments

During my assignment of putting together a career development program for employees (physicists, engineers, secretaries, technicians, administrators, craft workers, etc.) at Lawrence Livermore National Laboratory, I found that many assessment instruments then in popular use were not appropriate for working adults. Specifically, when I decided it was important to identify employees' career values, the instruments that I had been exposed to in graduate school were inadequate, One popular instrument had only six values. Another had dozens of values and was standardized on Peace Corps volunteers (hardly a mainstream sample). In my course work in clinical psychology, I had been introduced to the Q-sort method of identifying levels of pain or depression.

I decided to adapt that technique and printed a list of 41 career values and their definitions on a set of 3″ x 5″ cards. I then printed five category cards (Always Valued, Often Valued, Sometimes Valued, Seldom Valued, and Never Valued) and started using them with employees in career counseling sessions and workshops. Employees found them very easy to use and were impressed with the accuracy of the results.

I began demonstrating and discussing the Career Values Card Sort instrument with other counselors at local, regional, and national conferences and was impressed by the high level of interest from peers who found the instrument user-friendly. Consequently, I developed a Career Values manual and a set of cards that I began selling commercially. This card sort, and three others that I subsequently developed, have been translated into nine languages and have sold over 500,000 copies to career professionals around the world. The card sort instrument clearly filled a need that was recognized. To accomplish this entrepreneurial project, I used the Motivated Skills of innovating, designing, developing, producing, teaching, training, promoting, marketing, and selling.

1977: Career Planning & Adult Development Network

During the second half of the 1970s, I was a frequent speaker at local, regional, and national conferences for counselors, human resource professionals, and trainers. My topics usually involved providing career development for employees in the workplace, a very new arena for professional career counselors. At the conclusion of each presentation, I was "mobbed" by counselors who wanted to learn more about employee career development and how they might obtain employment in industrial organizations. Consequently, I started to collect business cards from counselors with the intention of duplicating materials that came across my desk and sending the copies on to each of them. The large number of business cards and mountains of material coming across my desk forced me to come up with a more manageable process.

I decided create a new association. It would be for career professionals (not just counselors) who worked with adults (not children in schools) who were in job or career transition. That organization became the Career Planning & Adult Development Network, now in its 28th year. As a vehicle to promote communication between career professionals, two colleagues and I designed a monthly newsletter (now bimonthly, in both e-mail and hard copy format) with information on conferences, workshops, books, instruments, new techniques, and ideas that would be of interest to career practitioners. The need was for an organization and publication for career practitioners who worked with normal adults. The Motivated Skills I used were observing, intuiting, innovating, designing, developing, organizing, arranging, creating, and implementing.

1977-1995: Services to Specific Niches

Lawyers populated the first really lucrative entrepreneurial niche that I developed. My first contact with attorneys involved being called by a family law attorney who had a client going through a divorce and was certain that she was "unemployable." The attorney had found my name in the yellow pages under career counselors and thought that I might be able to help her. She was a 40-year-old mother of two high school students who had never worked outside of the home. She had spent the last 20+ years raising her children and keeping house for her high tech executive husband. It didn't take long for her to realize that she had many skills as a wife and mother that were readily transferable to paid employment. Even though the person I was working with was very similar to the housewives that had been the focus of my private career counseling practice established in 1971, the woman was not my client. My client, as an entrepreneur, is the one who is paying me – in this case, it is the lawyer who is paying me. And, even more significant, the lawyer is paying me with other people's money. If I am very successful with the displaced homemaker I am working with, I will get no repeat business. She won't need my help after she gets on with her life and career. But, if I do a good job with the individual sent to me by a lawyer, I will get plenty of repeat business from the lawyer.

About three years after getting my first piece of business from the family law attorney, California introduced "No Fault Divorce," which replaced divorce with "marital dissolution" and alimony with "spousal support." With no fault insurance, the spouses who had put their career aside during the marriage could apply for spousal support to assist them in returning to an appropriate level of employment. The courts then established that any party who is asked for spousal support (usually the husband) can require that the spouse undergo a vocational evaluation to be performed by a vocational evaluator (career counselor). These evaluations could involve four to six individual counseling sessions, several assessment instruments, and a written report that documents the individual's current and potential earning ability and a step-by-step plan to get to career independence. The evaluation could cost several hundred dollars. I quickly saw a need for this service and wanted to fill the need. I decided to move aggressively into this arena.

Through the Career Planning & Adult Development Network, the nonprofit professional association that I had founded in 1978, I decided to host a presentation for family law attorneys on "What is Involved in a Vocational Evaluation for Spousal Support Determination." The presentation was set for a Thursday afternoon from 5:00 pm to 7:00 pm at a hotel two blocks from the county courthouse. We charged $25 to attend and provided wine and cheese and a formal one-hour presentation. The presentation involved a panel comprised of the chief judge in the family law court, a well-respected family law attorney, and a professional career counselor (me). We sent a letter inviting the 85 family law attorneys listed in the county bar association directory and 75 showed up. I had prepared a four-page paper entitled "How to Choose a Vocational Evaluator for Spousal Support Determination" and made sure it was handed out to each attendee. Although this was an objective paper on vocational evaluations, I emphasized "National Certified Career Counselors (NCCC) had excellent training and education to conduct vocational evaluations." Of course, the paper had my name with the NCCC designation, my organization's name, address, telephone number, and fax number placed at the end of the paper. My office received an endless stream of requests for evaluations from family law attorneys who had attended the presentation. By the early 1980s, I had two other contract career counselors assisting me in conducting vocational evaluations for spousal support. We even put a one-page ad in the annual county bar association directory describing our services of evaluations and expert testimony. In the process of filling this need, I discovered other needs of lawyers.

The more I interacted with lawyers as a vocational evaluator and expert witness, the more I learned about their own career concerns. Some lawyers found the actual practice of law very different than their notions of the profession before going to law school. But, since they had invested so much time, energy, and money in getting there, they were sticking with it because they couldn't see any way out. In addition, most lawyers have learned to play their cards very close to their chests, and are cautious about admitting any career insecurity or concerns. But, once they got to know me, many were able to share their concerns and became private career development or career change clients. Finally, this relationship eventually resulted in my very lucrative practice of providing expert testimony as an employment expert in medical malpractice, wrongful termination, and personal injury cases as well as the less lucrative family law cases. I successfully met the needs of lawyers by using the Motivated Skills of organizing, developing, promoting, selling, writing, and implementing.

1980: National Workshops for Career Counselors

In 1980, the Veterans Administration discontinued their local guidance centers, so I had fewer balls to juggle. I was also able to modify my job hours at Lawrence Livermore National Laboratory, where I moved from full-time to four days per week. This permitted me to start offering professional development workshops for career counselors throughout the country on topics such as Career Development in Business, Industry and Government; Career Assessment Techniques; Providing Expert Testimony; and Establishing a Private Career Counseling Practice.

I successfully met the needs of professional counselors to obtain practical training in the new profession of "career" counseling by using the Motivated Skills of organizing, developing, promoting, selling, writing, and implementing.

1980-2003: Career Practitioners' Resource Store

In conducting these seminars, I found that I could sell my card sort assessment instruments at the back of the room. Consequently, I developed a one-page (printed on both sides) flyer describing these instruments and sent them to counselors who couldn't attend the workshops. The card sort instrument sales took off. I received single orders for as many as 20,000 sets of Motivated Skill Card Sorts at a time. Since I had a little space left on the product flyer, I decided to include the 200-page "Professional Job Search Manual" that I had developed for use with my private practice clients. This manual was enclosed in a three-ring binder. I included the manual because so many career counselors that I met at professional conferences wanted to purchase copies of my manual rather than write their own. When I first put the manual in the flyer, I listed the price as $25 each and steadily sold several copies each week. Imagine my surprise when I raised the price to $45 each and resulting orders doubled. This level of product sales continued so I expanded the flyer to a larger (11″ x 17″) single sheet and included a listing of skill building workshops for career counselors that I was conducting across the country.

I have always saved catalogs and flyers that included career development and job search books and materials that crossed my desk (I might need them sometime). I noted that there were about 75 or 80 publishers' catalogs that I needed to look through in order to find the few career development or job search books that they carried. Wouldn't it be easier to go to just one "Career Development" catalog instead of 75 or 80 generic book catalogs? Consequently, I started contacting publishers who carried some career development titles in their catalogs and learned that I could purchase books from them at wholesale prices and resell them at retail prices. Some publishers would sell me as few as two or three books at 35% or 40% off. When I purchased larger quantities (10 or more), it was common to receive a 50% discount.

I had now reached a point where my materials sales exceeded my income from counseling services. The need for a "one-stop" mail order career bookstore (with a 64-page catalog) was recognized and filled. The bookstore eventually went on-line two years ago and merged with another on-line bookstore. This 20+ years in growing the Career Practitioners Resource Store is a clear example of recognizing a need and moving to fill that need. The Motivated Skills used were gathering and reviewing information, negotiating, planning, organizing, coordinating, promoting, selling, and implementing the project.

1984-2005: California Career Conference/International Career Development Conference

In late 1983, I was serving as the President of the California Career Development Association. In that role, I was on the planning committee for the conference of our parent association, the California Counseling and Development Association. My fellow career counselors and I were very frustrated by the content of concurrent workshops that were offered at our parent organization's annual conference. Even though our division (careers) was the second largest division of the state association, we only had one of 14 votes for programs to include in the conference. Each division or special interest group received one vote. A special interest group with 10 members had as many votes as our 500-member division. Consequently, very few of the concurrent workshop at the conference were of interest to career counselors that worked with mainstream clients.

Consequently, two colleagues and I decided to put on a freestanding career-development conference to provide exposure to excellent ideas and programs for working career-development professionals. The Career Planning and Adult Development Network, the California Career Development Association and EUREKA Career Information System chose a date, contracted with a local hotel, selected keynote speakers, and recruited concurrent workshop presenters. We hoped to attract 200 interested career professionals. To our surprise, over 500 career practitioners filled the first California Career Conference to overflowing. The conference would continue to grow and draw attendees from throughout the country and the world, resulting in changing the name to International Career Development Conference. We had clearly identified a need for a conference with practical information for career counselors and filled it. The Motivated Skills I used were needs assessment, designing, developing, planning, organizing, negotiating, recruiting, promoting, teaching, training, and selling.

1985-1987: Corporate Executive Outplacement Firm

In the 1970s, at Lawrence Livermore National Laboratory, I had been exposed to corporate outplacement (where a company pays a consulting firm to assist employees that it terminates or lays off to obtain new employment). I researched outplacement techniques that we wanted to use with valued scientific employees whose jobs disappeared as nuclear weapons testing went out of favor. I was exposed to it again in the early 1980s when the Silicon Valley firm where I was Employee Development and Training Manager went out of business (I conducted outplacement workshops for the staff and then turned off the lights). With the number of managers being laid off by Silicon Valley firms increasing and the common practice of new CEOs needing to replace executives with "their own" people, it looked like there would be plenty of business.

In 1985, the only outplacement firms doing significant business in the Silicon Valley were Drake Beam Morin and Right Associates. These were national firms, operated out of New York and Chicago. Often, when they received a contract from a local company, they would fly in an outplacement consultant (who had "Vice President" on his card) to provide the service. If my two colleagues and I decided to go into this business, these two firms would be our competition. One of my colleagues, a former employee of Drake Beam Morin, decided to call on human resource directors at Silicon Valley firms and ask them if they were satisfied with the outplacement services they were currently receiving. They all responded that yes, they were satisfied. So, how could we get their business if they were satisfied with our competitors?

We decided to differentiate our firm from our competitors. We explained to potential clients that if a company did business with either of our competitors, they would not receive services from the person "whose name was on the door." They would not know who would be delivering the service. Our company, Knowdell-Martin-Hagberg, Inc. was local, and the principals would be delivering the services. We then asked the human resource directors to just try us the next time they had a need for outplacement services. It worked. We started to get a number of executives from these companies. At the time we entered the field, the standard fee for executive outplacement was 15% of the executive's salary for the past year. That resulted in a fee between $10,000 and $15,000 for each executive.

In order to increase our segment of the business, we decided to offer a different pricing structure. We now offered our service for a flat fee of $7,500 for any executive. This quickly increased the flow of candidates into our firm. By the time we sold the firm three years later, we had contracts with 51 Silicon Valley firms to provide executive outplacement. Again, we a recognized a need and built an organization to fill that need. The Motivated Skills that I used were assessing needs, planning, organizing, coordinating, developing, negotiating, teaching and training.

1992-2006: Job & Career Transition Coach Training and Certification

Three significant events led to my development of the Job & Career Transition Coach training and certification program.

First, in the early 1990s, the U.S. Forest Service decided to place a "career counselor" in each national forest on the west coast. The agency was having difficulty in getting women and minorities promoted into the more desirable jobs and was looking for a way to train some of their personnel specialists as career counselors. When I explained to them that a two-year master's degree would be required to become a career counselor, they indicated an interest in exploring other methods of obtaining appropriate training. When I was busy training and supervising professional career counselors in business and industry in the 1970s and 1980s, we tended to limit the career counseling for each employee to four sessions. Being trained in "brief therapy," I viewed the employee career counseling process as "active problem solving," where we would identify the problem, consider several solutions, choose a solution, and then set a follow-up session. This process was very similar to "coaching". Consequently, I suggested that I could train a group of Forest Service personnel specialists in one week to be competent "career coaches". The one week of training consisted of day one on the U.S. Forest Service occupational structure and days two, three, and four on a simple four-stage career transition process and on specific coaching skills. Day five was focused on transfer, promotion and compensations policies of the U.S. Forest Service. I trained three dozen personnel specialists who proved to be excellent "career coaches" in their work settings.

Secondly, in the early 1990s, the National Board for Certified Counselors (NBCC) made significant changes in the requirement for qualifying to become a National Certified Counselor (NCC) and subsequently a National Certified Career Counselor (NCCC). The requirements for qualifying were raised to require a two-year master's degree in counseling and 3,000 hours of counseling supervised by a board-qualified counselor (NCCC was eventually discontinued).

Thirdly, the decade of the 1990s saw the rise of the new and controversial profession of coaching. Hundreds of coaches, some with Ph.D. degrees, and many with no education at all, were "coming out of the

woodwork." They were "life coaches," "financial coaches," physical conditioning coaches," "executive coaches," and "career coaches." What they seemed to have in common was working very quickly, prescribing specific activities for the client to engage in, and charging high fees. Most important, there did not appear to be any government (licensing) or professional (credentialing) regulations for coaching.

Consequently, based on (a) the effectiveness of a short and intensive career- transition coach training process, (b) the barriers faced by career counselors seeking certification, and (c) the current lack of creditable credentialing programs for career coaches, my organization, the Career Planning & Adult Development Network, decided to develop the Job & Career Transition Coach training and certification program.

Since I had been training career counselors and career technicians in small and intensive group workshops for several years, I decided to base the training on this model. I limit the group to 24 students and conduct the training on three consecutive eight-hour days. The training starts with an overview of the changing nature of work, jobs and careers, comments on the emotional impact of career transition, and then quickly moves into a four-step transition model:

1. Assessment
2. Exploration
3. Focus
4. Strategy Implementation

The bulk of the workshop involves active participation in the assessment, group exercises, and coaching skills that are introduced to the students. Each student is required to develop his or her own job or career transition plan that is used in coach practice session where each individual coaches another student, receives coaching on his/her transition plan, and observes and evaluates another student doing coaching.

Grades are pass or fail and are based on each student's active use of the coaching process and skills. Instead of placing rigid educational requirements on applicants to the certification program, the sole prerequisite is that successful applicants must be in an assignment where they are expected to provide career counseling, career coaching, career advisement, or job search training to adults.

A typical "open" workshop is comprised of two or three professional counselors trained at the Ph.D. level and with 20+ years or experience and two or three military career-transition advisors with no education or training in career development who had just been assigned transition advising duties. Those in between include private-practice executive coaches, college and university career counselors, employee development specialists, outplacement consultants, welfare-to-work case managers, and resume writers.

The Network currently conducts six open or public programs around the U.S. each year and about six "closed" programs for government organizations or professional associations. I am currently teaching all of these certification workshops and hope to add other trainers during coming years. There is clearly a need to train and certify career practitioners to provide career and job transition coaching to adults throughout the English-speaking world. We have filled that need by training and certifying over 3,000 career practitioners in Europe, Asia, Africa, Australia, North America, and South America during the last 14 years. I used my Motivated Skills of assessing needs, designing, organizing, planning, teaching, training, selling, and promoting.

As I come to the end of this paper, I am not yet at the end of being an entrepreneur. I am currently developing two projects that I hope will meet the needs of people willing to pay for the services that I plan to provide. And yes, they are both in the career development field and involve the use of my Motivated Skills of recognizing a need, designing a program, planning, coordinating, organizing, negotiating, building, promoting, teaching, and selling.

Resources

Shenson, H.L. & Anderson, T.D.. (1988, 2005). *The entrepreneurial style and success indicator.* Abbotsford, BC, Canada: Consulting Resource Group International.

Knowdell, R.L. (1977, 2005). *Motivated skills card sort.* Fountain Valley, CA:. Retrieved September 2, 2006: http://www.careertrainer.com.

Bolles, R.N. (2006). *What color is your parachute?* Berkeley, CA: Ten Speed Press.

The motivated skills card sort on-line version. Retrieved September 2, 2006: http://www.careertrainer.com.

The Entrepreneurial style and success indicator. Retrieved September 2, 2006: http://www.crgleader.com.

Editor's Note: Where Do You Go From Here?

Sally Gelardin, Ed.D.

There are no guarantees in life. The only guarantee is that doing nothing will get you nowhere. (Krumboltz, 2005).

Now that you have read the career entrepreneurs' words of wisdom on how to start and grow a career business and completed some of their thought-provoking activities, where do you go from here? Rather than leave you stranded in the entrepreneurial forest, which is often quite lonely, I offer you the opportunity to respond to the following questions that I asked experts who contributed to this monograph:

- What is motivating you to start a business?
- What entrepreneurial strengths do you have?
- What are your business vision and mission?
- How can you grow your practice with purpose?
- What are your sources of external and internal support?
- What is your strategic plan?
- What challenges have you encountered? How can you meet future challenges?
- How do you evaluate what you've accomplished and what more you need to do to reach your goals?
- Do you have an exit plan? If so, describe.
- In your opinion, what has made (or "will make") you a great entrepreneur?

Strategies For Starting and Building a Business

No one can predict the future. Unexpected events are inevitable. But if you are alert, you can make the most out of them when they happen. (Krumboltz, 2005).

Krumboltz (2005) asserted that an occupational choice is the result of a lifelong sequence of learning experiences. As you consider starting a business, or if you are in the midst of developing an existing business, you can apply what you learned from the stories of career entrepreneurs. In addition, you can further your knowledge through in-person training programs, professional career conferences and meetings, webinars, teleseminars, and other delivery systems. Research what interests you and apply what you learn, read entrepreneur books and do Internet searches on entrepreneur-related subjects. Experience career entrepreneur products and services; gather ideas for products and services from other industries. Reach your own conclusions.

Explore the print and/or online resources provided by the experts in this monograph. Read their books, seek their advice, take their trainings, try out their products. Read their biographies in Appendix B to learn more about them. Contact those who could mentor you. I not only became, and remain, active in career organizations, I have earned eight career certificates and continue to take training programs provided by NCDA and the contributors to this monograph, such as NCDA's Career Development Facilitator Instructor and eLearning training, ReadyMinds' Distance Counseling Certification, Dick Knowdell's Job and Life Transition Coaching workshop, Lynn Joseph's Job Loss Recovery trainer workshop (offered in conjunction with Parachute), Dan Geller's Instant Strategist business seminar, and Susan Whitcomb's Career Master Institute (CMI) webinars and teleseminars.

From each experience, you can pick up new business ideas, many of which you can apply to your own business. For example, after participating in a CMI webinar, I offered to present a webinar for CMI on "ePortfolios are Replacing Resumes." Subsequently, I invited Susan Whitcomb to be a guest lecturer for a CDF telesession on "Converting Resumes for Emailing and Web-Posting" (Whitcomb, 2005). I subsequently converted the recording of her presentation into an audio interview (Gelardin, 2005).

After reading several of Bob Chope's books and articles and attending his workshops and professional development institutes, I found myself attracted to his "whole person" approach to career counseling and invited him to present workshops with me on family influences on career development at the National Career Development Association (NCDA) annual conference, American Counseling Association (ACA) annual convention, and the International Career Development Conference (ICDC). This collaboration led to larger presentations and paid speaking engagements, both with Bob, and on my own. In addition, I often invite graduate students, counselors from other countries, and new counselors to present workshops with me.

Following is a summary of ways that you can continue down the entrepreneurial path:

- Participate in professional associations;

- Enlist the support of mentors;
- Research what interests you and apply what you learn;
- Organize your business on your computer;
- Create an Internet presence for your business;
- Join an in-person or virtual entrepreneur community;
- Take time to perform the exercises in Appendix A.

Participate in Professional Associations

Become active in professional associations, such as the National Career Development Association (NCDA). By attending workshops on workforce trends, you can discover what niche needs to be filled for career professionals and/or their clients, and how you can best meet that need.

I have attended presentations at national conferences and regional events featuring each contributor to this book, read their books, and use Richard Knowdell's card sorts and Carolyn Kalil's True Colors assessment cards with my master's in counseling students and with my Global Career Development Facilitator students - from San Francisco to Istanbul.

After hearing Ron Elsdon speak about workplace affiliation and reading his book on that topic, I invited Ron to lunch and asked him for permission to include his concepts in my online employability skills course. I was so impressed by his concept of affiliation that I changed the name of the lesson on job retention to "Workplace Affiliation," and encouraged him to submit a proposal for a NCDA Professional Development Institute.

Join and become active in professional associations such as the following, to network with the entrepreneurs featured in this book and with other career entrepreneurs. Here is a sampling of organizations that sponsor conferences, teleconferences, webinars, and regional meetings, where you can network with career entrepreneurs:

- National Career Development Association, http://www.ncda.org
- International Career Development Conference, http://www.careerccc.com (sponsored by the California Career Development Association (CCDA), the Career and Adult Development NETWORK, and EUREKA, The California Career Information System)
- Career Masters Institute, http://www.cminstitute.com
- Career Coach Institute, http://www.careercoachinstitute.com

Enlist the Support of Mentors

As you have learned from the contributors' stories, identifying mentors is an important part of succeeding as an entrepreneur. Joan Quintanar said, "When I am counseling students who have already decided their career path, I always encourage them to shadow three different people in that profession" (Quintanar, 2005). Find mentors among the contributors to this monograph and through your own network.

Gail Liebhaber asked me to be her mentor through NCDA's mentoring program. I asked her what burning questions she had. She asked, "How can I give back to other career professionals?" As our relationship developed, we began to talk about doing workshops together. I invited her to present with me at the Career Masters Institute (CMI) annual conference, to participate as an author in Café Philo (philosophy café at an NCDA conference), to become an active member of the NCDA Professional Development Committee, and to offer career tips with Richard Bolles and me at Café Vitae, my career service to attendees at the Professional Businesswomen of California Conference. Though she is younger than I, Gail became as much as a mentor to me as I to her and has referred me to serve as a keynote speaker for organizations. Gail is much more practical than I am. She keeps me grounded and I encourage her to take risks.

Martha Russell has been a mentor to me throughout my career as a counselor/educator. In addition to following her path as president of the California Career Development Association, over the years I have observed closely her presentation and leadership skills as she ascended the organizational ladder to become NCDA president. Martha is a down-to-earth, warm-hearted community builder. She offers me heart-felt advice and feedback.

Learn what you "need," not necessarily "want" to learn from mentors. The character played by Emma Thompson, in the movie *Nanny McPhee* (2006), says to the children for whom she cares, "When you **need me,** but **do not want me,** then I will stay. When you **want me,** but **do not need me,** then I have to go." You can apply this concept of what you "need" both to solve business problems and to create a mission statement.

For example, my personal mission is to balance my needs with the needs of others. It's not that I especially want to live a balanced life. I enjoy following my passions and serving others. However, I am aware that I need to pace myself, to be at peace with myself, and be aware of each precious moment, instead of just planning for the future or looking back at the past. Yoga and Pilates movements may be uncomfortable at times, but that's what my body needs, to keep me in good physical and mental shape.

I created an online course so that I could operate my business out of my home office or from anywhere in the world. As an extension of my personal mission, I provide a service that others need through an online course that they can log on from anywhere they have Internet access and any time that is convenient to them. Both my clients and I gain peace of mind, so ephemeral a concept in Western society, where we are inundated with information.

I used to think Jack Chapman was too promotional. When I took his workshop and became better acquainted with him, I found he had much to offer. That's when the "need to learn" kicked in, as opposed to the "like to learn." I needed to learn about the more practical aspects of running a business to balance my creative, missionary side, and Jack is the perfect mentor on this subject. He is very bottom-line profit-oriented.

Another of my profit-oriented mentors is Dan Geller. I discovered him through Small Business Development Center (SBDC), a division of the U.S. Small Business Administration (Retrieved September 21, 2006: http://www.sba.gov). SBDC is a free/low-fee service offered to entrepreneurs by the U.S. Government, in collaboration with local community programs. Dan also runs Instant Strategist, a strategic business planning training and advising company. I consult with Dan several times a month on business issues.

Apply What You Learn

Information abounds, but until you digest it and put it to good use, it is useless. For example, when I began teaching the Career Development Facilitator (CDF) curriculum, I became overwhelmed with the information available on the topic. Career information sites and how-to books were plentiful, except I could not absorb all the material. Instead, I turned off. I didn't want to look at another list of resume tips – and I was supposed to teach my students how to resource career information!

The only way I could think of absorbing this information and passing it on to my students was to create an online job-search skills course with built-in self-assessment tools. In addition, I added activities for learners to perform in each lesson. To create this e-course, I did years of research. Since it is an online course, I continually update the course, which is essential, since information is constantly changing.

My business model was unique – an online, lifelong employability skills course, available to workers in transition, from high school on up, and a distance delivered *Job Search Practitioner Manual* and training for career advisors and educators. I believe that job seekers and career advisors should be able to access job search strategies from anywhere in the world community (i.e., at an Internet café, in transit, or wherever they have access to the Internet), not just in the career center or counselor's office. The e-course can supplement career-advising services. In Exercise 1 of Appendix A, you are welcome to try a variation of a job search exercise from my e-course by organizing your business on your computer.

Creating my own career course was a great way to expand my knowledge base and keep myself current. I invite you to create your own career course and learn through the act of creating a course. If you create your own classroom or online course, I offer to make my lifelong employability e-course available to you as online licensed material. Let's break out of the rigid concept that courses have to be taught in a prescribed way. I believe that the primary goal of courses, for both student and instructor, is to expand one's knowledge base and increase one's ability to think, act, and be fully engaged in life, which includes acquiring, synthesizing, and analyzing information, coming to conclusions, taking action, and sharing knowledge with others to make the world a better place. If you recognize the value of learning, as opposed to the first step of gathering information, I welcome you to join me!

Organize Your Business Plan on Your Computer

Why set up paper files when you can organize your business plan and strategies on your computer? View Activity 1 in Appendix A to discover an easy way to set up computer folders using the chapters of this book. Perform the exercises in this monograph and keep notes in your folders, along with a journal of your progress, key contacts, and a list of resources and articles for each topic.

Join An In-Person Or Virtual Entrepreneur Community

Let's take this monograph forward by continuing the learning and sharing process. Join a free, open-source "Entrepreneur" web-based community, http://www.lifeworkps.com/entrepreneur, described in Exercise 2 of Appendix A.

Alternatively, create an in-person or distance-delivered Career Entrepreneur Lifework Book Club based upon the 10 questions at the beginning of this section. Create a topic for discussion in each book club session based on the chapter heading questions and use the wealth of resources provided at the end of the chapters in this monograph. If you are currently working for a college or university, you can use the same technical features as are available on lifeworkps.com to set up an entrepreneur book club or entrepreneur e-community through

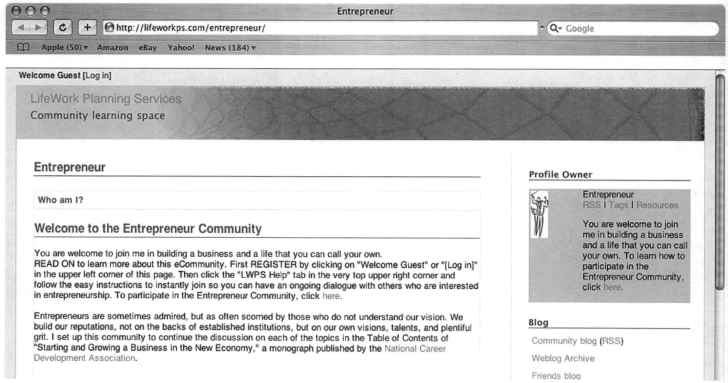

WebCT/Blackboard. Elgg, the technology source, provides an opportunity for instructors and institutions to function outside the boundaries of an individual course through blogging and social networking. An Entrepreneur eCommunity would be an interesting way for a Family Business Program at a university to support a learning community and groups. "Learning groups can be created across multiple sections, multiple courses, and even across departments." (Downes, 2006).

Reach Your Own Conclusions

Think for yourself. After you have listened to the wisdom of others, draw your own conclusions. At some  point, you will challenge your mentors. Just like separating from a parent, you will find solutions and conduct your business in a way that is best for you. For example, I worked for years with Fanita English (English, 1998) on applying her motivational theory (all individuals are motivated to make decisions, first by survival, and next by three categories of "drives" – service, passion, and quiescence). Then I developed my own model, incorporating her motivational theory into the Tightrope Artist's Career Decision-Making Model (Gelardin, 2006), that includes identifying one's learning styles, as well as one's preferred motivations, along with more frequently used self-awareness indicators: interests, skills,

values, personality traits, family influences, and environmental preferences.

The Job Juggler, my Internet-based employability program (Gelardin, 2004), incorporates learning styles that employ both sides of the brain – progress, review, and discussion questions that appeal to logic and memory, along with career expert audios that appeal to sense of sound, and online courses that appeal to senses of sight and touch. In support of my mission to balance my needs with the needs of others (and to help others manage this balancing act), I infuse into my services and products awareness of the present (often measured by physical and sensory variables), while preparing for the future and reflecting upon the past. This concept is the origin of my business trademark, "The Job Juggler," a metaphor for juggling or balancing job search balls, multiple jobs, work and home, needs of others with one's own needs, and other lifework-balancing concepts.

The ball is in your field now. Don't drop it. You have plenty of support. Buckminster Fuller failed in the real estate business and spent a year without talking to anyone before he designed his famous geodesic domes. You may strike out several times before hitting a home run. Becoming an entrepreneur involves risk. However, as leading career expert John Krumboltz said, "There are no guarantees in life. The only guarantee is that doing nothing will get you nowhere."

If you embark on an entrepreneurial journey, don't lose a sense of balance and become sick or ignore your family and friends. Entrepreneurs tend to work long hours. Heed the following statistics presented by the Herman Group (2005) on U.S. workers: "The vacations of U.S. workers are the shortest in the industrialized world – only 8.1 days after one year on the job (Bureau of Labor Statistics). European workers take four to six weeks vacation a year, and Chinese workers get three weeks off." According to a Boston College survey, 26 percent of Americans take no vacation at all. The International Labor Organization (ILO) reports that Americans work up to 12 weeks more in total hours annually than their European counterparts. Entrepreneurs generally work even harder than other workers.

On the other hand, not enough work has its toll, too. According to the Hermans (2006), "The least satisfied workers actually wanted more work; they did not want to feel mediocre, ineffective, or less than valuable to their employer and the world." Therefore, if you are going to go into business for yourself, choose a business that you enjoy, because you'll probably spend a good deal of sleeping time, as well as waking time, immersed in your business. Be fully present in the "here and now" as you plan your business. Take frequent short breaks to revitalize yourself. Enlist the support of, and create alliances with, people with whom you want to do business. Whether you go into business for yourself or work as a consultant or full-time employee of an organization, you can benefit by reading about the experiences of successful entrepreneurs, implementing their exercises, and participating in live and online entrepreneurial dialogues.

Life is a juggling act in the fast-moving 21st century. Juggling job responsibilities, work and home responsibilities, wage and age – it's all a juggling act. Successful entrepreneurs don't become obsessed with dropping the ball because they know they can try again. May you find joy, fulfillment, and peace within the rising and falling.

References

Downes, S. (2006). Curverider and Aperto work on integrating WebCT and Elgg. Retrieved September 17, 2006 from: http://www.downes.ca/cgi-bin/page.cgi?action=conversation&link=54932.

English, F. (1998). *The Forces within us* (Videotape). Oakland, CA: International Transactional Analysis Association.

Gelardin, S. 2004. *The mother-daughter relationship: Activities for promoting lifework success.* CAPS Press. Retrieved September 2, 2006: http://www.askdrsal.com.

Gelardin, S. 2004-2006. The Job Juggler web-based job search strategies program. Retrieved September 2, 2006: http://www.jobjuggler.net/

Gelardin, S. 2004-2006. Lesson 1 Demo. Retrieved September 2, 2006: http://www.jobjuggler.net/jobseekers.html.

Gelardin, S. 2004-2006. Content Orientation, Job Juggler *Practitioner Manual,* Retrieved September 2, 2006: Retrieved September 2, 2006: http://www.jobjuggler.net/careerprofessionals.html#. Click on "free demo."

Gelardin, S. (2006). Tightrope Artist's Career Decision-Making Model. Retrieved September 17, 2006: http://www.lifeworkps.com/Creativity.

Gelardin, S. (2006). Entrepreneur blogging and networking e-community. (2006). Retrieved September 2, 2006: Retrieved September 2, 2006: http://www.lifeworkps.com/entrepreneur.

Herman Trend Alerts. Retrieved September 2, 2006: http://www.hermangroup.com.

Krumboltz, J. (October 18, 2005). Email conversation with author.

Whitcomb, S. (October 21, 2005). Career expert interview: *Converting resumes for emailing and web-posting.* Audio recording. Retrieved September 17, 2006: http://jobjuggler.net/careerexpertaudios.html.

APPENDIX A:

EXERCISES

Exercise 1: Organize Your Business Strategy on Your Computer

Sally Gelardin, Ed.D.

Purpose

To help potential and current entrepreneurs organize their strategies for growing a business on the Internet.

Learning Objectives

- To create an Entrepreneur Folder on your computer for organizing your business
- To network with other career entrepreneurs who can support you and whom you can support in the entrepreneurial process

Target Population

Current or aspiring entrepreneurs

Rationale

If you are ready to proceed with developing your business, the Internet is an excellent resource. However, it can exhaust and overwhelm you and create frustration unless you know how to navigate through it effectively. Organizing the entrepreneurial process on your computer can help keep you organized.

Participants

The Entrepreneur Folder can be organized independently, unless one is technically challenged. In that case, seek the assistance of a person who understands how to insert documents into computer folders.

Setting

Any place where you can concentrate

Time Required

Initial set-up of files takes less than ½ hour. Inserting documents and folders into master folders is ongoing. You can create folders as needed. The time required varies, depending how much material you choose to collect and organize on your computer.

Materials

Computer and Internet connection (preferably high-speed)

Instructions

Set up an Entrepreneur Folder on your computer. Create 10 folders and insert into your Entrepreneur Folder. Label each of the 10 folders with a monograph chapter heading. Create four document or folders to insert into each chapter folder: (a) Journal (document), (b) Resource list (document), (c) Exercise/s (folder), (d) Articles (folder). Following is an example, based on Chapter 1:

1. What motivated me (or "is motivating me") to start a business (folder)?

   a. Motivation Journal (document – include reflections, thoughts, feelings, and insights)

   b. Motivation Resource List (document – note websites, reports, books, and other media resources; annotate each resource to remind you why the resource is valuable)

   c. Motivation Exercise/s (folder – insert your responses to exercises from book that relate to Bob Chope's "motivation" chapter; add other exercises)

   d. Motivation Articles (folder – insert documents that relate to "motivation")

Discussion

As an alternative, or in addition, to setting up your career business on your computer, you can set up your career business on the Internet. Learn more by joining a "Starting a Business" discussion on the Internet. View a free Internet learning community, http://www.lifeworkps.com/entrepreneur. Join me and other career entrepreneurs to continue the discussion. Learn how to participate in this online discussion in the next exercise.

Assessment

You have set up an Entrepreneur Folder on your computer and created 10 folders to insert into your Entrepreneur Folder. Each of the 10 folders is labeled with a monograph chapter heading. You have inserted the following four documents or folders into each chapter folder: (a) Journal (document), (b) Resource List (document), (c) Exercise/s (folder), (d) Articles (folder). As you build your business, add material to each document and folder. You will know if you reached the outcomes of the exercise if you can easily access the material in your Entrepreneur Folder and put it to use to help build your business.

Exercise 2: Participate in an Internet-based Entrepreneur Community

Sally Gelardin, Ed.D.

Purpose

To provide an Internet-based community for potential and current entrepreneurs to share strategies for starting and growing a business

Rationale

Reading a monograph about starting a career development business is a good way to jump-start your business. In addition, the continued support of other entrepreneurs can help you through the building process. A no-fee Internet-based entrepreneurial community allows you to participate at your convenience. This exercise gives you an opportunity to participate in an online discussion with contributors to this monograph and other career entrepreneurs.

Learning Objectives

- To join and participate in a free Entrepreneur Community on a Web-based platform.
- To network with other career entrepreneurs asynchronically (without regard to time or place).
- To give and receive support in the entrepreneurial process.

Target Population

Current, aspiring, and experienced entrepreneurs

Instructions

Instructions for joining a free Internet-based Entrepreneurship Community can be found at http://www.lifeworkps.com/entrepreneur/weblog/835.html. I have purposefully referred you to the free Entrepreneurship Community rather than providing instructions in this monograph because the best way that you can learn about joining the Community is by doing it.

Assessment

You will know that you are a full participant in the Entrepreneur Community when you have joined the eCommunity and have viewed a post and posted a response in the Entrepreneur Community. You now have the basic technical skills needed to participate in the Entrepreneurship Community. Note: This e-community can be viewed by the public, so write only what you choose to share with the public. If you would like to learn how to restrict access to selected viewers, click on "LWPS Help" at the top of any page on http://www.lifeworkps.com, then click on "Lesson 1."

After performing this exercise, you will know how to (a) register, (b) create your e-profile, (c) find the Entrepreneur Community, (d) reply to a post in the Entrepreneur Community, (e) use access restriction function.

Exercise 3: Creative Thinking

Robert Chope, Ph.D.

Purpose of Exercise
To help you quickly assess your divergent thinking, or how well you think "out of the box."

Learning Objective
 • To discover how imaginative you can be.

Target Entrepreneur Population
Aspiring entrepreneurs

Participants
Readers of the chapter

Setting
Home or office

Time Required
Three minutes for the exercise, one minute for evaluation

Materials
Stop watch or watch with a second hand, paper, and pencil

Instructions
On a sheet of paper, jot down all of the probable and improbable uses you can imagine for a brick. Be a little zany with the exercise and stretch your imagination. Count the possibilities when the three minutes are up.

Discussion
How many uses did you jot down? Building is something that most people use a brick for. But did you consider its utility as a measuring device or weapon or means of percussion?

References
You may read further about the exercise in *Dancing Naked* (Chope, 2000). (A copyright transfer is not needed.)

Assessment
If you came up with more than 10 uses, your divergent thinking and potential to be creative in developing your business are in good shape. If you had less than five uses you might want to try other exercises that can help stimulate your imagination.

Now, try the next exercise.

Exercise 4: New Idea, New Business

Robert Chope, Ph.D.

Purpose of Exercise
To give you an opportunity to discover new and different career counseling services you might offer.

Learning Objective
- To become aware of business possibilities that are everywhere around you

Target Entrepreneur Population
Aspiring and recently launched professionals, although even seasoned professionals may find this to be useful.

Participants
The reader and possibility the reader's network of supporters

Setting
Home or office

Time Required
Two to three hours minimum

Materials
Newspapers, computer with web access, paper, and pencil

Instructions
Get three or four newspapers at a local newsstand and read them thoroughly. Then view five of your favorite Internet websites and five new ones and spend more time exploring the sites than you usually do. From these two sets of resources, the Internet and the print media, what type of service needs do you become aware of with regard to developing a private counseling business? Make a list of these.

What type of clients emerge that seem to be in need of assistance? Make a list of these. Now create a brand new idea for a business and write this down along with the names of people who could help you take this further. Afterwards, determine what new information is needed to launch this business. Then, try to create a vision of a counseling prototype. If you are this far along in the exercise, you have the enthusiasm and curiosity to start your own business.

Assessment
It might be useful for me to share some of the more unusual contacts that I have had as a career counselor that have generated substantial income, and have been challenging and even intriguing. View these contacts below:
- Consultant to airlines to help business travelers overcome fears of flying
- Consultant to banking industry to counsel bank employees who have been robbed
- Counselor for corporate leaders who have speaking phobias or social phobias
- Consultant to fire departments integrating women into the firehouses
- Consultant to police departments trying to create affirmative action programs
- Consultant on toxic coworkers for many corporations
- Counselor for employees who work with extraordinarily angry clients
- Career counselor for people who can't pass state bar examinations
- Career counselor for injured dancers of a ballet regarding new careers
- Outplacement counselor for public and private clients
- Keynote speaker for corporate conferences, spiritual organizations and civic clubs

If you have come up with several ideas like these, you may be well on your way to entrepreneurial success.

Exercise 5: Values Clarification

Jennifer Kahnweiler, Ph.D.

Purpose

To provide a forced ranking of values that inspires prospective or current entrepreneurs to take actiions that reflect their priorities, satisfy their most important values, and gain fulfillment.

Learning Objectives

- To become aware of the need to make trade-offs.
- To clarify how you are living your values now.
- To become aware of how consistent your values are with the role of an entrepreneur.

Target Population

Current or aspiring entrepreneurs

Participants

Readers. Follow up with a partner or career coach suggested.

Setting

Any quiet place

Time Required

Thirty minutes to complete and discuss with entrepreneurial mentors or associates

Materials

Handout below

Continued on next page.

Instructions

Place an "X" in the column that most closely describes the strength of each value below. Try to distribute your responses fairly evenly among the four levels of value strength. Be sure to avoid marking an abundance of items "Always Valued." Total the number of X's you have in the Always Valued column. Circle the top 5 values from that list.

VALUE	Always Valued	Often Valued	Sometimes Valued	Rarely Valued
PERSONAL GROWTH: Develop my potential and use my talents				
ACHIEVEMENT: Have a sense of accomplishment and mastery				
KNOWLEDGE: Develop and use specific knowledge and expertise				
STATUS: Hold a position of recognized importance in the organization				
COMPETITION: Engage in activities in which people must compete against each other				
CHANGE AND VARIETY: Have job responsibilities with varied tasks				
SERVICE TO SOCIETY: Contribute to a better society				
INDEPENDENCE: Control my own work/schedule				
LEADERSHIP: Influence others to achieve results				
CREATIVE EXPRESSION: Express my creativity and imagination in my work				
CHALLENGE: Find work that mentally stimulates me				
MONEY: Reap significant financial rewards				
MANAGEMENT: Achieve work goals as a result of others' efforts				
WORK WITH OTHERS: Belong to a satisfying work group or team				
POWER: Have control over resources at work				
INTEGRITY: Work ethically and honestly				
BALANCE: Achieve the right proportion between my personal life and professional responsibilities				
FRIENDSHIP: Develop social/personal friendships with work colleagues				
CAREER ADVANCEMENT: Be promotable within the organization				
DETAIL WORK: Deal with tasks that must meet specifications requiring careful and accurate attention to detail				
HELPING OTHERS: Involve myself in helping other people				
LOCATION: Live in a convenient community				
RECOGNITION: Receive credit for work well done				
EXCITEMENT: Experience frequent novelty and drama				
MORAL FULFILLMENT: Contribute to moral ideals				
AESTHETICS: Appreciate the beauty of things and ideas				
HEALTH: Be physically and mentally fit				

Discussion

Ask yourself and discuss with a partner or career coach:

- How closely are you living the values you have ranked the highest in your current work?
- How aligned are these with the entrepreneurial role you are in or are considering?
- What tradeoffs will you have to make in order to better incorporate these values in your work?
- What value conflicts do you currently experience?
- How have your values changed in the last 3 years? 6 years?
- What value conflicts do you see in the future?

Assessment

You will know if you reached the outcomes of the exercise if you can clearly articulate your values and your values tradeoffs. You will also be able to refer back to your top five values on a regular basis to see if you are in synch with what you have expressed.

Exercise 6: Building on Your Strengths

Carolyn Kalil

Purpose of Exercise

To assist you in creating a business that is built on your expressing who you are and doing what you do well and feel passionate about.

Learning Objectives

- To clarify your personality preferences and unique talents
- To write an intention statement that delineates your strengths on which you can build your business

Target Entrepreneur Population

It is best for those who are developing a new business, but it can also be helpful for entrepreneurs who want to re-evaluate their roles in their business.

Participants

This exercise is designed for you, the reader. You may want to share with others interested in becoming entrepreneurs.

Setting

Pick a favorite place that opens you up to your creativity. I can work in coffee shops in spite of the noise but you may prefer someplace more peaceful such as the beach, a park, or the library.

Time Required

Proceed at whatever pace works for you. It depends on how aware you already are of your personality preferences and talents.

Materials

These are optional if you already have the information. Book: *Follow Your True Colors To The Work You Love* (Kalil, C., 1998) or MBTI or Keirsey Temperament Sorter.

Instructions

Make a list of five of your positive personality traits if you already know them. If not, you can take the True Colors Assessment and find a list of these traits based on your first color in Follow Your True Colors To The Work You Love. You can find the same information from your MBTI or Keirsey Temperaments.

Next, make a list of five things that you do particularly well — your talents.

From your lists of personality traits and talents, which two traits and which two talents do you feel the most passionate about? In other words, which ones give you the greatest satisfaction or sense of excitement?

Who needs a service using your particular traits and talents (e.g., students, job seekers, career coaches, and others)?

Write an intention statement that includes the four steps above. Example: "I intend to use compassion and my desire to help people reach their potential to inspire and train professionals to better prepare job seekers in finding fulfilling and rewarding careers." Write your intention statement: "I intend to use (list two of your major personality traits) to (list two of your special talents) (what audience for what purpose)."

Focus your attention on your intention by reading your statement daily until you actualize it. This is exactly what Jack Canfield and Mark Victor Hansen, authors of *Chicken Soup for the Soul,* did. Their book was turned down by all of the major New York publishers but they didn't let that stop them. Two years before their book became a best seller, I visited their office in Southern California. They had posted all over the walls "Chicken Soup for the Soul, #1 New York Times Best Seller." They believed in the idea so strongly that they wrote it down and focused their attention on what they wanted daily. Within two years they turned that book and many others into New York Times #1 Best Sellers. Like them, don't allow any obstacles or challenges of any kind deter your efforts to be successful. Build your business on your strengths.

Discussion Questions

- Are you open to introspection and discovering your true self?
- What brings you satisfaction at a soul level?
- How can you turn your strengths and passion into a service for others?
- What are people looking for that you can provide in a unique way?
- Is there a need for a partner and what strengths could they add that compliment yours?
- Who would make good mentors?
- Are you willing to stretch yourself and take some risks?

Assessment

Did you clearly state your personality traits and unique talents?
Did you write an intention statement that explains how you will use your personality strengths and talents to build your business?

Exercise 7: Writing a Business Statement

Marcia Bench, J.D.

Purpose of Exercise
To help you develop a clear business mission statement

Learning Objectives
- To clarify your personal life purpose
- To identify your business mission
- To clarify the work the business will be doing
- To align your business mission with your personal life purpose

Target Entrepreneur Population
Aspiring, just launched, or in process

Participants
Reader only

Setting
Can be done anywhere you can relax and concentrate

Time Required
30-60 minutes
Materials
The form below and a writing tool

Instructions
If you are not sure what your life purpose is, answer the following ten questions to guide you. Your business mission (which follows this exercise) should align with your life purpose. Read the instructions and fill in the blanks, then reflect upon what you have written.

Ten Clues To Discover Your Life Purpose
1. What do you love to do, whether in your spare time or at work?
2. What parts of your present job or life activities do you thoroughly enjoy?
3. What do you naturally do well?
4. What are your ten greatest successes to date (in your eyes)?
5. Is there a cause about which you feel passionate?
6. What are the ten most important lessons you have learned in your life?
7. Are there some issues or perceived problems that have occurred over and over again?
8. What do you daydream about doing?
9. Imagine you are writing your epitaph. What things do you want to be remembered for at the end of your life?
10. What would you do if you knew you could not fail?

Themes in my answers:

_____

_____

_____

_____

My life purpose is to:

_____

_____

through (list life and work activities here)

1. _____

2. _____

3. _____

Other_____

Please complete the following items as best you can with what you know now.

My business mission (identity/purpose) is

_____

_____

My business philosophy is

_____

_____

Business elaborated purpose (three points)

My principal business objectives or functions are:

1. _____

2. _____

3. _____

My business mission is consistent with my life purpose in these ways:

1. _____

2. _____

3. _____

Other_____

Assessment

Does your business mission align with your life purpose? If not, go back and try again to choose a business mission that does align with your life purpose.

Exercise 8: How to Recover Your Old Dreams

Donna Christner-Lile

Purpose of Exercise

To assist you in planning a business by revisiting dreams and activities that gave you a sense of happiness and fulfillment in the past

Learning Objectives

- To reflect upon your past influences
- To determine what activities gave you a sense of happiness and fulfillment
- To become aware of dreams that have not yet materialized
- To envision a business in which you can fulfill those dreams by doing activities that you enjoy

Target Entrepreneur Population

This exercise is best done with adults who are 40+ years. The reason that the exercise is more difficult to do with younger adults is that younger adults often seek fulfilling careers more than personal fulfillment.

Participants

The reader

Setting

Choose a place and time where you can reflect on your past influences and answer the following questions.

Time Required

Proceed at your own pace.

Materials

Tool to write with and notebook on which to write

Instructions

Dreams are often lost in everyday events. In your notebook, write three stories:

- Story #1 is about your life from age 5-13.
- Story #2 is about your life from ages 14-18.
- Story #3 is about your life from 19-30.

In those stories, identify the places you best remember, the people you were most with and the activities that gave you the greatest pleasure. Think of the aromas, sounds, and details about the environment.

Be sure to include any work, life role, or career thoughts you had at that time and where those thoughts came from. Was it your idea or someone else's?

Go back over the stories and read them once with your head, and a second time with your heart.

After you have finished reading, write down any recurring themes in the environment, as well as activities, people, or places that made you the happiest.

Take time to ponder the common themes from these three stages of your life. Make a special note of those things dreamed about and not yet fulfilled.

Try to identify a career that encompasses many of those common themes. If you cannot readily identify the career yourself, take your stories to a career counselor for help in identifying the careers most suited to your desires.

Discussion Questions

- What were your favorite memories?
- What have you yet to complete in your life?
- What work would allow you to do that which gave you the most joy in the past, and at the same time, allow you to complete something that is important to you?

Assessment of Exercise

If you can write the stories, analyze, and answer the discussion questions, and explain how these themes fit together, then you are well on your way to creating a viable business and a satisfying life.

Resource

True Colors Free personality assessment. Retrieved September 2, 2006: http://www.truecolorscareer.com.

Exercise 9: Creating Your Special Statement of Purpose

Ron Elsdon, Ph.D.

Purpose of Exercise

To give you the tools to write a statement of purpose for your practice and describe how your practice will be different and special for your clients and customers

Learning Objectives

- To clearly state what you and your practice stand for
- To describe how your practice is different and brings special value to clients and customers

Target Entrepreneur Population

While this is a particularly valuable exercise for those creating a new practice, it is also useful to revisit on a regular basis both to renew your enthusiasm and to decide if your statement of purpose needs to change and evolve as your practice grows.

Participant(s)

You are the primary participant guiding this exercise, but it also affords an excellent opportunity to link with mentors and existing or prospective customers/clients for their perspective.

Setting

Since this is a reflective process, some may find a quiet, peaceful setting helpful in creating the initial draft of purpose, others may find the process catalyzed by conversation. In either case, view this as taking steps along a path that expresses the wonder of who you and those around you are, through your and their contributions.

Discussion

- What kind of environment will you create to foster growth of your practice?
- Are you open to learning, to new ideas, to serendipity and to responding rapidly to opportunities?
- Are you inclusive and do you welcome different points of view?
- Can you create a nurturing, trusting environment that values collaboration?
- Will you let customers guide and support development?
- Can you choose the right time to grow?
- Can you avoid applying old rules to new situations?
- How can you build a strategy that forms the foundation for success?
- What are the core differentiating aspects of your practice?
- What components should you include in the portfolio that constitutes your practice?
- What types of customer are you seeking?
- What skills do you need to be effective in your practice (e.g., content knowledge, consulting capability, effective selling, financial and business acumen, marketing capability, time allocation, managing your costs and determining your fee structure, deciding on partners, giving how and to whom)?

Assessment of Learning Outcomes

- Did you clearly state what you and your practice stand for?
- Did you describe how your practice is different and brings special value to clients and customers?
- Is your statement of purpose integrated into your marketing materials, such as your web site and brochures, and are you able to bring it to life for others?

Exercise 10: Professional Development Pulse for Private Practitioners

Edward Anthony Colozzi, Ed.D.

Purpose of Exercise
To help you identify areas of your professional development that can be improved

Learning Objectives
- To become aware of specific areas of professional development that can increase self-efficacy
- To receive feedback from self-reflection and meeting with mentors/peers
- To set specific action goals and timelines for accomplishing goals

Rationale
Research indicates self-efficacy beliefs are acquired and modified through four primary information sources (Lent & Brown, 1996):

1. personal performance accomplishments
2. vicarious learning
3. social persuasion
4. physiological states and reactions

It is possible to create opportunities that encourage involvement with these sources of efficacy information. Through self-reflection and small group interaction, counselors can discuss their career journey (obstacles and accomplishments) and experience appropriate modeling interventions from their peers. This approach would also permit counselors to deal effectively with feelings (anxiety, fear, and doubt) and receive feedback and encouragement. Such an approach may contribute significantly to the modification of career efficacy beliefs and serve as a useful intervention to assist with setting goals to initiate a private practice or related business venture.

Target Entrepreneur Population
Aspiring, just launched, and in process

Setting
Quiet time/space for initial reflection and appropriate small group setting.

Time Required
30-60 minutes for initial reflection and 1 to 2 hours for small group sharing. Ideally, repeat the exercise every 3 to 6 months.

Materials
Paper and pen, your favorite beverage, and perhaps a candle and quiet music playing during your reflection. Provide a pot of coffee or tea and light refreshments for your support group of mentors/peers.

Instructions
Simply follow the instructions provided on the Exercise Sheet.

Discussion
Once you have completed the Exercise Sheet, ask yourself, "What is there about your stated concerns that seem to be causes for low involvement in the specific areas covered?" Identify any feelings related to your observations. Which feelings are your strongest and why? Are the action items and timelines appropriate for effecting change? How will you be able to measure success?

Assessment of Learning Outcomes
Counselors will be able to easily observe any changes and improvement by re-visiting the exercise and entering new ratings and comments every 3-6 months after the initial exercise is completed.

Exercise Sheet: Professional Development Pulse for Private Practitioners

Reflect on each of the areas below; be honest in your ratings. Fill in the "concerns and comments for action" section indicating concerns, activities, and timelines that best support your professional development. Check below, using a scale of "+", "0" or "-" to indicate your level of involvement with the following areas.

　　　"+" rating = high degree of active involvement;

　　　"0" = moderate degree of involvement and some improvement may be needed;

　　　"-" = little or no involvement and some action is needed.

Use the results to reflect on specific areas you want to address that will support your own professional development. Find an appropriate mentor, peer, or small group of colleagues to share your comments and receive feedback. Repeat every 3 to 6 months.

I take time to read the journals and/or the NCDA web materials (*Career Developments* or *Career Convergence*) – at least the articles and research that are relevant to the clients I serve.

"+"___; "0"___; "-"___

Concerns and Comments for Action _____

Realistic Timeline _____

I take time to write an article about a topic that holds my interest so that I share my ideas with other colleagues and stimulate a dialogue. This might be for NCDA, the local newspaper, or an appropriate magazine or other publication.

"+"___; "0"___; "-"___

Concerns and Comments for Action _____

Realistic Timeline _____

I plan and budget to attend conferences so that I can network with other professionals, take workshops for professional improvement and provide myself the important social contact with my colleagues.

"+"___; "0"___; "-"___

Concerns and Comments for Action _____

Realistic Timeline _____

I take the time to develop a program proposal for either local or national conferences to share my ideas with colleagues and stimulate a dialogue about my particular areas of interest.

"+"___; "0"___; "-"___

Concerns and Comments for Action _____

Realistic Timeline _____

I volunteer my time appropriately to gain visibility for the profession and increase the public's awareness of the benefits of career counseling and my own business throughout my local community. This could involve NCDA at the national level (e.g. joining a committee, serving as a mentor, participating in the Each One Reach One (EORO) Program under Membership at http://www.ncda.org), your local state career development association level, or some other community organization.

"+"___; "0"___; "-"___

Concerns and Comments for Action _____

Realistic Timeline _____

I take the time to evaluate my services; modify, innovate, and explore techniques that challenge existing theories and practices; and "grow" the profession and my business. This includes marketing my services regularly.

"+"___; "0"___; "-"___

Concerns and Comments for Action _____

Realistic Timeline _____

Exercise 11: A Gap Analysis – What Do You Need To Feel Supported?

Gail Liebhaber

The following exercise provides a tool that you can use to assess your current sources of support and what you can do to close the gap.

Purpose of Exercise

To improve your self-awareness and provide a process for moving your plan into action. Taking the time to do a gap analysis helps you become clear on key information required to achieve your goals.

Learning Objectives

- To identify your strengths and weaknesses in as much detail as possible
- To evaluate your current resources for support, both internal and external

Target Entrepreneur Population

Aspiring, just launched, in process

Participants

Anyone interested in analyzing his or her support sources

Setting

None prescribed

Time Required

30 minutes

Materials

Pen or pencil and paper

Instructions

Start to analyze your sources of support. Do not be limited by the space provided. Use additional paper.

List your current sources of support.

Internal: _____

_____

_____

_____

_____

External: _____

_____

_____

_____

_____

For the questions below, circle one whatever choice feels most applicable.

1. I am satisfied with the amount of support I have in my life.

   (1) strongly agree, (2) agree somewhat, (3) undecided, (4) disagree, (5) strongly disagree

2. I am satisfied with the quality of the support that I have in my life.

   (1) strongly agree, (2) agree somewhat, (3) undecided, (4) disagree, (5) strongly disagree

3. I have well-developed support in terms of variety and availability.

   (1) strongly agree, (2) agree somewhat, (3) undecided, (4) disagree, (5) strongly disagree

4. I am satisfied with the benefits that my sources bring me.

   (1) strongly agree, (2) agree somewhat, (3) undecided, (4) disagree, (5) strongly disagree

5. I believe that I am getting the best support possible.

   (1) strongly agree, (2) agree somewhat, (3) undecided, (4) disagree, (5) strongly disagree

Take a look at your scores. Anything above a score of 8 could benefit from some attention.

Analyze

What are your gaps? Are you willing to develop more or different resources?:

_____

_____

_____

How will you develop your weaknesses to bridge the gap? Think of friends, activities, and solo pursuits.

_____

_____

_____

Prioritize

While making your list, decide how many things you can expect to accomplish in a reasonable amount of time and what results you can expect in that amount of time. As you fill this section out, consider who or what can help you with this process.

What steps will be required?	Completion date

Assessment of Learning Outcomes

Explain what you learned about your self.
Describe what you learned about your resources.

Discussion

Take a moment to remember why it is important for you to have these sources of support.

Exercise 12: Position Yourself To Be Successful

Randy Miller

Purpose

To assist you in determining the role that you will play in your business

Rationale

The concept is to help you understand not only your strategic plan, but the role that YOU will play in achieving it. Know Thyself! Often, we lose touch with our identity and position in the workplace. Knowing who you are and your role in the business promotes understanding and efficiency throughout.

Learning Objectives

- To identify your strengths (personal and work skills)
- To describe what business needs you can fill
- To explain what personal needs you fill through the business
- To examine how you contribute to key sectors of the business
- To identify your weaknesses

Target Entrepreneur Population

Entrepreneurs, you (and possibly your partner, if applicable)

Setting

Choose a quiet location by yourself – no distractions (this includes computer and phone). I suggest a Saturday or Sunday when you have private time. Locate a park bench, recliner, scenic overlook, convertible, garden, etc.

Time Required

One hour to three days. I suggest that these exercises take place near water (fountain, river, lake, or ocean), as many key decisions have positive outcomes if made near water, which has a meditative, calming effect on the brain. Requiring a time limit for personal thought and reflection is restrictive and counterproductive to the entire concept. Indulge in yourself for as long or as short a time as you wish.

Materials

Paper, pen, and clear mind. The absence of tangible items is important. Bring your thoughts, goals, ideas, and inspiration.

Instruction for Activity

Go with the flow. Think without thinking. What might be helpful here is to give an example of a strategic plan, and the role that you or another entrepreneur played in the plan. Traditionally, ideas start in your head, and are then translated to paper. Often, things are lost in the translation. Don't limit your role in the organization to a job description printed out on company stationary. You are the entrepreneur. These are your ideas. They were incubated in your mind, now nurture them to maturity.

Assessment

Assess the completion of each Learning Objective from the onset by answering the following questions:

- What are your personal and work skills?
- What business needs can you can fill?
- What personal needs do you fill through the business? (Do you embrace your truth? Do you admire yourself? Do you influence the outcome?)
- How do you contribute to key sectors of the business without being overbearing or spreading yourself too thin?

- What are your weaknesses, and do you outsource when the need for a specialist's assistance is present? Do you know when to get help?

Discussion

Following are more detailed questions to answer:

- What are your revenue streams?
- Do you have your pricing, your costs, your projected profit?
- How will you implement your business plan?
- Who are your current mentors?

Exercise 13: Developing a Competitive Advantage

Dan Geller

Purpose

To provide tools for you to identify your competitive advantage. In business, just like in physics, everything is relative. Your customers evaluate your business relative to your competition. Therefore, your competitive advantage should be developed relative to your competitors and not in a vacuum. Your competitive advantage should target the weakest point(s) of your competitive set (weakest points of your business compared to that of your main competitors). The way to validate your competitive advantage is to ask, "Will this (plan, part of plan, advantage) bring me customers AND will it bring customers to me rather than to my competitors?

Learning Objectives

- To understand the principle of competitive advantage
- To learn to identify the weaknesses of your competitive set
- To develop your competitive advantage relative to the weakness of your competitors

Target Audience

Pre-business: use this exercise to develop your competitive advantage.

In business: use this exercise to review the validity of your competitive advantage.

Participants

Person who is involved in setting up the strategy for the business. Others, such as mentors or marketing personnel, may join.

Setting

Person(s) conducting this exercise should have a computer with Internet connection and Excel application.

Time Required

Exercise can be completed in one to two hours.

Instructions

In the table below, list the five most threatening competitors to your business. This group is called your competitive set.

Competitive Matrix

Competitive Set	Connectivity	Inter-exercise	Speed	Ease	Simplicity	Selection	Availability	Flexibility	Other
Competitor One									
Competitor Two									
Competitor Three									
Competitor Four									
Competitor Five									

If you do not know your competitive set, go online, choose a search engine such as "Google," and enter a key word or key phrase that defines your business. For example, if you are in the book publishing business, enter "book publisher" in the search box.

On the right-hand side of the Google screen, you will see advertisers. These are your competitors (companies that have money to advertise are the most threatening to you).

Review the websites of about 10 to 15 competitors, and select the five that are the most threatening.

Evaluate each of them in accordance with the criteria in the competitive matrix above. If a competitor satisfies a criteria, enter "yes" in the space under that category. If not, enter "no".

Then, for each of the criteria, highlight the columns that have the most and the second most "noes." This means that one should focus on these columns because they contain the weakest elements of the competitor and an opportunity for the business to excel in that category.

See example below:

Competitive Matrix

Competitive Set	Connectivity	Inter-exercise	Speed	Ease	Simplicity	Selection	Availability	Flexibility	Other
Competitor One	Yes	Yes	Yes	Yes	Yes	No	Yes	No	Yes
Competitor Two	Yes	No	Yes	Yes	Yes	No	Yes	No	
Competitor Three	Yes	Yes	Yes	Yes	No	No	Yes	No	
Competitor Four	Yes	Yes	No	Yes	Yes	No	Yes	No	
Competitor Five	Yes	Yes	Yes	No	Yes	No	No	No	

Based on the example above, the primary competitive advantage should be "selection", and the secondary competitive advantage should be "flexibility".

Make sure that you incorporate your primary and secondary competitive advantages into your business strategy.

Never select a competitive advantage that is the same as your competitive set. In such a case, you and your competitors will spend lots of money and effort, and there will be no clear winners in the market place. In the example given above, the competitive advantage that is the same as your competitive set is "connectivity."

Discussion

In order to validate your selection for the primary and secondary competitive advantage, ask yourself (or the other participants): Would a potential customer choose to do business with me because of my competitive advantage? If the answer is yes, you may use the primary and secondary competitive advantages to differentiate your business from the competition. If the answer is no, you need to change the categories of the competitive matrix, and start the process all over again. Good luck!

Exercise 14: Get Ready, Get Set, Go! Overcoming "I'm Not Ready"

Jack Chapman

Purpose

- To give career practitioners an opportunity to become aware of overcoming their fear of failing in private practice

Learning Objectives

- To distinguish between real and imaginary fears
- To determine personal success criteria
- To create a plan for succeeding in your private practice

Audience

- Career practitioners in a full-time position, not ready to start a private practice
- Career practitioners in a part-time job, not ready to go into private practice full-time
- Career practitioners in private practice, ready but anxious about earning $100,000 or more in their practice

Equipment

Word processor or paper and pen

Instructions

Make three columns on a sheet of paper.

In column 1, finish the sentence, "I'm not ready yet, because…." with 10 or more endings. Notice if the items you listed in column 1 describes things that you lack. For example, you might have completed one sentence as follows: "Im not ready yet, because I don't have an office."

In the second column, write what you do have in relation to each of the 10 sentences. For example, "What I do have is a telephone book and some thoughts about shared office space." For each of the 10 sentence completions, in column 2, write "What more I need is ….

In Column 3, write what you need to deal with to be ready. For example, you might say, "I'll be ready when I have "$2000 in the bank to pay rent for one month." Summarize Column 3 by saying, "Here are the things I choose to have to be ready." Review Column 3. Mark each item with: (a) nice to have and (b) need to have. Pick from Column 3 the things that you absolutely need to have to be ready and make a plan to get there.

Assessment of Learning Objectives

Review what you filled out for columns 1 to 3. Column 1 is imaginary; Column 3 is real.

Review the items that you distinguished as "need to have" or "nice to have." Those items listed as "need to have" are your personal success criteria.

Exercise 15: Transforming Entrepreneurial Challenges into Opportunities

Susan Whitcomb

Purpose of Exercise

To identify and overcome your entrepreneurial challenges

Learning Objectives

- To identify specific challenges associated with their business
- To develop action steps to address each challenge based on the four components of the "I CAN" model
- To demonstrate behavior that addresses both the "Mindset" and "Mechanics" to transform challenges into opportunities

Target Entrepreneur Population

This activity is helpful for both start-up and experienced entrepreneurs.

Participants

The entrepreneur is the primary participant in this activity, although it may be helpful to engage the input of trusted colleagues or friends who can contribute ideas to overcoming your entrepreneurial challenges.

Setting

Choose a setting that is conducive to focusing on you and your entrepreneurial dreams. For most people, that means a setting away from your office where there are few distractions!

Time Required

It is recommended that you set aside a minimum of two hours of uninterrupted time for this exercise. Ideally, a half or full day devoted just to you and your entrepreneurial advancement can bring new insights and breakthroughs.

Materials

The only materials are pen and paper or journal or a computer to capture your thoughts

Instructions for Conducting the Activity

Use the "Transforming Challenges into Opportunities" form below and answer on a separate piece of paper (or your computer) some of the entrepreneurial challenges that you are currently facing. Refer to the categories in the "I CAN" Entrepreneur Diagram (see Chapter 7, p. 49) to identify which areas are presenting the biggest challenges/opportunities for you. After identifying your challenges, read The Mindset below and answer the various questions throughout that section.

Discussion

Answering the questions in the "Transforming Challenges into Opportunities" form and reviewing the categories in the "I CAN" Entrepreneur diagram will help you identify some of the entrepreneurial challenges that you are currently facing. Which areas are presenting the biggest challenges/opportunities for you?

Continued on next page.

Transforming Challenges into Opportunities

Questions to Identify Challenges	Example Responses Linked to Categories in the "I CAN Entrepreneur" Diagram
If you could change just one thing about your business that would make a world of difference to your success, what would it be?	#8: Prioritize, Manage Time, Develop Self-Discipline: I would be able to say "no" to projects and people that aren't aligned with my business mission, or say "wait" to projects that look great but won't fit into my personal bandwidth at the moment.
As you think about leveraging your strengths and delegating tasks that someone else could do, what aspects of your business do you need the most support in?	#2: Leverage Strengths & Delegate to Support Team: Administration, specifically answering email.
What area(s) of your business do you procrastinate on?	#4 and #2: Network and Delegate: Tasks that are outside of my comfort zone, like calling people I don't know and asking for help.
What takes your attention away from priorities that will impact your bottom-line profit?	#8: Prioritize: Volunteering for a school committee that I should have said no to.
What are the triggers that cause you to lose focus, courage, and momentum?	#8: Self-Care: Not getting enough rest; not allowing space to recharge after traveling to conferences; cluttered workspace.

Tip: Virtually every entrepreneur I've spoken with has mentioned lack of support as a challenge in their business. If you're just starting out and carefully watching cash flow, look for opportunities to barter for services such as administrative support, computer repairs, etc. More established entrepreneurs may benefit from a virtual assistant who works as little or as much as you need. For resources on finding certified virtual assistants, see References and Resources in my contribution to Chapter 7: What Challenges Have Your Encountered?

The Mindset

Now let's look at the second part of the success equation: Mindset. Henry Ford quipped: "If you think you can or can't, you're right" (emphasis added). A recent Wall Street Journal article revealed how the significance of our beliefs, mental modes, and mindset shape our behavior. According to psychologists interviewed for the piece, we act and perform according to the beliefs these models tell us is true. For example, if you don't think that there are enough clients to create a sustainable career-consulting business, you will not find them. Conversely, if you believe there is a niche of clientele out there who need you desperately and would love to pay for your services, you will find them.

Mindset can sink or support you. It is the one single factor that can transform every problem into an opportunity. How do you make that shift? By acting on the I CAN acronym, which stands for:

- I – Inspire Daily
- C – Control the Controllables
- A – Act Now
- N – Never Give Up!

Having seen career clients struggle with resiliency during challenging job searches, I developed the "I CAN" acronym for the *Interview Magic* and *Job Search Magic* books published by JIST. Reprinted with permission (and edited for entrepreneurs), I'll present the four steps to this model in condensed format. As you read through them, take time to answer the coaching questions found within the steps and tips.

STEP 1: I = INSPIRE DAILY

Recall a time when you felt remarkably inspired, ready to take on the world, confident that everything would work out for the best. What would your business look like if you could have that emotional strength on a daily basis?

Not weekly, not monthly, not annually ... daily! Tasks would get tackled immediately, people would want to have you on their team, ideas would flow, and energy would be focused on what really matters. Successful people have mastered the art of recharging themselves. Here are some tips for daily inspiration.

Tip 1: Master the Law of Inner Action

The Law of Inner Action is simply a variation on the adage, you reap what you sow. Thoughts and choices, or inner action, precede outer action. To get to action that will bolster your inspiration, you must first bolster your thought life. Thoughts and choices either empower or impale you. Convert every self-defeating thought to a self-supporting thought, as this before-and-after example illustrates:

- BEFORE: Self-Defeating Thought: My to-do list is overwhelming. I'll never get this all done. I'm feeling crushed. I should have said "no" to serving on that committee.
- AFTER: Self-Supporting Thought: I am committed to tackling these tasks in priority order. I am learning to give myself permission to let go of the low-priority items. I will ask Joe for help on a couple of these tasks.

Tip 2: Put Yourself in Charge of your Own Inspiration

Inspiration starts with the letter i, reminding us that I alone am in charge of inspiring myself. No one else can do this for you. Take the first two letters of the word "in" and realize that you must also internalize the inspirational message for it to shift from head to heart. Be aware of and choose activities that inspire you every day of your life.

Here's a starting list for inspirational activities: Attending workshops (industry conferences, meetings with motivational speakers); talking with others who have persevered and succeeded; recalling your past successes; journaling about what you'd like to accomplish in the future; setting specific goals; meeting small or big goals; learning something new; exercising; taking action; reading inspirational material; attending religious services; praying or meditating; getting away to refresh and reinvigorate. What will you select from or add to this list to tailor it to your needs?

Tip 3: Keep a Future Focus

Victor Frankl, psychiatrist and survivor of a Nazi concentration camp, chronicles his Auschwitz experience in Man's Search for Meaning. Beyond the despicable deeds done, the dehumanization, and the loss of touch with loved ones, Frankl describes the psychological severity of not knowing when, or if, the imprisonment would end. In order to bear the terrible how of his existence, Frankl looked for a why - an aim - that brought meaning. As part of Frankl's future focus while imprisoned, he pictured how he would someday stand in front of audiences and lecture on his experiences -a vision that became reality. What vision do you want to become reality? Complete this future-focus sentence: Next year at this time, I will _____.

STEP 2: C = CONTROL THE CONTROLLABLES

One of the secrets of successful people is that they have a strong internal locus of control (see Resources at the end of my contribution to Chapter 7: What Challenges Have Your Encountered? for links to free, online loci of control instruments). Select one of the business challenges that you listed previously and concentrate on what you can control about that situation! For instance, if Networking is a challenge for you, recognize that you can't control whether networking contacts will refer clients to you. But, you can control how frequently you network, whom you will network with, and how positive an experience you will create for those who refer clients to you. Here are three basic tips for controlling the controllables.

Tip 1: Control the Basics

Control the basics in both your career and your personal life. The controllables for your career might include the number of hours you spend on marketing, working smarter instead of harder, putting a viable economic business model in place, and participating in professional associations to increase your visibility. On the personal front, the controllables may be as simple as the amount of exercise, rest, and nutrition you give yourself. Another controllable might be the type or amount of news and media you allow yourself to consume. Notice whether the input inspires you and helps you stay focused on your ideal circumstances. What are the basics you want to control in your life?

Tip 2: Find Bone-Marrow People

Bone marrow is where life is produced. Diseased marrow is a death sentence. Cancer victims who have a successful marrow transfusion are able to regenerate new, healthy blood cells. Just as bone marrow creates life for your body, Bone-Marrow People create life for your mind and spirit. When you've been in the presence of Bone-Marrow People, you become more, not less … closer to, not farther from, your ideal self. If you're a solopreneur, reaching out to like-minded entrepreneurs is invaluable. One of the resources of Career Masters Institute is its teleseminars and webinars. One track is the Entrepreneurial Eagles, devoted specifically to entrepreneurial matters, where you can congregate with other entrepreneurs who are committed to helping each other soar. (See the Resources at the end of my contribution to Chapter 7: What Challenges Have Your Encountered? for links to Career Masters Institute entrepreneurial teleseminars). Who is on your bone-marrow list?

Tip 3: Maintain an Attitude of Gratitude

Instead of focusing on the things that have gone wrong (the roadblocks with marketing or the prospective client who decided to use another service, etc.), be grateful for what has gone right (e.g., the chance to ask precision questions to close the sale so that you're more prepared for the next one). Attitude is a controllable. What are you thankful for? Consider starting a "Joy Journal" in which the only things you can pen are things for which you're grateful.

STEP 3: A = ACT NOW

If we were as relentless in our commitment and action as life is in its daily demands, success would be certain. Act. Persist. Success doesn't happen in your head! Consider these three tips for action.

Tip 1: The 80/20 Principle

Choose your actions wisely. Devote the greatest part of your energy to that which yields the greatest results. The 80/20 principle recognizes that it is the minority (20%) of the effort that yields the majority (80%) of results. For instance, in many companies in corporate America, roughly 80% of a company's profits come from 20% of its customers.

Tip 2: Act Successful

Kurt Vonnegut, Jr. said, "We are what we pretend to be, so we must be careful what we pretend to be." Act AS IF. Act as if you already have the business success you want. Attitudes, actions, vocabulary, dress, posture, knowledge, habits, self-talk, and mindset all play a part. How do you need to act to personify success in your business?

Tip 3: Pump up Another Part of your Life

Do you sometimes feel that all you do is live and breathe work? If so, it may be helpful to step back and pump up some other part of your life. Now may be the perfect time to start a self-improvement project, rekindle a relationship, pick up an old or new hobby, or tend to some other area of your life that has been neglected. You may think that this will give you less time to work on your business. It may, but it has a more important effect: Less time at work means you'll need to make smart, focused choices about work. Greater creativity and energy at work are often by-products of pumping up another part of your life.

STEP 4: N = NEVER GIVE UP!

This past year I worked with a life and nutrition coach to help me stop munching my way through every roadblock that crossed my path, including frustrating or confusing circumstances and over commitments that I had a tendency to make. Several months into our work together, I came to a turning point where I shifted from "I will never conquer this" to "I will never give up." Now, when I see old habits trying to creep back in, I remind myself that I will never give up, which frees me to focus on the new me. What do you need to "never give up" on? Is it your business success? Your marketing? Your "I CAN" attitude? Three tips for never giving up include:

Tip 1: Persevere

Thomas Edison noted, "Genius is 1% inspiration and 99% perspiration," while Woody Allen quipped, "80% of success is showing up." Nothing substitutes for hard (and smart) work. Enough said!

Tip 2: Don't Take Things Personally

"I've decided to work with a different career consultant." If you hear this response when closing a sale, don't take it personally. If you do, it can send you into a downward spiral of discouraging self-doubt. Although you must control the controllables in terms of training and service delivery, you must also remember that rejection doesn't have to be associated with your value. Eleanor Roosevelt once said, "No one can make you feel inferior without your consent." Don't let your clients, or you, give consent!

Tip 3: Listen for the Leading

Television executive Squire Rushnell writes in his delightful book *When God Winks* that "Coincidence – God Winks – are little messages to you on your journey through life, nudging you along the grand path that has been designed especially for you." In the Introduction to his book, Rushnell tells of his own God Wink that helped confirm the direction his career would take. At the youthful age of 15, his dream was to be a radio announcer. A job interview 10 miles away with the general manager of a local television station required that he hitchhike, a relatively safe undertaking in those days. The traffic on his rural road was sparse. Every car passed him by. Fearful that he hadn't left enough time to get to his appointment, he began to lose faith. Eventually, the car that did stop to scoop him up was driven by none other than his favorite disc jockey, his pop hero at the time. The DJ knew the general manager with whom Rushnell would be interviewing, and asked Rushnell to pass along a hello. Rushnell made it on time and he got the job. That first position eventually led the wannabe radio announcer to an award-winning, 20-year career as an executive with the ABC Television Network. As you think about never giving up, what events, places, or persons have been encouraging signs along your way?

After implementing these four steps, I'd love for you to share with me any interesting stories about what happened when you (or your clients) shifted from "I CAN'T" to "I CAN!" Mastering this mindset will enable you and your business to grow and thrive and prosper, and is guaranteed to move your start-up or stuck to significantly successful!

Assessment

Entrepreneurs will be successful at this activity when they have:

- Identified and prioritized a list of specific challenges associated with their business.
- Developed and committed to making action steps to address each challenge based on the four components of the "I CAN" model. These commitments might take the form of writing activities in their calendar and being accountable to a colleague or supporter.
- Demonstrated behavior that addresses both the "Mindset" and "Mechanics" to transform challenges into opportunities. Specifically, challenges that were present will no longer be present!

Exercise 16: Annual Business Check-Up

Martha Russell

Purpose of Exercise

To help you conduct an annual check-up on your business. Just as career counselors encourage clients to conduct an annual career check-up, entrepreneurs will benefit from the same process.

Learning Objectives

- To evaluate where you and your business are at the present time
- To develop a framework for future planning
- To determine whether you are in an expansion or maintenance stage

Target Entrepreneur Population

This exercise is great for those who are reevaluating the business they are in, in progress after at least one year in business, and most effective at the end of the third year and beyond.

Participants

The individual business owner and individuals who support that person, who can be either partners, resource individuals, or family members who agree to support and challenge the person.

Setting

Anywhere that supports focus on the annual check-up with few distractions and promotes encouragement of dreaming, planning, and focusing.

Time Required

This process may take place in stages. It works well if the person begins in the last quarter of the year and either completes this in one to three segments.

Materials

Journal, notes, notebook or flipchart, computer, and whatever else you use to help organize your thoughts. Colored folders, note cards, index cards, and/or post-it notes can also be helpful.

Instructions

Answer the following questions, on an annual basis.

Annual Check-up Questions

Focus on the desired segment of the market.

- Who is the intended recipient of the services that you want to deliver?
- How have client needs changed during this past year?
- What do clients wanting more of? Less of?
- Who are your competitors in meeting the needs of clients?

Focus on Yourself.

- What is it that YOU want from your business? Consider you lifestyle and your own needs. What is it you want to do more of? What is it you want to do less of? What new opportunities do you want to explore?
- What services do you want to provide?
- What energizes and motivates you?
- As you look back on the past year, where has the focus of your business been?
- What challenges have you been faced with?

- What new skills have you developed?
- What motivated you to go into your own business? Have those motivators changed? How?

Focus on Goals.

- What are your overall business goals for the year?
- What do you need to do to reach those goals?
- What does this mean in terms of marketing efforts?

Focus on Evaluation.

- How will you determine whether your efforts are paying off?
- How will you redirect your efforts to increase or decrease your exercise?
- What are some ways you might terminate or let go if your plans are not working?
- How will you celebrate your successes?

Discussion

For each section of the annual checkup you may find it helpful to go through the process of reflecting on the question and the responses, outlining the major points and developing a plan. For example, when you outline specific goals, you might select a specific goal of "increased revenue from workshops."

Outline a strategic marketing plan for each goal. This plan needs to be specific with action item, resource needs, and timeline.

For example, in order to reach my goal of "increased revenue from workshops," I may need to do the following:

- Write a monthly article to publicize my workshop topics (and my expertise in those topics).
- Connect with a community resource center to offer workshops through their established program.
- Offer a brown bag lunch to an organization (at a reduced or waived fee).
- Review conference presentations that I might make during this next year.
- Develop a written or electronic marketing piece that publicizes my workshops.
- Put together a catalogue of workshops I offer.

Assessment of Learning Objectives

- Evaluate where you and your business are at the present time.
- Develop a framework for future planning.
- Determine whether you are in an expansion or maintenance stage.

Exercise 17: Clarify Your Business Vision and Mission

Lynn Joseph, Ph.D.

Purpose

To provide a helpful exercise in which you will experience relaxing and inspiring guided Mental Image Technology (MIT). This exercise can help you clarify your mission and vision, and inspire you to set lofty goals around building a successful practice.

Learning Objective

To bring greater clarity and focus of intention to a positive vision for your practice in order to deepen desire and enhance expectation of success.

Note: If you have more than one direction for your practice that you would like to "try on," do a separate exercise with each one. Then determine which one you are more drawn to.

Setting

Find a quiet setting where you will not be disturbed, and either sit or recline comfortably. You may want to record the MIT script in your own voice along with relaxing background music of your choice, and then experience the exercise as the recording plays.

Assessment of Learning Outcomes

Before beginning the exercise, do the following: Note on a scale of 1 to 10 with 10 being highest, how clear and focused your vision is for your future practice. After completing the exercise, note again on the same scale how clear and focused your vision is for your practice. Measure your progress in this way each time you do the exercise.

Exercise: Light Your Fire—With MIT

Find a comfortable position . . . Gently close your eyes. Begin by focusing on your breathing - inhaling deeply and exhaling fully . . . Allow your abdomen to expand and contract as you breathe deep into the diaphragm . . . And again . . . breathing in relaxation . . . and breathing out any tension in your body . . . relaxing more and more . . . becoming more calm with every breath . . . Imagine any distracting thoughts drifting away . . . For the moment your mind is still . . . feeling calm and relaxed now . . . inhaling deeply . . . and exhaling.

Enjoy these few moments in peacefulness . . . Notice the heaviness as your muscles begin to relax . . . As I count down from five to one, allow yourself to become more and more relaxed . . . Imagine all the anxiety flowing out of you as you relax deeper and deeper . . . Five . . . four . . . going deeper . . . three . . . two . . . even deeper . . . and one . . . Allow these feelings of tranquility to spread through your body . . . You may notice a warm, heavy feeling coming over you, a sign of deep relaxation.

Move your attention to your feet . . . Feel all the muscles in your feet and toes slowly relax, and begin to feel very loose and warm . . . Allow the relaxation to spread into your calves as these muscles begin to feel loose, warm, and heavy . . . Now release any tension you feel in your knees . . . Now your thigh muscles begin to relax, all the tension releasing down, out of your feet, and into the earth . . . This relaxing, peaceful feeling is a gift you're giving to yourself.

Focus on your hips and abdomen . . . Feel all the muscles loosening and relaxing . . . Release any tension held there, allowing it to flow down and out of your body . . . Now your back muscles are loosening, feeling warm . . . Your neck and shoulders, a favorite place to hold burdens, are loosening and releasing any knots blocking you. . . Continue to relax as you go deeper and deeper.

Move your attention to your arms, your upper and lower arms, and your hands . . . Let go of any burdens and responsibilities. You can pick them up again later . . . Sense your hands relaxing and warming as the tension flows out through your fingers . . . Your jaw is now becoming loose and relaxed . . . Your face is relaxing, feeling warm and heavy . . . all the muscles around your eyes, relaxing . . . all around your head, loosening and relaxing . . . Feel the muscles releasing their knots, the anxiety and tension flowing down and out . . .Take a few moments to scan through your body, noticing any remaining tension . . . Release it now, letting it flow down and out . . . Allow yourself to enjoy this relaxation and peacefulness.

Go even deeper into your inner world . . . Imagine yourself in a very special and safe place where you can be alone and at peace . . . You can create your safe place and change it any way you like at any time . . . Maybe it's a secluded place in nature, such as an ocean beach with gentle waves lapping at the shore, or a forest clearing with the comforting sounds of birds . . . or perhaps a mountain meadow with a soft breeze whispering through the wildflowers . . . any place where you feel comfortable and safe.

Look around your safe place . . . Sense the shapes and colors coming into focus, becoming more and more clear . . . Notice what time of day it is – perhaps the soft light or mist of morning or the colorful setting sun at day's end . . . Listen to the sounds of nature around you . . . Notice a hint of fragrance in the air, perhaps pine or wildflowers . . . Feel the solid earth under your feet, or run your fingers through the pool of water or waterfalls that might be there.

Make any changes you like; this is your place . . . No one can come here without your invitation . . . You are in control . . . Notice how good it feels . . . Let any distracting thoughts float away, as you go even deeper.

Now bring your dream - your vision - to mind. What is it that you want to create for yourself and for your business? Imagine what it will look like when you have achieved it.... Bring a picture of it to mind and sense it in as much detail as you can, with all the desire you have . . . How will you feel? Feel it now . . .

Begin thinking about the events that occurred or would likely have occurred in your life to lead you to the success you desire . . . Mentally travel back into your past to observe or line up the events that would have made it so . . . (pause). We most often remember best the traumas and challenges of our past, while forgetting many of the positive, supportive events. If you have difficulty identifying positive events at this time, simply imagine that they did occur. Follow the timeline of your life up to the present.

Now move ahead to once again vision your dream accomplished . . . Imagine what it will look like when you have achieved it . . . Bring a picture of it to mind and sense it in as much detail as you can, with all the desire you have . . . How will you feel? Feel it now . . .

Shift your attention further into the future to see what your life will look like well after you have achieved the success you desire and are now living it out. What are the results of your success . . .What will you have and do? . . .How will you be with others and how will they respond to you?.... What will it all mean to you and for you and your loved ones? . . . Hold the vision with all the desire, spirit, and passion you can . . . Feel powerful, free, valuable and valued, loving and loved! Think of your safe place once again, and find yourself there . . . In a moment, you will come back to full awareness of the room where your journey began, feeling relaxed and refreshed. . . . The count from five to one will help you return . . . Five . . . beginning to return . . . four . . . sensing the feelings in your body . . . three . . . sensing the environment around you . . . two . . . beginning to move around . . . and one. When you are ready, open your eyes and return, feeling awake and refreshed . . . Take a few slow, deep breaths . . .

Exercise 18: Do You Have an Exit Plan?

Michael Shahnasarian

Purpose of Exercise

To give you an opportunity to consider your ideal transition from your private practice and draft your current exit plan

Learning Objectives

- To determine why you are exiting your practice
- To decide what you will do - both professionally and personally – after your exit
- To figure out how you will implement your exit plan
- To carefully consider the questions posed at the beginning of Chapter 9
- To think through the details necessary to realize your exit plan objectives

Target Entrepreneur Population

Practitioners who have already established a practice and are considering an exit will find this exercise thought provoking and facilitative. Those in the maintenance and withdrawal phases of their career development will likely benefit most.

Participant(s)

The practitioner considering an exit is the key individual to the exercise. Others to involve include mentors and trusted colleagues; family members/significant others; shareholders, associates, and employees of the private practice; and primary clients and customers.

Setting

You will need a quiet place where you can discern and process your objectives in exiting your practice, consult necessary business records, and draft your exit plan. Access to the participants identified above can prove invaluable.

Time Required

I recommend that you write out your exit plan and put it aside for one week before revisiting it. Then, review it with one or two trusted individuals who know you and your practice well. This process will make the exercise more meaningful than just mentally thinking through an exit plan.

Materials

Exit planning is a dynamic, ongoing process. Your preparation for the process can be greatly facilitated by engaging the types of self-assessment activities and using career information that counselors use with their clients to facilitate career decision making. You may wish to consult the references and resources listed at the end of *Chapter 9: Do You Have an Exit Plan?* Access to financial, production, employee, and other practice business records also may be in order. Another necessary item is a recording device to draft the exit plan.

Instructions

Before you begin work on your exit plan, review the sample exit plan below to consider the questions posed at the beginning of this chapter, and review business records necessary to provide a perspective on how your practice evolved to its present state. Then, begin drafting a plan similar in structure to the sample. I recommend that your exit plan include the following specific details:

- your analysis of the current state of your practice
- your exit plan objectives
- specific actions necessary to attain your objectives, with associated rationale statements
- a summary of your overall exit plan strategy

Assessment

After you have completed your exit plan, present it to someone who is both familiar with your practice and qualified to provide sage analysis. Together, review the plan and ponder the following questions: Are objectives clearly stated and attainable? Are timeframes for attaining various milestones realistic? Will the steps you outlined likely lead to the attainment of your exit plan objectives? What contingency actions will be available to you if one or more of your action plan steps prove less effective than you anticipated?

Sample Exit Plan

Practice Background

Franklin Parsons, Ph.D., founded Metropolitan Career Services (MCS) in 1976. He operated the business with his wife, who provided support services, for several years. As the practice grew, Dr. Parsons began employing associates. Today, MCS employs 10 full-time staff members. Four staff members hold graduate degrees in counseling or psychology; the others provide technical and support services. Dr. Parsons is the practice's only shareholder.

MCS's revenues have been consistent during the past 5 years, with annual billings of approximately $1.5 million. In addition to Dr. Parsons' recognized expertise as an organizational consultant, the practice's major assets include a 3,000 square-foot building in an excellent suburban location, experienced staff, a diverse and well-established referral base, established practice areas and processes, and lack of debt. The areas in which the practice specializes include organizational consulting and private career counseling.

Ironically, among the factors that have most contributed to the practice's success -namely, Dr. Parson's reputation for providing specialized, high-quality services, albeit at a high billing rate - is also one of the factors that pose the biggest challenges to his exit from MCS. The practice's other counselors have yet to establish the referral base, advanced technical skill set, and business acumen necessary to sustain the practice.

Although Dr. Parsons has four adult children, none will likely pursue his or her career development as counselors. Because of MCS's success, Dr. Parsons, age 58, has attained a level of personal financial security that has prompted him to consider his exit from the practice so he can pursue other career objectives, including expanding his career-related writing interests and establishing another separate specialized business.

Exit Plan Objectives

The exit that Dr. Parsons plans has two phases.

Phase I involves a significant diminution in his MCS participation within the next 3 years, with an associated transition in his role from practitioner/managing officer to managing partner/mentor, with modest involvement as a practitioner.

Phase II involves Dr. Parsons' complete exit from MCS. He is deferring a specified timeframe to implement this latter phase, as he does not believe he is ready to contemplate leaving his practice entirely, and he acknowledges that exit-planning adjustments will likely occur as his exit plan evolves.

- In planning his exit from MCS, Dr. Parsons aims to position both himself and the practice by pursuing the following objectives:
- To significantly reduce the practice's dependence on him by developing his counselors' technical skill sets and referral base.
- To reduce his future level of practice involvement from 75% to 25% in the next three years.
- To maintain or increase MCS's current levels of practice service and revenues.
- Transfer ownership, in part, to MCS staff members.
- Establish MCS as a self-sufficient practice able to continue to operate without his participation at an unspecified future date.

Dr. Parsons believes his success in realizing the proposed transition relies largely on his ability to develop his staff's capacity to assume the role and functions he has been performing during the past 30 years. Also, he acknowledges that his proficiency and productivity will not be easily replaced – an especially important consideration in view of an ambitious goal to maintain or increase levels of practice service and revenues.

As part of his counseling staff analysis, Dr. Parsons is mindful that his successors have career profiles that are different from his – including different work values, interests, personal circumstances, and interests. Accordingly, his exit plan is not necessarily one they will readily embrace or aggressively pursue.

Exit Plan Details

Foreseeing all of the details and unanticipated challenges that inevitably occur during a transition, especially one protracted, is obviously impossible. The seven action steps below were selected to facilitate Dr. Parsons' exit plan objectives. A formal reassessment midway (18 months) through the plan's development, accompanied by ongoing honing of the action steps, is anticipated.

Action Step 1: Increase Dr. Parsons' hourly billing and daily billing rates approximately 40%. Correspondingly, offer prospective MCS customers, as an alternative to retaining Dr. Parsons, the significantly lower billing rates of MCS's other counselors.

Rationale for Action Step 1: While Dr. Parsons anticipates that a core group of MCS clients (20% to 30% of existing clients) will continue to retain him regardless of a 40% or more increase in his fees, he also anticipates that most clients will balk or be dissuaded. This gives Dr. Parsons a prime opportunity to refer and offer as an alternative his staff counselors, less experienced but billing at a much lower rate, with a commitment to clients of overseeing the staff's work.

Action Step 2: Contract a salesperson to promote services that have traditionally been less dependent on Dr. Parsons and, as new business evolves, delegate the work to MCS staff.

Rationale for Action Step 2: Expanding on established, proven areas of practice proficiency and profitability that have not required Dr. Parsons' involvement will help mitigate the loss of his contributions, while leveraging the talents of his counseling staff.

Action Step 3: Hire another counselor, ideally, one with solid experience in organizational consulting. This is an area in which Dr. Parsons is most competent and that has proved to be profitable.

Rationale for Action Step 3: It is unrealistic to assume MCS can maintain its productivity and profitability while experiencing a 70% to 80% diminution in Dr. Parsons' practice involvement. Hiring one or two additional counselors may be necessary; of course, like contracting a salesperson, this will increase practice operating costs.

Action Step 4: Hold individual conferences with staff members to assess their concordance with the exit plan and, accordingly, draft individual development plans to facilitate their transitions into their new roles. Below are brief profiles of four MCS staff members that include an assessment of developmental needs during the 3toyear transition period.

Action Step 4A: Mary (career counselor, age 43, six years of service with MCS). Mary's development is central to Dr. Parsons' exit plan. She has obtained the necessary credentialing and has a good grasp on the overall career counseling process. Additionally, she has been responsible for the day-to-day operations of MCS during the past three years. Areas necessary to Mary's development include significantly improving analytical abilities related to the assessment of career options, demonstrating greater initiative, improving writing skills and proficiency, committing more time to the practice, and increasing day-to-day productivity. Mary also needs to work on serving as a motivating force for staff, developing a business frame of reference in her practice work (including valuing her and others' time, and leveraging times to maximize profits), and pursuing professional activities to enhance her stature as a community leader. Dr. Parsons' prognosis for Mary realizing these developmental goals to the degree necessary to fulfill the exit plan is good.

Action Step 4B: Bill (career counselor, age 28, three years with MCS). His growth and assimilation into the practice has been average. Bill's background is in psychology, and he is continuing to become familiar with career assessment instruments and the use of career information. Work tasks he completes - although generally well done - are slow. He will need to grow considerably in the next 18 months to realize his part of the succession process and exit plan. His prime contribution to the exit plan could be to help manage the practice and provide technical support services.

Action Step 4C: Melissa (psychologist, age 53, 12 years with MCS). A replacement for Melissa will likely be necessary in the next 3 to 5 years. Melissa performs her job well, but she could be more productive and involved in other practice work, Her future replacement likely will.

Action Step 4D: Rita (general counselor, age 62, 18 years with MCS). A replacement for Rita will likely be necessary within the next 2 years. This will be a moderately difficult position to replace, given the diverse tasks Rita performs; however, her productivity and motivation have diminished over the years. Her departure from the practice will present an opportunity to increase the position's associated work output.

Rationale for Action Step 4: The development of staff in a manner that offsets Dr. Parsons' diminished involvement in MCS is critical to fulfilling the exit plan.

Action Step 5: Commit to a two-to-three year lease of 500 to 1,000 square feet of space to accommodate new staff.

Rationale for Action Step 5: MCS is already tight on space, and additional staff will make space problems more acute. Dr. Parsons believes a decision about MCS's long-term space needs should be deferred until after his 3toyear exit plan.

Action Step 6: Conduct a formal, comprehensive 18-month progress review, including assessments of staff development, practice profitability, and the success of Dr. Parsons' planned exit, and make necessary exit plan adjustments.

Rationale for Action Step 6: Depending on success in realizing pre-established exit- plan benchmarks, significant adjustments may be needed. The formal 18-month review also provides an opportunity to refocus all involved on the primary objectives associated with Dr. Parsons' exit plan.

Action Step 7: Depending on progress in implementing the exit plan at the time of the 18-month review, consult with a financial planner about making partnership opportunities available to staff members.

Rationale for Action Step 7: The midpoint review promises to be a defining point in the evolution of Dr. Parsons' exit plan. The prospect of partnership in MCS and the opportunity to assume significantly higher levels of career advancement, Dr. Parsons hopes, will motivate MCS staff to fulfill his exit plan.

Summary and Analysis

Like all plans subject to scrutiny and change, Dr. Parsons' exit plan requires ongoing evaluation, adjustment, and nurturing. While developing his exit plan, Dr. Parsons ruled out attempting to sell the practice, ceding it to family members, and gradually dissolving it.

Because of the practice's strong reliance upon him, Dr. Parsons understands that a lengthy transition period will be necessary if he is to realize his objective of positioning MCS so it can persevere without him. Likewise, he appreciates that his objective, at least in the short term, will require him to invest in additional staff, space, and other resources. Further, strategically shifting the focus from Dr. Parsons' specialty and MCS's current mainstay, organizational consulting, to areas in which his counselors are already adept enhances the practice's opportunities to supplant Dr. Parsons' absence with new sources of revenue.

Exercise 19: Entrepreneurial Skills Assessment

Richard Knowdell

Purpose

To give you an opportunity to assess your preferred style, what Motivated Skills you will strive to employ and how your background compares with the backgrounds of successful entrepreneurs

Learning Objectives

- To determine what type of entrepreneur fits your unique personality
- To delineate what Motivated Skills you will need to become successful
- To compare your background with the backgrounds of successful entrepreneurs

Target Population

This exercise is important to any aspiring entrepreneur.

Participants

This exercise can be completed alone or in a group setting with other individuals undergoing a career evaluation.

Setting

This exercise can be accomplished in a classroom, private office, or at home.

Time Required

While I am sure that some individuals could successfully complete this exercise in a single day, it is best to spread the exercise over several two-hour sessions, perhaps every Saturday afternoon for a month in order to digest and incorporate the results into a realistic career strategy plan.

Materials

A copy of the Entrepreneurial Style and Success Indicator (ESSI) and a set of Motivated Skills Cards with a Matrix Sheet and instructions. In addition, a copy of *What Color is Your Parachute?* (any edition) could be substituted for the Motivated Skills Card Sort. Both the ESSI and the Motivated Skills Card Sort instrument are available in on-line versions (see the reference section in *Chapter 10: What, in Your Opinion, Has Made You a Great Entrepreneur?*).

The ESSI is available for purchase as a hard copy or can be taken on-line (for a fee) at http://www.crgleader.com.

The Motivated Skills Card Sort instrument can be found in the back of *Building a Career Development Program: Nine Steps for Successful Implementation* by Richard L. Knowdell, 1996, Davies-Black Publishing (Palo Alto, CA). Alternatively, the Motivated Skills Card Sort can be taken on-line (for a fee) or purchased in hard copy from CareerTrainer by going to the web site, http://www.careertrainer.com. The author of the Motivated Skills Card Sort would be pleased to provide a complimentary copy of the Motivated Skills Card Sort to graduate students or career practitioners who cannot afford to purchase the instrument. Just contact me at dick@careertrainer.com. You can record all of your skills in the 15 cells provided on the following worksheet.

Instructions

One method of determining your Motivated Skills and your preferred personality style is to write an autobiography of your past achievements. By "achievements," I mean distinct accomplishments that you enjoyed doing, believed you did them well, and are proud of. An example of an *autobiography* would be the 16 stories in *Chapter 10: What, in Your Opinion, Has Made You a Great Entrepreneur?*. You should be able to look at each of the accomplishments in your autobiography and see a clear pattern of your Motivated Skills, as well as the goals that you accomplished. You can find a more detailed description of this method of identifying your Motivated Skills in any edition of Richard Bolles' bestseller, *What color is your parachute?*

The Entrepreneurial Style and Success Indicator (ESSI) Instrument

Complete the 24-page ESSI, which takes about 60 minutes to obtain results. The first part of the ESSI contains 16 items. Each item contains four descriptive words that the individual must rank order in terms of how accurate each word is in describing him or her. This is a forced choice instrument and each item must be completed. The instrument is based on a four-quadrant view of personality preferences. The results present the individual with a paragraph that describes that individual's probable "style" of attempting to be an entrepreneur. These 21 different styles have titles such as Directing, Astute, Networking, Freelancing, and Persuasive. The second part of the ESSI has 28 statements. The individual is asked to indicate how well the statement describes him or her on a scale of one to ten. An example statement is "I was an early self-starter: I had an income-producing job or had my own business before age 15." From the resulting scores, individuals can see how similar or different their background is to successful entrepreneurs. In the interpretation section of the ESSI, each statement that the individual rated is followed with a paragraph outlining how that experience relates to those of successful entrepreneurs.

The Motivated Skills Card Sort Instrument

Complete the Motivated Skills Card Sort. This instrument contains 52 cards, each with the name and brief description of a generic transferable skill. Examples are: organize, strategize, analyze, sell, teach, etc. The individual places five category cards (Total Delight in Using, Enjoy Using Very Much, Like Using, Prefer Not to Use, and Strongly Dislike Using) in a vertical column on their left. The "Totally Delight in Using" card goes at the top and the "Strongly Dislike Using" card is placed at the bottom. They are then asked to sort the entire deck of skill cards into five stacks to the immediate right of each of the five category cards. Each of the five stacks must contain a minimum of five cards. When all of the cards have been assigned to the five categories, the individual then turns all five category cards over so they appear blank.

The individual then places three additional category cards horizontally across the top of the work space with the "Highly Proficient" card above the five stacks of cards, the "Competent" category card to the immediate right of the "Highly Proficient" card, and finally the "Lack Desired Skill Level" card to the immediate right of the "Competent" card. The individual is now asked to sort the five stacks of cards (one stack at a time) to the right into three stacks according to the individual's competence at each skill. Each skill card must be compared only to other cards in that stack and at least one card needs to go into each of the three positions on the first row. The individual then goes to the next stack of cards and sorts it to the right, being sure to only compare the skills cards with others in its stack, and not those in the row above. The individual continues sorting each row of cards until there are 15 stacks of cards that form a matrix that is five stacks high and three stacks wide.

Motivated Skills Matrix Worksheet

Preferences	Highly Proficient	Competent	Lack Desired Skill Level
Total Delight in Using			
Enjoy Using Very Much			
Like Using			
Prefer Not To Use			
Strongly Dislike Using			

Interpretation

The Motivated Skills matrix shows the individual's skills on a two-dimensional matrix with his/her motivation to use the skills on the vertical axis and the individual's competency at using the skills on the horizontal matrix. Those skills on the cards in the upper left hand corner (High Motivation and High Competency) are his/her "Motivated" skills, those skills that he or she enjoys using, does very well and seeks every opportunity to use at work or in leisure activities. These are the skills that will be used in any successful entrepreneurial venture. The skills in the lower left hand corner are "burnout" skills, those skills that the individual is very good at but dislikes doing. If the entrepreneurial venture requires the use of these skills, the individual will suffer "job burn out" and the venture will probably fail. Finally, skills in the upper right hand corner are his or her "Developmental" skills, skills the individual loves to use but at which he or she is not as competent. These are skills that require training and development and that can eventually lead to success.

Assessment

When you compare your "preferred" work style results from the ESSI with the most appropriate work style for the self-employment exercise that you are considering, you should have a good idea of how good a fit there is between you and the self-employment exercise and setting.

When you have compared your Motivated Skills with the skills necessary for success in the self-employment exercise that you are considering, you should be able to determine if you will be able to use most of your Motivated Skills in the exercise (the more you can use, the more motivated you will be to succeed) and if any of your "Burnout" skills are critical to the exercise. It is often important to avoid using your "Burnout" skills since that will result in failure.

When you compare your background score with the scores of successful entrepreneurs on the ESSI, you should be able to determine how similar or different your background is to those who were successful in their own businesses. While being different from most entrepreneurs doesn't mean you couldn't succeed, it may mean you would find the necessary tasks uncomfortable or difficult.

Discussion

When individuals are aware of their entrepreneurial style preference and their Motivated Skills, they should be able to look back at their life and see where they have succeeded in activities that required their Motivated Skills and failed in activities that required their burnout skills. This would be a good time for the individual to turn to the "Seven Stories" section in *What Color is Your Parachute?* and complete that exercise.

APPENDIX B:
CONTRIBUTORS
WHO WE ARE

Sally D. Gelardin, Ed.D., Editor

Dr. Sally Gelardin is founder of The Job Juggler (Employability Is Job #1). She is a career expert who speaks internationally on the topics of employability and personal development. Having operated a profitable retail business in the 1980s and 1990s, she shares her expertise and experience by counseling entrepreneurs in a variety of business categories. Through e-learning curriculum design, career expert audio interviews, presentations, radio and television interviews, and publications for print and electronic media, Dr. Gelardin demonstrates ways workers can develop lifelong employability skills.

Dr. Gelardin is a career development facilitator instructor (CDFI) with an e-learning specialty, approved NBCC provider of the global CDF curriculum, national certified counselor, distance credentialed counselor, and job and career transition coach. She is a career educator, serving as women's studies portfolio evaluator at the University of San Francisco. She is past-president of the California Career Development Association (CCDA). Dr. Gelardin is an active member of the National Career Development Association's (NCDA) first Leadership Academy. In addition, Dr. Gelardin serves on the advisory board of the Redwood Empire Small Business Development Center and owns several career-related e-communities (http://www.lifeworkps.com/sallyg; view "Owned Communities"). She was awarded the NCDA Merit Award for significant contributions to the field of career development. Dr. Gelardin is author of *The mother-daughter relationship: Activities for promoting lifework success,* guest editor of the *Career and Adult Development Journal,* and contributor to Barron's *The Complete job search guide for Latinos.*

Dr. Gelardin earned a doctorate in international and multicultural education and two masters' degrees (in urban teaching and life transitions counseling). Contact: Dr. Sally D. Gelardin. Phone: (415) 461.4097. Websites: http://www.JobJuggler.net, http://www.lifeworkps.com/sallyg, http://www.AskDrSal.com. Email: sal@jobjuggler.net.

Marcia Bench, J.D.

Marcia Bench is a expert in the field of career and life coaching. A master certified career coach and nationally respected expert in the job/career transition field, she has been coaching and consulting both individual and corporate clients since 1986. She is founder and director of Career Coach Institute, LLC, http://www.careercoachinstitute.com, Retirement Coach Institute, http://www.retirementcoachinstitute.com, and Schools of Career Coaching, http://www.schoolsofcareercoaching.com.

A former attorney, Marcia has authored 18 books, including *Career coaching: An insider's guide* (Davies-Black, 2003) plus the corresponding workbooks and CDs; *Retire Your Way!;* and more. Recently she completed two series of three books each: the *Job/career design series*, designed for individuals in transition; and the *Practice-building for coaches series* for coaches desiring to launch and build their businesses. Ms. Bench has been a featured speaker/trainer at over 450 local, regional, and national conferences, as well as a guest on numerous television and radio programs. Her mission is to help individuals and organizations chart their own unique course for success. Her coaching experience includes work with managers and executives from Fortune 500 firms in a variety of industries, as well as dozens of military officers entering the civilian workforce and business owners and other professionals.

Ms. Bench was senior vice president of a dotcom career management firm. She spent ten years as president of a business and consulting firm that she founded. Ms. Bench developed her expertise in business startup and management in part through her four years as a practicing attorney specializing in business and employment issues. She is a current member of the International Coach Federation. Her education includes a JD and a bachelor of science in psychology. In addition, she is a certified career management practitioner through the International Board of Career Management Certification, a certified business coach, a certified teleleader, and a master certified career coach. Contact: Marcia Bench. Address: Career Coach Institute, LLC, PO Box 5778, Lake Havasu City, AZ 86404, Ph/Fax: (866) 226-2244. Email: coach@careercoachinstitute.com. Website: http://www.careercoachinstitute.com.

Jack Chapman

Jack Chapman is a 25-year seasoned veteran of the career-coaching field. He is the director of the International Guild of Career Excellence, an international mastermind group of independent career advisors who work closely with each other in creating and delivering the most cutting edge, innovative, effective career coaching in the world. In addition to authoring the best-selling "bible" of salary negotiations, *Negotiating your salary; How to make $1000 a minute*, Jack has developed and published innovative approaches to the career search coaching field, including: *Special reports: Amazing new job search tool that gets ten times the response and a hundred times the impact of [even the best] resume and cover letter, The twelve biggest mistakes job hunters and career changers make and how to avoid them, Tripartite model for a networking campaign: Three distinctions that double networking confidence and effectiveness, Streetwise guide to job interviewing: How to gain an (almost unfair) advantage in job interviewing*, and *How to earn $100,000+ in private practice career consulting and still be a decent human being.*

Mr. Chapman moved from his initial (struggling) private practice to join, and then own, the Chicago/Milwaukee territory of the oldest and largest executive career consulting firm in the U.S. He grew it from one office to four offices, managing 22 staff, 8 career advisors and all administrative personnel. He left that in 1996 to return to private practice, and founded the GUILD in 1997. He has personally coached, one on one, many career advisors in private practice to significantly expand their practices and income. His group presentations are engaging, practical, inspiring, provocative, and motivating. Contact Jack Chapman, Lucrative Careers, Inc. Author: *Negotiating your salary, how to make $1000 a minute, providing lasting and lucrative career solutions for people*. Address: 511 Maple Avenue, Wilmette, IL 60091. Website: http://www.salarynegotiations.com. Phone: (847) 251-4727. Fax: (847) 256-4690. Email: jkchapman@aol.com.

Robert Chope, Ph.D.

Robert Chope is Professor of Counseling at San Francisco State University where he founded the Career Counseling Program. He is also the founder of the Career and Personal Development Institute in San Francisco, a practice that he has had for over 27 years. Dr. Chope received his Ph.D. in Counseling Psychology. His dissertation advisor was David P. Campbell of the Strong-Campbell and Campbell Interest and Skills Inventory fame. He was heavily influenced and mentored by B.F. Skinner in his undergraduate work.

Dr. Chope is a licensed psychologist and a licensed marriage and family therapist. He is the author of *Dancing naked: Breaking through the emotional limits that keep you from the job you want and Shared confinement: Healing options for you and the agoraphobic in your life,* both published by New Harbinger Publications and *Family matters: The influence of the family in career decision making* published by Pro-Ed, as well as 40 other refereed papers. He has been heard on over 100 radio and television shows around the country and is regularly featured in newspapers and on-line journals.

Dr. Chope is a National Career Development Association (NCDA) Fellow, a winner of the Robert Swan Lifetime Achievement in Career Counseling Award, a winner of the 2004 NCDA Outstanding Career Practitioner of the Year Award, and the 2005 winner of the Morgan Vail Award for Contributions to the Counseling and Development Profession in California. He is most interested in the integration of personality and family influences on career decision-making. Contact: Dr. Robert Chope. Email: rcchope@sfsu.edu. Address: Department of Counseling, San Francisco State University, San Francisco, CA 94132. Phone: (415) 338-1496 or Address: Career and Personal Development Institute, 582 Market Street, Suite 410, San Francisco, CA 94104. Phone: (415) 982-2636. Website: http:www.cpdicareercounseling.com.

Donna Christner-Lile

Donna Christner-Lile, CPC, NCC, DCC, SRES, is an energetic life transitions counselor, who has presented on talk shows and has been featured in professional publications, such as the American Counseling Association's *Counseling Today*, *Thrivent Magazine*, and public media. She successfully has combined her experience and education from two life careers into an outstanding planning resource for boomers, caregivers, and elders. Finding herself with extra time and burned out from real estate sales, she went back to school for her Masters in Counseling, and opened her own practice, Christner-Lile Consulting. She has balanced two careers while providing care to her 92-year old mother. With increasing numbers of boomers facing caregiver stress, downsizing, and retirement issues, as well as elders choosing to remain in their homes, Ms. Christner-Lile is uniquely positional to provide services and resources.

Highlights of her career include a master's degree in life transitions counseling and a bachelor's of arts degree in lifespan development. She is a national certified counselor; California professional counselor; distance credentialed counselor; owner, Christner-Lile Consulting; director of Charitable Life Consulting; broker and owner of Pacific Real Estate Services; and senior advantage real estate specialist (SRES). She is author of an upcoming book, *Aging in Place: Let's Chat, A Simple, No-Nonsense Book About How You Can Live in Your Own Home Forever*.

Contact: Donna Christner-Lile, MA, NCC, SRES, Life Transitions Counselor/Broker Owner, Christner-Lile Consulting. Address: 6150 Stoneridge Mall Rd., Ste. 105, Pleasanton, CA 94588. Phone: (866) 463-0302. Website: http://www.mentorcentral.com. Email: 2mentor@mentorcentral.com.

Ron Elsdon, Ph.D.

Ron Elsdon brings a wealth of experience to workforce development, organizational consulting, and individual career counseling and coaching. His organizational consulting practice, Elsdon Organizational Renewal (EOR), integrates organizational assessment processes with workforce and leadership development approaches to strengthen and revitalize organizations. His career counseling and coaching practice, New Beginnings Career and College Guidance, provides caring and personalized support to individuals in creating a meaningful path forward.

Ron's organizational consulting and individual career counseling and coaching work includes his private practices, corporate, nonprofit, and public sector settings and extends to public speaking, publishing and lecturing. Dr. Elsdon and his co-author were awarded the Walker prize by the Human Resource Planning Society for the paper that best advances state-of-the-art thinking or practices in human resources. He is author of *Affiliation in the workplace: Value creation in the new organization,* published by Praeger (2003).

Dr. Elsdon has more than 20 years of leadership experience working with U.S. and international organizations in a broad range of sectors (e.g., public sector, biotechnology, semiconductors, chemicals, healthcare, energy, and textiles). He founded or led practices for Drake Beam Morin (DBM), a human resource consulting firm, where he supported organizations in improving workforce and leadership effectiveness and provided services to senior executives in transition. Dr. Elsdon is an adjunct faculty member at John F. Kennedy University, has been on the adjunct faculty of Santa Clara University, and is affiliated with Vanderbilt University. He holds a Ph.D. in chemical engineering, a master's degree in career development and a first-class honors degree in chemical engineering. Contact: Ron Elsdon. Website: http://www.elsdon.com/. Phone: (925) 838-2362. Email: renewal@elsdon.com.

Edward Anthony Colozzi, Ed.D.

Edward Anthony Colozzi, Ed.D., is the owner of Career Development and Counseling Services in Winchester, MA, and provides corporate training, individual counseling, career coaching, and motivational speeches. He has served in numerous teaching, counseling, and career development center coordinator positions at both graduate and undergraduate levels for approximately 30 years. He has developed cost-effective systematic models of career guidance that emphasize a career/life focus in many traditional counseling programs. His work with "discovering client callings" involves Depth Oriented Values Extraction (DOVE) and is being prepared for publication as a monograph by the National Career Development Association.

Dr. Colozzi has published book chapters and articles on these and related topics. He wrote and produced a video, "Making Choices," for use with high school and college students, and his self-paced workbook, "Creating Careers with Confidence," was selected for publication in Braille and is presently being prepared for publication by Prentice Hall with a CD-ROM option. He has created guidance materials for students in K-12 and post-secondary settings, including a career game for middle school students for JA Worldwide (Junior Achievement). He is currently writing a research article focusing on the spiritual dimensions of career counseling. Dr. Colozzi received his undergraduate education in psychology and master's and a doctorate degree in education and a second master's degree in counseling psychology. He is a licensed mental health counselor, a national certified counselor, a master career counselor, and an NCDA fellow. Contact: Edward Anthony Colozzi, Ed.D., Owner, Career Development and Counseling Services. Address: 165 Washington Street, Winchester, MA 01890 USA. Phone: (781) 721-1200. Website: http://www.lifeworkps.com/edwardc. Email: edcolozzi@verizon.net.

Jennifer Kahnweiler, Ph.D.

Jennifer B. Kahnweiler, Ph.D. is founder and owner of AboutYOU, Inc. an Atlanta-based firm specializing in providing career management expertise to professionals, organizations, and the media. She has over 25 years experience in consulting across a wide range of industries and has helped thousands of individuals resolve their career challenges. She is also an associate of Parachute, Inc., a leading provider of career transition services. As an active faculty member of the American Management Association and an instructor in Emory University's Institute for Professional Learning, Jennifer delivers a wide array of career development and leadership courses.

Dr. Kahnweiler is co-author with Dr. Bill Kahnweiler of a book for Human Resource (HR) professionals called *Shaping Your HR Role: Succeeding in today's organizations* (Elsevier, 2005), a results-driven guide for crafting a successful HR career. As a media expert, Dr. Kahnweiler writes the Advisor column in the award winning Navigator section of *AARP The Magazine* and recently appeared as a featured career expert on the national show *Movie and a Makeover* on WTBS. She has been a guest host on the syndicated *Job Talk* radio show and has been a keynote speaker for many local and national organizations. She has been published in over 20 trade and professional publications and has been quoted in the *Wall Street Journal*, *New York Times*, and *Washington Post*.

Dr. Kahnweiler earned her Ph.D. in counseling and human systems from Florida State University. She received her master's degee in counseling and bachelor's in sociology from Washington University, St. Louis. She holds master career counselor (MCC), national certified counselor (NCC), and licensed professional counselor (LPC) certifications and has served on the boards of the National Career Development Association (NCDA) and the Georgia Executive Women's Network. She was awarded the Outstanding Career Practitioner of the Year by NCDA in 2005. Contact: Jennifer Kahnweiler. Website: http://www.aboutyouinc.com or http://www.myhrsuccess.com. Email: jennifer@aboutyouinc.com.

Carolyn Kalil

Carolyn Kalil is a counselor, a speaker, and the author of the best selling book, *Follow your true color to the work you love*. She is on a mission to inspire and assist others in discovering and using their unique gifts and talents. She has spoken to audiences throughout the United States and internationally on a variety of topics including career, parenting, team building, relationships, and individual diversity.

In 1989, Ms. Kalil wrote a workbook, *How to express your natural skills and talent in a career* using Don Lowry's True Colors Personality System. Since publication of this book, she has collected and published the results of research in *Follow your true colors to the work you love*. This book is the 7th best selling career book in the U.S. and is used in colleges, high schools, and industry. Fortune 500 companies (e.g., Cisco Systems, Warner Brothers) use it for managerial training and team building.

In addition to being active in the professional career development field, she is a sought after and highly rated speaker. She has delivered keynote speeches, workshops and certification trainings. Ms. Kalil earned her bachelor's degree in elementary teaching in 1970 and her master's degree in counseling. She taught elementary school for two years in South Central Los Angeles, and then began her 30-year counseling career at UCLA and El Camino Community College. Contact Carolyn Kalil. Address: PO Box 2804, Malibu, CA 90265. Phone: (310) 993-2164. Email: CKalil@truecolorscareer.com. Website: http://www.truecolorscareer.com.

Dan Geller

Dan Geller is an expert strategist specializing in business-strategy formulation for small and micro-companies. He is the founder and president of Instant Strategist, a strategic planning, training, and counseling company based in San Rafael, California. In his capacity as trainer and counselor, Dan has helped hundreds of business people develop a valid strategy for their new or existing businesses.

Realizing that most small-business owners do not have, or are not engaged in, formalized planning, Mr. Geller has devoted five years to researching this topic, and to formulating a strategic planning methodology that allows small-business owners to develop a quick and easy strategy for their business. He continues his research in this area through his doctoral dissertation work at Touro University International. Dan is a professor of business strategy at the Graduate Business School of Dominican University of California. He is also a business advisor with the Small Business Development Center (SBDC), where he helps small-business owners with their business-strategy needs and other planning issues. In addition, Mr. Geller conducts strategic planning workshops for clients of the SBDC. He is a frequent speaker on the topic of strategic planning, and has appeared on national shows, such as World Business Review hosted by Casper Weinberger. He is the author of the book *Instant strategist* (WizBizWeb publication). Contact Dan Geller. Email: dan@instantstrategist.com, Phone: (866) 343-5537, Website: http://www.instantstrategist.com.

Lynn Joseph, Ph.D.

Lynn Joseph, Ph.D., is a recognized transition specialist and author of the highly acclaimed book, *The Job-loss recovery guide: A proven program for getting back to work – fast!* As former senior vice president, Career and Life Transition Programs, Parachute, Inc., Dr. Joseph co-developed The Parachute Career Transition Program in 2004, an innovative approach to helping individuals facing career transition. She also developed and delivered trauma recovery workshops for hurricane disaster survivors in the New Orleans and Gulf Coast area. Dr. Joseph has worked for many years with Fortune 100 companies, such as Johnson & Johnson and Abbott Laboratories, in managerial positions in sales training and human resources, and was also an executive search consultant. She later earned a doctorate in psychology and founded Discovery Dynamics Incorporated, a company dedicated to providing people with the mental and emotional tools to reclaim inner calm and clarity, while at the same time boosting morale and productivity during stressful organizational change and life transition events.

Dr. Joseph developed and scientifically tested a career-transition program based on Mental Image Technology (MIT). The resulting breakthrough study was published in the prestigious *Consulting Psychology Journal*, a peer-reviewed journal of the American Psychological Association, and the successful study protocol is the basis of *The Job-loss recovery guide* (New Harbinger Publications, June 2003), as well as a companion MIT program recording. The Job-Loss Recovery Program received an award of distinction from the U.S. Department of Health and Human Services. Dr. Joseph has been featured on hundreds of national radio and TV programs and was also profiled by Fortune magazine. Contact Dr. Lynn Joseph. Email: DrJoseph@DiscoveryDynamics.net. Phone: (951) 780-7374. Website: http://www.JobLossRecovery.com.

Richard Knowdell

During a 35-year career, Richard L. Knowdell established one of America's first successful corporate career development programs, directed a regional Veterans Administration Guidance Center, instituted an internal employee assistance program at a national laboratory, directed a Silicon Valley corporate training and employee development department, established an executive outplacement consulting firm, and served as an executive coach. Mr. Knowdell holds a master of science degree in counseling psychology and is a National Certified Career Counselor and a Charter Career Management Fellow. He is the president of Career Research & Testing, Inc., author of *Building a career development program: Nine steps for effective implementation* (1996) and co-author of *From downsizing to recovery: Strategic transition options for organizations and individuals* (1994). In 1994, President Clinton appointed him to the Board of Examiners of the United States Foreign Service.

He has developed four popular career assessment instruments that have been translated into Russian, Spanish, German, Japanese, Dutch, Swedish, French, Vietnamese, and Icelandic. In 1979, he founded the Career Planning & Adult Development Network, and has edited the organization's newsletter and journal, and developed its Job & Career Transition Coach Certification program. He was the recipient of the Robert Wegmann Professionalism Award from the Association of Job Search Trainers (AJST) and the 2000 Generosity of Spirit Award from the International Career Development Conference. He is a frequent presenter at local, regional, national and international career conferences. Contact: Richard L. Knowdell, Executive Director, Career Planning & Adult Development Network. Address: P.O. Box 611930, San Jose, CA 95161to1930 USA, (408) 272-3085. Fax: (408) 272-8851. Email: dick@careertrainer.com, Website: http://www.careernetwork.org.

Gail Liebhaber

Gail Liebhaber has been involved in the field of career development for 25 years as a trainer, consultant, coach and counselor. In addition to her private practice, Ms. Liebhaber was the director of career services for the Harvard Graduate School of Design in Cambridge from 1997-2002 and currently holds the same position at the Harvard Divinity School. Her previous organizational roles have included: organizational consultant and staff training coordinator for the Department of Employment and Training for the Commonwealth of Massachusetts; adjunct faculty at Bay State College; recruitment program director at Jewish Vocational Services; sales associate for the Software Council Fellowship Program; and director of Metro South/West Career Center, a publicly funded outplacement agency serving laid-off professional, managerial, and technical workers from the Greater Boston area.

Ms. Liebhaber established her own firm, Career Directions, in Lexington, MA in 1993, dedicated to the mission of coaching adults and organizations through career transitions with effective and empowering results. In her private practice, she counsels clients individually in life/work planning, job search strategies, and work enhancement. As an executive coach, she employs the Myers Briggs Type Indicator, the FIRO-B and The Career Architect to increase effective communication skills, develop leadership potential, and enhance career development. Ms. Liebhaber facilitates a wide spectrum of career related workshops, advising participants in career management and lifework balance concerns. She is the author of the 2004 book, *Purposeful listening: Spiritual coaching techniques for career development practitioners*. Contact Gail Liebhaber, 40 Cottage St, Lexington, MA 02420. Phone: (781) 861-9949. Cell: (781) 820-5310. Fax: (781) 863-5965. Email: gliebhaber@rcn.com. Website: http://www.yourcareerdirection.com/.

Randy Miller

Randy Miller founded Ready & Motivated Minds (ReadyMinds) in 1997 to improve the way individuals think about their personal and career growth. His philosophy was to focus on providing a quality distance career counseling program designed to maximize each client's opportunity to determine and secure an occupation best suited to their particular talents, needs, and life goals.

Mr. Miller spent five years studying the industry, financing proprietary research, and recruiting experts in career counseling, education, business, and human resources. With 18 years experience in strategic business planning, identifying new market opportunities, and management expertise, Mr. Miller has created a first-class organization that has developed the resources to enhance the way clients select, prepare for, and manage their careers, while aiding them in achieving personal fulfillment through career success. Mr. Miller realized early in life the benefit of personal mentoring and professional career counseling. He currently oversees corporate strategy, long-range planning, marketing and finance.

Prior to founding the company, Mr. Miller was vice president and member of the board of directors of a New York manufacturing company he co-founded in 1989 and grew into a multi-million-dollar business. He graduated in business administration with a BS degree in marketing and management and a concentration in psychology.

Throughout his career, Mr. Miller has sought to share his knowledge and experiences with others. He has served as a mentor, teacher, and motivational speaker on numerous college campuses, helping individuals gain a better understanding of themselves and their career interests. He currently speaks to businesses nationwide and presents at national education conferences and higher ed forums on topics related to the distance career-counseling field. Contact: Randy Miller. Phone: (888) 225-8248. Email: helpdesk@readyminds.com. Website: http://www.readyminds.com.

Martha Russell

Martha Russell, NCC, is a career consultant and owner of Russell Career Services, currently located in Battle Ground, WA. Established in 1987 in Sacramento, CA, her career consulting practice includes staff development and career issues work with corporate clients, public agencies, and individuals seeking career guidance and life planning.

Ms. Russell is a frequent speaker and workshop facilitator on career management including professional growth and workplace alignment issues. She has designed and facilitated workshops both nationally and internationally. Her international work has included developing alliances and training career professionals in the former Soviet Union and Asia, with training in China scheduled in 2006. She has also presented at international conferences in Australia and within the U.S.

Ms. Russell was the 2005-2006 president of the National Career Development Association. She was the 1993 president of the California Career Development Association and a past president of the Sacramento, CA chapter of the American Society of Training and Development. With an undergraduate degree in the field of speech/theatre, she went on to complete her master's degree in career counseling. She currently serves as an adjunct faculty member for John F. Kennedy University in California and City University in Washington. Contact: Martha M. Russell, MS, MCC, NCC, Russell Career Services – Connecting People with Purpose. Address: PO Box 2647, Battle Ground, WA 98604, Office Phone: (360) 686-1924, Office Fax: (360) 686-1925, Email: RCareer@aol.com.

Michael Shahnasarian, Ph.D.

Michael Shahnasarian, Ph.D., founded Career Consultants of America (CCA) in 1986. The practice, based in Tampa, Florida, now employs 10 individuals. Its services include private career counseling, organizational consulting (including employee selection and staffing, establishing mentoring programs, and outplacement), forensic consultation, and vocational rehabilitation.

As his practice developed, Dr. Shahnasarian became particularly recognized for his expertise in providing expert insight in lawsuits involving career-related disputes. Over the years, Dr. Shahnasarian has testified as a forensic expert in more than 1,000 civil and federal court cases throughout the United States and Caribbean. CCA's corporate clients have included manufacturing organizations, business service firms, maritime organizations, and various government agencies.

Dr. Shahnasarian is a past president of the National Career Development Association (NCDA). The organization named him a Fellow in 2002, the same year it selected him as Outstanding Practitioner of the Year. Dr. Shahnasarian currently serves on the editorial board of the *Career Development Quarterly.* NCDA published his most recent book, *Decision time: A guide to career enhancement, 3rd edition*, in 2006. Dr. Shahnasarian has served on numerous NCDA committees during the past three decades. In addition to his service with NCDA, two Florida governors appointed Dr. Shahnasarian to career-related advisory boards. During his service on the National Board for Certified Counselors, Dr. Shahnasarian was chair of the Career Academy. His publications include six books and approximately 50 articles and book chapters. Contact: Dr. Michael Shahnasarian through Todd Wilber Career Consultants of America. Address: 11019 N Dale Mabry Hwy, Tampa, FL 33618. Phone: (813) 265-9262, Fax: (813) 265-4226.

Susan Britton Whitcomb

Susan Britton Whitcomb is a career and life coach and author with more than 20 years' experience in the careers industry. She has been a careers columnist and featured chat guest for Monster.com and America Online and, as an industry expert, has been cited in *U.S. News & World Report*, cbs.marketwatch.com/, the Dow Jones' *National business employment weekly*, and numerous national publications. She is author of the best-selling "Magic Series" published by JIST, including *Resume magic; Interview magic;* and *Job search magic.* Ms. Whitcomb is co-author of *eResumes* (McGrawtoHill), and author of *Career magic,* a 400-page reference accompanying the Certified Career Management Coach program offered through Career Coach Academy.

In addition to founding Career Coach Academy, http://www.CareerCoach Academy.com, Ms. Whitcomb is executive director of Career Masters Institute, a global association of leading career professionals. Career Masters Institute is dedicated to innovational career tools and strategies, transformational training for professional and personal growth, and an inspirational community of support and networking for its members. Contact Susan B. Whitcomb, CCMC, CCM, NCRW, MRW, Career Masters Institute. Address: 757 East Hampton Way, Fresno, CA 93704. Phone: (559) 222-7474, Fax: (888) 795-2725, Email: swhitcomb@cminstitute.com. Website: http://www.cminstitute.com.